The Surprising Life and Times of a Dominican Sister

Judith Ann Brady

authorHOUSE

AuthorHouse™
1663 Liberty Drive
Bloomington, IN 47403
www.authorhouse.com
Phone: 1 (800) 839-8640

© *2018 Judith Ann Brady. All rights reserved.*

No part of this book may be reproduced, stored in a retrieval system, or transmitted by any means without the written permission of the author.

Published by AuthorHouse 01/15/2019

ISBN: 978-1-5462-6155-1 (sc)
ISBN: 978-1-5462-6153-7 (hc)
ISBN: 978-1-5462-6154-4 (e)

Library of Congress Control Number: 2018911455

Print information available on the last page.

Cover photo: Courtesy of **The Times-Herald Record**

Any people depicted in stock imagery provided by Getty Images are models, and such images are being used for illustrative purposes only. Certain stock imagery © Getty Images.

This book is printed on acid-free paper.

Because of the dynamic nature of the Internet, any web addresses or links contained in this book may have changed since publication and may no longer be valid. The views expressed in this work are solely those of the author and do not necessarily reflect the views of the publisher, and the publisher hereby disclaims any responsibility for them.

New American Standard Bible (NASB)

Copyright © 1960, 1962, 1963, 1968, 1971, 1972, 1973, 1975, 1977, 1995 by The Lockman Foundation

Table of Contents

Dedication vii
Acknowledgements ix
Chapter 1   Double Dutch 1
Chapter 2   Marriage Changed Everything 16
Chapter 3   I Have Called You Friends 27
Chapter 4   Here I Am, Lord 44
Chapter 5   Change Ahead 91
Chapter 6   Party, Where's the Party? 124
Chapter 7   Sisterly Love 154
Chapter 8   Mother Dear 178
Chapter 9   The Joys of Convent Living 207
Chapter 10 The Hundredfold 219
Appendix 227

Dedication

To my sisters, Sr. Joan Dolores (Joan Marie Willemse),
Margaret (Geri) Toal, and Clare Brady Johnson

Acknowledgements

Many years ago I left home to become a Sister. One of many young women whom God called, I was in good company as I learned the customs of the Dominican Sisters and most importantly, prayed in community for the intentions of the world. After wearing the black dress of the postulant, we received the white habit and veil of a novice. When we professed our vows of poverty, chastity, and obedience we received the black veil of a professed Sister and a gold ring, a symbol of God's love. My desire to share the wonder of being called and becoming a bride of Christ led me to write this book.

How to proceed? I needed a new approach, different from the academic papers that I had written. A doctor whom I respect for his insights suggested writing a memoir. How could I do that? "Take a course so you can learn how to write a memoir." Before long I searched and found courses offered by colleges and independent schools. June 2013 I discovered Gotham Writers' Workshop that offered courses in Manhattan.

Many have helped me to persevere in writing this memoir. Anna Bartley funded me so I could work with Gotham Writers. Ryan C. Britt who taught the Memoir course was a breath of fresh air. He encouraged us to read all we could. I followed his advice and read many memoirs. Ryan accepted us, his students, and appreciated who we were; he sensed what was important in our lives. Thank you, Ryan, for inspiring me to write and yes, to read aloud in class.

I connected with Bette-Jane Raphael, a journalist and author in her own right. She worked with me in refining and editing various chapters. Under her guidance I was able to submit two essays: *My Great Aunt Nellie* and *Calling All Names, Calling...* that were published in *Visible Ink* 2014 and 2015. Special thanks to those who read the entire manuscript and offered precious insights, especially Anna Kantor, Maryann Fallek, Sr. Angelique Dryden, and Rev. John Allard.

I am grateful to my mother, Margaret J. Brady for saving the letters I wrote home when I was at Nazareth College of Rochester (1959-1961) and during the Novitiate and year in Formation (1961-1964) at Sparkill. These provided details that I would never have recalled and helped me relive days from long ago. Thank you to Sr. Margaret Palliser for her dedicated research re. copyrights and to Sr. Maureen Foy who provided access to our Archives at the Motherhouse in Sparkill so I could verify information leading up to the Chapter of Affairs (1969). Thanks to Joe Vanderhoof, President/Publisher of Times Herald-Record, who located the photo that appeared on the front page of their paper on 9/7/67; thanks to his staff for making a digital copy available for use in my book. Sincere thanks to Heather Hill and Mary Kohl at the Faculty Technology Center at Fordham University on the Rose Hill campus. Their technical assistance was invaluable for scanning and saving personal photos.

Special thanks to my congregation, the Dominican Sisters of Sparkill who sponsored me for the Parable Tour to Guatemala and El Salvador (August 1991); there I met the peacemakers who were advocates for the poor in the midst of conflict. I was humbled by the loving tenacity of these advocates for social justice. Their words and deeds inspired me to share their dedication to human rights and belief in a loving God who is with us as we work to bring peace and social justice to the poor and oppressed.

The story begins with the life of a young immigrant from the Netherlands, Cornelius Willemse, jumping ship to get to lower Manhattan. Come and read the adventures of my paternal grandfather…

Chapter 1

DOUBLE DUTCH

The lions looked straight ahead as I slowly climbed the stairs. "'Better not disturb them," I thought. I have great respect for large animals even when they are made of marble and in a resting position. They guard the entrance to the New York Public Library on Fifth Avenue at 42nd Street and I feared that they might come to life. They were witnesses of this special day when I would search for the books that my paternal grandfather had written. All my life my family had said that he had written two books. Today was the day I would finally hold them in my hands and discover what they could tell me about him.

The card catalog helped me access vital data: author's name: Willemse, Cornelius W.; title: *Behind the Green Lights* (1931) and *A Cop Remembers* (1933). I filled out a request and waited. The books arrived each enclosed in a zip-lock plastic bag as if they needed to be preserved and protected from overzealous readers. I handled them carefully for I knew that they would reveal the legacy of my Dutch roots. Two hours, only two hours for me to read and digest all the facts in those books for they could not be signed out, not even by me, his granddaughter.

Why had he left his home in the Netherlands? How did he get to New York? These were some of the questions that I wanted to be answered. In 1888 Cornelius Willemse, age 15, left the Netherlands and set sail for the United States. He left behind his parents and five sisters. Understanding why he left is more complicated; for this I needed to know who he was from his birth. When he was two months old, his mother was so seriously burned that she was unable to care for him. He was sent to live with his grandmother in Oosterhout, North Brabant near the Belgian border. Cornelius was the center of attention at his grandmother's home. He attended private schools thanks to his grandmother and heard tales of valor from his granduncle who had been a cavalryman and served under Napoleon Bonaparte in thirteen major battles. On the one hand he was spoiled by his grandmother and on the other encouraged to fight. He thrived in this atmosphere that instilled courage and the ability to endure hardship. How would a boy with a head filled with tales of adventure and a penchant for languages (he could read, write, and speak English, German, Dutch, French, and Flemish) settle down and work as a baker in the family-owned business in Rotterdam? When his grandmother died, Cornelius, age 11, had to return to his birth family. He was as much a stranger to his parents and his younger sisters as they were to him; he even spoke with a Belgian accent. He acted in ways that irritated his father: he did not accept correction when he was sent to another uncle to learn how to be a butcher; he was only interested in learning history, geography, and languages. While he seemed unable or unwilling to learn any family business, he spent every available moment at the Rotterdam docks listening to the sailors' exploits. Gradually he became a rebel with a cause. He devised a plan to escape: he forged his father's signature to sign on as a cook's mate on a ship sailing from Rotterdam to New York. By the time they landed in New Jersey, he devised another plan. With two friends, he jumped ship, hid out in a field, slept two nights up in a tree to avoid capture until he crossed over by ferry to Manhattan.

Strong and tall for his age, Cornelius worked a variety of jobs trying to keep hunger and homelessness at bay. He longed to follow in the footsteps of his granduncle and live a life of adventure, but his early days in New York were more about survival. It required intelligence and brawn to work in the Bowery, but he had grander ambitions. In 1896 at age 24 he became a citizen and applied to become a police officer. Theodore Roosevelt, then Police Commissioner, would not hire him because he worked in an establishment that sold liquor. Cornelius Willemse did not give up. In the fall of 1898 he passed the civil service examination for the Police Department and a year later was called to take the physical which he passed with flying colors. Cornelius was sworn in as a New York Police Officer in February 1900. His finely tuned ability to observe and adapt to new situations proved invaluable as he worked in different precincts in Lower Manhattan: the San Juan district on the West Side and the West 20th Street police station. After seven years as a police officer and many months studying, he took the examination and earned the rank of sergeant. In 1913 Willemse became a detective in the Homicide Division and eventually commanded the plainclothes forces in all police stations between East 14th and 42nd Streets. He relished the job and shared stories of how he investigated crimes and brought criminals to justice.

One thing that puzzled me about my grandfather was the fact that when I visited my parents' graves in Woodlawn cemetery, I saw a metal plaque bearing his name. I wondered, "Why is there a plaque from the King of Belgium?" It seemed so out of place that I almost removed it. At the last minute I let it be— firmly implanted in the soil in front of the gravestone that bore his name. *Behind the Green Lights* revealed how and why this plaque was conferred on my grandfather. In 1914 while visiting relatives in Belgium, he saw how civilians were fleeing for their lives to the Netherlands as the German armies advanced into Belgium. With few possessions and far from home, they needed food, clothing, and shelter. Cornelius Willemse returned to New York and began collecting police uniforms, a charity that grew exponentially when the NYPD updated their uniforms and overcoats. The old uniforms were warm and in good shape. He had them shipped to his sister aboard Holland-American ships; she in turn gave them to Belgian organizations that distributed the clothing to those in need. He continued sending coats and uniforms over many years. As strange as it may have seemed to see NYPD uniforms without insignia, it was those coats and uniforms that saved many Belgian refugees from freezing to death.

Cornelius Willemse was in charge of security when President Woodrow Wilson came to New York City during World War I. In 1919 he was the personal guard for King Albert, Queen Elizabeth, and the Crown Prince Leopold of Belgium. King Albert had learned all that Captain Willemse had done for his people during the war. As a token of their appreciation and in honor of my grandfather's dedicated charity, the King decorated Cornelius W. Willemse with the gold medal of the Order of the Crown. For once he was speechless. At the end of their visit, in recognition of his service as bodyguard to the royal family, Cornelius W. Willemse was also made a Chevalier of the Order of Leopold II.

Having my grandfather's books in my hands whetted my appetite to know more. My friend, Judy Donaldson located the books on the internet and before long I had both books in my possession. The stories of his childhood drew me in: how he was pampered by his grandmother and after her death, returned to his parents and five sisters only to feel like a stranger, and left home to follow his dream of living an exciting life only to endure hardships as a teenager living from hand to mouth in the late 1800's. He had a native intelligence and a facility with languages that served him well in New York City where there were immigrants from around the world. My grandfather was a man whose stories had such vivid details that it seemed as if all of Manhattan became his friends. He learned from adversity when he was on his own working for a butcher. He got blood poisoning from a wound that became infected because of contact with a rusty meat hook. He was hospitalized first at Bellevue Hospital and then, City Hospital on Blackwell's Island (later renamed Roosevelt Island). When he was released in November, he had only the clothes he had worn going into the hospital, but they were flea infested when he found them thrown on the floor of a closet. He returned to the house where he had lived, but the owner had moved away. No one knew him; he lost his meager possessions and rented room, and was forced to live on the streets for the next five months. Cold and hungry, weak from his hospitalizations, Cornelius became a shadow of his former self. Good fortune returned when William Pilgrim, a man who had worked for his family in Holland recognized him on the street. It was a chance encounter, but it rescued him from homelessness. Mr. Pilgrim bought him new clothes, paid for him to get a haircut, a shave, and luxury of luxuries, a long, hot bath. They went to a restaurant where Cornelius ate to his heart's content; Mr. Pilgrim paid for a room where he got a good night's rest, and extended a loan. Once he was clean and well dressed, Cornelius Willemse could again get work first, as a delivery man for a butcher's shop on First Avenue. At that point he met a patrolman, John Cray whose enthusiasm for police work encouraged him to join the force.

Cornelius needed to build himself up so he joined an athletic club. Once he learned how to wrestle, he worked as a bouncer in the Bowery, good preparation for becoming a cop. Over the years he rose to the rank of Acting Captain of the First Detective Division and after retiring from the NYPD wrote two books in which he recorded his adventures as a Dutchman in a police force dominated by Irish Americans. He joined the NYPD after civil service examinations provided the opportunity for men of all nationalities to join the NYPD. When my grandfather first joined the police department, they were on reserve 67 of 96 hours; as needed they had to respond to situations requiring more patrolmen. At the end of their shift, they would sleep upstairs in the dormitory above the station house. In that crowded, poorly ventilated space new members were initiated by the veterans and pranks were commonplace. He took this in stride and made the best of what came his way. He was in a unique position to know how it felt to be an outsider so he looked out for other men new to the force especially those of different nationalities and religions. He made a point of saying that he avoided talk about politics and religion because these discussions easily ignited prejudices and led to full-blown fights. Hours of drudgery walking the beat were peppered with the thrill of hunting down and capturing criminals. When they were imprisoned and doing time, he often looked out for their mothers who had no income or relief, an action that earned the criminal's gratitude. Thanks to these books I met a man who had great empathy for those in need and who helped those who suffered hunger or pain. Because of his deeply felt charity and ingrained sense of justice, I was not only proud of my heritage but also sad to have missed him. I found his concern for the underdog especially appealing; it is a trait that I share with him though I never met my grandfather. If only he had lived longer! As *The New York Times* obituary recorded, Cornelius W. Willemse died on July 11, 1942 at the age of 70 after an emergency appendectomy. He left behind a widow, Mrs. Anna Elizabeth Willemse and two sons, Cornelius W. Jr. and George A. Willemse, my father. Judging from funerals for police officers in my time, I am sure that his comrades gathered at his wake and attended the funeral service at the Steven Merritt Chapel on Eighth Avenue and 22nd Street, for he had served in the NYPD for twenty-five years reaching the rank of Captain of Detectives.

His books had stories of his interactions with people great and small, but what endures for me is the fact that this was a deeply human man of great courage who recognized the humanity of others even as he worked in a profession that dealt with criminals of all social classes. This was indeed a man of honor not without fault. In his early days on the Bowery when he worked the lunch counter where his responsibility was to maintain order, he gave food to newly arrived immigrants who were unable to pay for he knew how it felt to be hungry and without funds. When discovered, he told his boss that these men would remember and return when they got work to the place that treated them well. All his life Cornelius Willemse fought to protect those who were preyed upon and brought to justice criminals and gang members of the early 1920's.

The summer of 1942 will always be remembered by my family. My father, George was mourning the unexpected death of his father when his family had to deal with another emergency. Our lovely garden apartment became a no-man's land when the sewers backed up and a toxic brew came streaming through the apartment. My father, George had acquired a carton of toilet tissue, no small feat after the USA had entered World War II and rationing was the norm. Someone told me that the rolls were floating through the apartment and that the precious possession was ruined. The person laughed and I suppose I did too, but upon reflection that was rude for George was sickly and really needed toilet tissue. Not only that, he became the person who would deal with the clean-up.

My mother, hugely pregnant with me, went to the country to stay with family friends. My sisters went to their paternal uncle's home in New Jersey. My sister Geri tells me now many years later that she wanted to stay there with her aunt, uncle, and cousin, and attend school. She felt loved and was treated well by the Willemse family. She knew instinctively that life in the Bronx was going to be difficult and would not measure up to life with Uncle Neal, Aunt Helen, and cousin Neal. How difficult she did not know, but was soon to find out.

Back in the Bronx, George was left to clean the apartment. Dealing with the realities of sewage and trying to salvage their meager possessions was an especially daunting task for my father. He was probably the last person who needed to be put in that position for he was sickly and had been dealing with stomach and GI issues over many years. Emergencies can bring forth the best and the worst in people. I can imagine his trying to rescue important papers and possessions, moving furniture to higher ground, and cleaning the fetid brew. In that long ago time, I have come to believe that with his compromised health he became sicker as a result of his cleaning out the apartment.

By the time I was born in late August they had a different apartment in the same low-rise complex. My mother had returned to the Bronx for my birth. Her sister, my Aunt Frances, went with her to Union Hospital where I was born on a pleasant Tuesday shortly after 1:00 PM, six days before my father's thirty-seventh birthday. Each year on my birthday my mother would tell me how the weather was perfect and that I weighed 6 pounds, 8 ounces and was pink and beautiful, not scrunched up like other newborns. In September life settled down: my father went to work, my mother cared for her new-born and the other members of the family, and my sisters attended school. Life had returned to normal.

My sister, Geri told me that on Halloween 1942 my mother was out with my older sister, Joan and me. Geri was home alone with our father when he doubled over in pain. She went with him to the drugstore to get over the counter medication to ease his discomfort. Nothing seemed to help. Geri got out the prayer book that she had received when she made her First Communion and read the prayers for the dying. When we finally arrived home it was apparent that our father was seriously ill. My mother called an ambulance and our father was taken to St. Clare's Hospital in mid-town Manhattan, the same hospital where his father had his appendectomy. The next few days were harrowing for both my parents. George was critically ill and there were no remedies that could help him. My mother was very upset. Surely the doctors could ease her husband's discomfort; surely they could administer some medicine or do some procedure that would bring him back to normal. George's condition worsened and on November 13 he died.

My father slipped away from us at an early age. He was young and handsome, beloved by my sisters, but a phantom for me. Like a blue sky with barely a cloud in sight, George A. Willemse lived a short life, loved his wife Margaret, procreated three children, worked as a stationery salesman, a job that my stepfather, Joe Brady told my mother, "was well below his exceptional abilities," had illnesses for which there were no cures, and left the earth. George was laid to rest in the family plot next to his father who predeceased him by four months. For me his life was a shadow, one that I would gladly have experienced, but family members shared very few memories of my father. He was really smart: he could mentally add up prices in the grocery store and tell the cashier he was a few cents off. My older sister, Joan remembered how he loved playing shuffle board, a skill she learned watching him and at which she too excelled. He planted and cared for the garden; during the war the garden apartment was more than a lovely name. Geri still remembers the juicy, red tomatoes that they harvested and ate.

Our father's death had immediate consequences. The family could no longer afford the rent for their apartment, so they had to move. Our mother had to work outside the home, but who would care for the infant and her daughters aged eight and ten? Aunt Nellie, my mother's maiden aunt came to the rescue. Nellie McDowell had worked all her life and never married. She was the go-to person when someone needed a baby-sitter or help, such as paying for my mother to take piano lessons as a young girl. She was in effect our family's social service agency. Whenever Aunt Nellie's name came up at family gatherings even years later, someone would say, "Aunt Nellie was a saint," for they knew that she would help anyone in need, no questions asked, with no fuss or bother.

And so we moved to a one-bedroom apartment on the fifth floor of a walk-up apartment at 282 East Gun Hill Road in the Bronx. The location was within walking distance of Aunt Nellie's furnished room on East 204th Street. We soon settled into a routine. Aunt Nellie stayed with us during the week and returned to her furnished room on the weekends. Over the next ten years she was our senior citizen in residence who came not to rest but to serve. My memories of her are of a buxom woman with white hair worn in a bun, wearing a dress and sensible black oxfords. She loved to sing but was hard of hearing. She was a second mother who nurtured and cared for me; my protector and advocate when disagreements arose between my sisters. She loved me with all her heart;

I was the child she never had. When I look at pictures of Aunt Nellie, she was no beauty, but to me Aunt Nellie was the most beautiful person in all the world. She was also a companion for my mother. My mother and Aunt Nellie would often relax over a glass of wine at night after we were settled in bed. Such moments were like an oasis that replenished each one's spirit.

As children it was easy to run up the stairs but for Aunt Nellie the stairs, two flights for each of the five floors were more than a challenge; for her it was like climbing Mount Everest. Geri tells me that when Aunt Nellie came she stayed upstairs for the week. Climbing the stairs was just too difficult. My sisters would pick up milk or bread from a local store. Aunt Nellie and my mother shared the cooking. They alternated making oat meal and Ralston; one had lumps, the other was smooth. I was never quite sure who did it better. By the time I turned five, they enrolled me in first grade at St. Ann's School. That eased the burden on Aunt Nellie, but proved a challenge for me. I remember being in a really large class when the principal came into the classroom. Everyone stood to greet her. "Good morning, Sister" they enthusiastically chimed. In the middle of the class one sole holdout, too scared to get out of her seat and join the others, sat quietly. It is far easier to do what the group is doing, but at that moment I was paralyzed —my body could not lift me up. There was no punishment, just the sense that I could not be or do at that moment what the other children seemed to do so naturally. I was a year younger than my classmates and had not been with other children my age so school was challenging. Gradually I fit in and had no problem doing what the class did. It was just a matter of time.

Aunt Nellie's respite came to an end shortly after Christmas. Each of the eight grades at St. Ann's had an act in the Christmas pageant. For weeks before we would go to the auditorium to practice. We knew it was special for we bought a costume and our parents came to attend the show. Aunt Nellie had her reservations about the costume: it was "too flimsy" as if she feared that something bad would happen. A black and white photo shows my class on stage; I am on the far right, three rows from the front. Like all the girls I wore a frilly dress and I was standing next to my chubby partner. It was a thrilling experience. By the time Christmas arrived, I had a cold. Had Aunt Nellie foreseen this? It lingered and then developed into measles, followed by mumps, and finally mastoiditis, a dangerous infection of the middle ear. I was a poster child for why immunizations were so badly needed. Those were the days before immunizations so these childhood diseases were common. After nights of excruciating pain that had me in tears with my mother at my side to comfort me, they brought me to St. Joseph's Hospital in Yonkers, NY. This hospitalization was costly and we had no health insurance. My mother would pay every month for many years. I was a teenager by the time the bill was paid in full.

I was in a ward with other children in beds that had slatted sides so high that we could not escape, but low enough to throw a toy to the child in the next bed. By day my grandmother and Aunt Nellie came to visit. They went to great lengths to cheer me up. I was glad to see them, but I wanted my mother. I was so anemic that over the course of a few days the doctor ordered three blood infusions. For one of these the nurse left me after inserting a needle into my arm. When she returned I was covered in blood. I watched in horror as the blood flowed over me and my clothes. I shivered in fear convinced that somehow it was my fault. At night, when I missed home the most, a nurse would come to the door and threaten us if we did not go to sleep. She was a silhouette, outlined by the hall light, and I wondered why she was so mean. As the days wore on and the ear infection did not improve, the doctor advised surgery that would have also caused severe hearing loss. As a last resort they decided to give me a relatively new drug, penicillin. It broke the fever and cleared the infection so surgery was no longer needed and even better, it left my hearing intact. For many years thereafter my mother said that it was a relic that she had pinned to my hospital gown that saved me. (Sad to say the relic disappeared; it went to the laundry when they changed the gown.) Whoever was responsible, I was so relieved that I could go home. It had only been a week, but it had felt like an eternity.

After so many illnesses and the hospitalization, I needed time to recuperate. Aunt Nellie was the person who wrestled with the problem of my snarled hair. After seven days in the hospital my long hair was a mess. She worked patiently over many hours to remove knots and tangles that at first sight had appeared to be an impossible task. It took the patience of a saint and the determination of a strong willed woman, but Aunt Nellie finally got my hair back to normal. Then my hair could be washed and worn in two long braids with bangs. There must have been a family council for soon I went to stay with my grandmother. She lived quite a distance from us on Middletown Road in the Bronx in a large house with her fourth husband, Louis Wienecke. (Her first husband was the father of my mother, Margaret, and my aunt, Dorothy. The second was the father of Aunt Frances. The third was the father of my three uncles, Henry, and fraternal twins, Alfred and Howard. I only knew Louis Wienecke. My grandmother had her hands full; these husbands died natural deaths and left her with children. I admire her perseverance. I am sure there were days when she felt like giving up, but she kept on going.) It was a treat to stay at my grandmother's house; she was funny and made me laugh. I spent many weeks eating and resting, and as winter melted into spring sitting outdoors on the steps of the house to get sun. I also saw Nana in a new light: as she shoveled coal into the cellar furnace, it belched huge flames. She never seemed concerned about her safety. My grandmother was a slight woman but she worked like a man dragging out buckets of ashes to the yard in addition to cooking, cleaning, and shopping. I shared a bedroom with her where she taught me to kneel and pray to God before going to bed. On the wall above the bed was a framed picture of Jesus praying in the Garden of Gethsemane. His was a comforting presence even though it was a sad time in his life, just before he would suffer and die for our sins.

After all the sicknesses, I never returned to first grade. There was work to make up and my older sister, Joan had to teach me. At first I was thrilled thinking that I would get more attention from Joan, who probably had much more interesting things to do than tutor her kid sister. It soon became apparent that my genius sister at age 16 had little patience for her kid sister. I remember trying to distract her and not wanting to do school work. She was intent on teaching me and did not appreciate my antics. Her/Our efforts must have been sufficient because I returned to St. Ann's in the fall and rejoined my classmates at the beginning of second grade. Life was back to normal.

School was certainly about learning even though the class size was well over sixty. There was safety in numbers and besides, the nuns kept the class in order. My favorite time was after lunch in good weather when we went out to play. The school sidewalk was our playground. As boys ran around, so did we girls. I invented a game: Horsey imitating the sounds and actions of horses. It was great fun to whinny and race around. Jump rope was another favorite as was Double Dutch. We took turns jumping and then being one of the two steady enders. It was much more fun to jump and run around than to be a steady ender. Double Dutch was a great challenge; it was a matter of timing to get into the ropes and then a matter of rhythm jumping quickly as the ropes were turned. Before we knew it, it was time to return to class. The afternoon went quickly and by 3:00 pm we were dismissed and walking home with our friends. Arlene Fanelli and I frequently walked together down East Gun Hill Road until we reached her street; then I continued another block or so to our apartment building. Since Arlene lived near me, sometimes I went to her apartment to play. Other times I played outside our apartment house with the Abbatte sisters who lived on the other side of our U shaped apartment building. It was amazing how we could play for hours with no props; we drew upon what we knew. It was role playing before we knew that term, reenacting what we had seen and heard at home, school and in church. When we played family, I was sometimes the father which was strange because I had no memories of my father. We also played church and practiced receiving Communion; we used white Necco wafers that were round like the host, though they were hard and sweet. I remember how happy I was when I redeemed an empty soda bottle for a nickel because then I would buy a Three Musketeers candy bar; it was easy to divide into three equal pieces, one for each of us, and it tasted so yummy.

On weekdays once homework was finished and I had time to play, I liked sewing clothes for my doll. My skill was limited to draping material around the doll, always a strapless gown because I did not know how to cut out sleeves or to sew them. Some afternoons I was alone. I would arrive home ahead of my sisters who were in high school and no one was there. As it got dark, I would listen to the radio. Two programs stand out: Sergeant Preston and Yukon King and the Lone Ranger. Each of these had a classical theme song that helped me to imagine the settings and the characters. If I got scared because I was alone, these characters became my surrogate family. What could go wrong when Sergeant

Preston would stop criminals with the help of his loyal dog, Yukon King? They took my mind off any problems I had and convinced me that the good guys were invincible. The Lone Ranger with his sidekick, Tonto had a resonant voice that calmed me. They would always get the bad guy and live to fight another day. When the Lone Ranger appeared on television a few years later, it had none of the power of the radio show. What flowed seamlessly on radio thanks to an imaginative mind and great sound effects seemed stilted and contrived on television.

Adults had a way of speaking that convinced me that what they said was true. I overheard someone say that when a person died, their feet turned black. That strange statement came to mind the day that I swallowed gum. Aunt Nellie had warned me not to chew gum and worse, not to swallow it. As the gum slid down my throat, I felt doomed. No one was with me and darkness was creeping through the windows. I did not know how to reverse what was about to happen. First, I took off my shoes and socks to check my feet; they were still flesh color. But wait, it probably took time so I sat and waited hoping that they would not turn black. If they did, of course, I would be dead. Time ticked by so slowly, a minute, then five and more. Nothing had happened. In fact I felt all right. Carefully, oh so carefully, I put my socks and shoes back on. Later I thought, "Adults don't always know what they are talking about. I will have to try to figure out when they are telling the truth and when they make things up," a task that I had not the slightest idea how to do. Life was confusing enough for a seven year old; why couldn't adults get it right?

My older sisters, Joan and Geri often had disagreements. Geri told me that once they were fighting over who could hold me—I was just a baby. Back and forth they passed me from one to the other. Aunt Nellie yelled for them to stop. They did at the exact, same moment and I fell to the floor. So much for sisterly love! Years later they were having a fight: was it the time Joan wanted more pancakes and Geri said that she was finished cooking and would not make any more? No, that time Joan tried to make the pancakes and when she ate them, she started to choke. She ran out of the apartment, across the hall to our neighbor, Mrs. O'Neill. Thank goodness she was able to help Joan cough up the pancake. Yet another time Joan and Geri were fighting and pushing each other around the living room. The next thing I knew one was pushed against the upright piano against the wall. One of the legs of the piano was dislodged and the poor piano needed repair. Once again Aunt Nellie yelled for them to stop. I was watching and was terrified that they would both be hurt. Somehow they stopped screaming and fighting and life returned to normal.

I always loved radio programs. My older sisters controlled the dial. They would tune into afternoon Yankee games and at night shows featuring songs of the 1940's. I loved *The Shadow* "Who knows what evil lurks in the hearts of men? The Shadow knows." It was scary, but my sisters were there so I felt safe. The great part of radio was being able to imagine what was happening; the sound effects helped immensely. I had a hard time with baseball because I could not picture what was happening, probably because I had not yet learned the rules of the game. When I looked at the headlines of *The Daily News* to see who won, they used exotic words like "trounced" that only confused me. Why couldn't they just say won or lost and keep it simple? I had to see the score to learn who had won.

As an adult I became a fan of National Public Radio. Radio never lost its charm. My tastes changed as I listened to other programs. Along the way I discovered Garrison Keillor's "Prairie Home Companion" broadcast every Saturday night since 1974, featuring the news from an imaginary town, Lake Woebegone, "where all the women are strong, the men are good looking and all the children are above-average." Garrison Keillor is an artist with words: his mastery of the written and spoken word is legendary. For over thirty years he created new versions based on a familiar framework. Live and listening audiences wait expectantly for what is new within the well known sketches. In addition he had a terrific sound effects man who could reproduce almost any sound. The Shoe Box Band along with local soloists provided rhythmic settings for songs whose lyrics Garrison Keillor adapted for the different cities where they performed live. This is an example of what radio does best: provide a communal setting that combines familiarity and novelty in just the right doses to keep listeners/fans hoping for more.

One afternoon when I was eight, I could not open the door to the apartment. Someone was home; I could hear voices. I called out, "Let me in. Please, let me in," but they ignored my pleas. My imagination went crazy. Was someone sick? Was there an accident and they did not want me to see? I ran upstairs to the roof where I could look down into the living room. Someone was arranging what looked like furniture. That was better than all the things I had imagined. Finally after what seemed like an eternity, they let me in. There in our living room was a brand new television. I had seen television in my Aunt Dorothy's and Uncle Bill's apartment. They were the first in our family to afford such a luxury. I wonder now how my mother could afford what was so expensive. Was it a gift? Did someone give my mother money toward its purchase? At the time I was just excited to see what was on. I soon learned the theme for the Howdy Doody Show and would sing along. I liked Princess SummerFallWinterSpring because her name was such fun to say. Evening shows had more variety: the Ed Sullivan Show on Sunday nights that featured all kinds of acts from animal acrobatics to singers hoping to break into the business; comedians Milton Berle, Jack Benny, Bob Hope, Red Skelton, Groucho Marx, Lucille Ball and Desie Arnaz; the Vaughn Monroe Show, Victor Borge Show, What's My Line? TV was fun, but it could never compare to radio.

Chapter 2

MARRIAGE CHANGED EVERYTHING

I overheard my mother and god father discussing their marriage plans in the kitchen of the old country house in Neversink as I played with my doll in the next room. It seemed strange to hear Joe Brady say, "Don't worry. She will learn so much living in the country." How could life in the country ace life in the Bronx?

The door opened. Oh good, finally we would get to eat. No, more conversation this time including me. "Judy, Uncle Joe and I are going to be married." My mother assured me that life in the country would be fun. I had heard enough to know that they were deeply into planning their/our new life. I had only known a single parent, my mother since shortly after I was born. Joe Brady was my godfather and had visited us on occasion in the Bronx, but that was *my* home. I responded, "Certainly." I had practiced what I would say knowing that sooner or later I would be brought into their conversation. Parents made decisions and children had to agree; this was the time when children were "seen and not heard." The part I had not really thought about was that their marriage would effectively end my family's life in the Bronx with my mother, Great Aunt Nellie, and my two sisters as well as easy access to Nana and other relatives for we would have to move upstate to the Catskills.

When I was six and my sisters, Joan and Geri sixteen and fourteen years old, we had visited the Brady family in Neversink, NY. In the summer there was swimming in the Neversink River where I could see groups of tiny fish moving quickly below the surface. Too bad I wasn't a large fish looking for a snack. In fact I needed to hold onto an inner tube lest I drown. I was jealous of their swimming ability. Occasionally we went berry picking. It was hot and muggy. Insects swarmed around our faces. The ground was uneven and overgrown with weeds so getting fresh berries was not so much fun. I preferred buying them in a store or at a roadside stand. One evening we took a car ride to buy ice cream. That was a mixed bag: trying to eat ice cream as it melted onto my hands and dripped onto my shorts. I was a slow eater so I felt the pressure to lick fast. Inevitably I ended up with sticky fingers and lips covered with the remnants of vanilla ice cream. Riding home in the back seat of the car made me nauseous. Honestly I would have preferred eating at home where the floor was stable and there would not be trees and fields whirling by.

Some nights, though, Joan and Geri went out with Tom and Joseph Brady who were the same ages as my sisters. I was left home with their sister, Clare Anne, three years younger than I. While they were out having fun, I had to go to bed while the sun was shining. Who went to bed so early? In the city that never happened, but here I was being treated like a baby. It was demeaning, a punishment, but there was no recourse. I had to bear it for the week. I wanted to say that I was homesick, but honestly I didn't know if that meant I was missing my home (what I wanted to say) or sick of home. Better to keep this to myself. Words could be so confusing.

Ten years after my father, George Willemse died and two years after Joe Brady's wife, Thelma died, Margaret and Joe would remarry and we would form a new family. The downside for me was not having my Aunt Nellie or older sisters to shield me. No, I would be on my own, the only child for the first year and then the older of two when my stepsister would join us the following year.

My introduction to country life began the day after they were married. We drove upstate to meet the movers. It was a long car ride during which my stepfather had severe cramps in his hands. I got scared: if he couldn't drive how would we get there? We stopped briefly so he could rest. Hours later we pulled into the driveway and behold, there was our house set back from massive maple trees with a mirror-image house next door. There was space, so much space: a huge field across from us where many sports teams could play. The house was an improvement over our crowded apartment in the Bronx: a large kitchen which opened onto a cozy living room, my parents' bedroom to the left and finally my/our bedroom off the foyer close to the bathroom. There were two entrances—one from the front porch through the smaller bedroom and another into the kitchen. It was September with abundant sunlight and the warmth of an autumnal afternoon. I was assigned to swat the large, lazy flies that were all over. Flies were way easier to kill than the ubiquitous roaches that had inhabited our apartment in the Bronx. Maybe this place would be better after all.

The house was a glorified bungalow on cinder blocks with a massive kerosene heater in the living room. The former owner had been a barber which explained the small building out back behind the house. It had a barber chair in front of a huge mirror and a counter for his tools; on the other side wooden shelves from floor to ceiling. Those shelves would prove useful over the years for storing items that did not fit into the house. Actually my stepfather called it the Climax, for it was where we stored the extras, those things not needed in the house, and not yet exiled to the attic. Initially the extra set of good dishes, each piece wrapped in newspaper inside a large egg carton and various odds 'n ends were stored in the Climax. It would also be a safe place when we got cats for them to give birth to kittens. The first time the new mother chose the egg crate with the good dishes each individually wrapped. That upset my mother big time. After that I lined a clean cardboard box with paper, then shred more newspaper, and placed the box on a shelf low enough for her to jump up and high enough to discourage unwanted visitors.

It was more than a week before I attended my new school. We visited it and met some of the nuns. Something strange happened when my mother met my teacher. It was one of those times when a look, an expression, and comments whispered so I would not hear clued me in that they knew more than they wanted me to know. It was many months later that I learned that my mother knew my teacher, really knew her from years ago. The big secret was that my mother had been a nun in the Dominican Sisters of Blauvelt. That sounds contradictory for sisters do not marry nor have children. But here I was, living proof that my mother may have been a sister, but she had left the convent and married. That was a huge revelation. It also made sense of a picture I had found in the top drawer of my mother's bureau of a young woman wearing a full length white habit and veil with a crown of thorns on her head. Now that was something! No name or date on the back so I had to piece together tidbits of information to make sense of it. But wait, we had just arrived upstate so let's resume that story.

I did not understand why I could not start school. It was all part of another earth shattering development: my name. One day we drove seven miles west on Rte. 52 to Jeffersonville, NY where my parents filed the papers for an official change in my last name. They had determined that it would be better if I had my stepfather's last name; it would stop people from whispering behind my back or questioning, "Who is her father?" So while I waited outside in the rear seat of the olive green Pontiac, my identity as a child of George Willemse was dissolved; I would now be considered a Brady. At first I thought that was no big deal, but over the years it made me feel as if I lost something special, one of the few connections to my father George: his surname. I felt like an imposter posing as a member of the Brady clan. They said it would be better for me, prevent problems. It was obvious to me that I had no real choice in the matter. Could I have stood up and cried, "Do not change my name." That was highly unlikely. Don't forget, my mother had already changed her name and was now Mrs. Brady so I had better follow suit. I remember the next time we received report cards. We sat at attention while the principal called each of us and gave us our report card. From first to fifth grades I could relax; it took some time to reach the end of the alphabet and besides, they stumbled over my last name. But now there was no daydreaming; I repeated my new name over and over to myself so I would react. Before I knew it, Brady was called and after that I could relax again. Is this how spies felt when they were strangers in a foreign land?

September 30 was my first day attending school at St. Peter's in Liberty. No walking to school as in the city. Instead I boarded a yellow school bus up on Rte. 52 across from the post office/general store. Five miles and many stops later to pick up other students we arrived in Liberty. For the return trip an hour after school was dismissed we had to get the bus in a large lot close to the public school. My memories of the commute center around the weather: wearing long pants under my uniform skirt during the cold months and still feeling cold. Sometimes I sat on the sunny side of the bus as it meandered toward White Sulphur Springs. There were puffy clouds through which the sun dramatically shone. It reminded me of pictures I had seen in religion books, and to be honest inspired me to admire God in all the wondrous beauty of creation. Those were brief but powerful moments.

St. Peter's in Liberty was a remarkably compact school: eight grades in four classrooms. Each classroom housed two grades. So there I was on one side of the room with my fellow sixth graders and on the other side were the fifth graders. It was a lesson in selective listening, knowing when to tune in and pay attention as opposed to ignoring what was not our lesson or concern. Years later when I taught a self-contained class I realized how extraordinary that was. As a teacher I found it difficult to prepare all the subjects: developing a teaching plan, inventing strategies, and anticipating questions that students might raise. How on earth did the Dominican sisters plan and teach two years in the same room? To this day I find this an amazing feat.

We had a fair amount of work especially for social studies and geography. There was a long list of questions covering the entire semester for which we wrote answers so we read and deciphered a great amount of material. The *Warps Review Book* in geography was a compendium of knowledge, but I found it the most boring of all books. It would be years before I recovered from being stuffed with facts like a turkey bound for the oven. As an adult I regained an interest in geography when I had the opportunity to travel to Spain, to Europe, to Mexico, and Central America. Geography needed the human touch—how lives were affected by their birthplace and how countries were limited or enhanced by the bounty of their terrain. Before and during trips abroad I read travel guides and learned about the culture of the places I visited. Lived experience trumped being stuffed with facts.

The teacher was paramount to the learning process. Over three years I had three Sisters with distinctly different personalities. Sixth grade we had a Cracker Jack teacher who excelled in teaching English grammar. We learned and loved diagramming sentences. That skill has stood me in good stead all these many years later. Seventh grade we had a teacher who inspired me to learn and more importantly, related to us as persons in our own right. She was also the principal so our parents got to know her. I was devastated when she was changed, a common practice when the principal was reassigned every six years. Our eight grade teacher was formal and cold. Yes, we learned what she taught and did well, but the joy of learning diminished like a tree withering in a drought.

There was no lunchroom so we ate lunch in the classroom. In good weather we went outside to play; there was even a field where we played baseball in the spring. One day a classmate asked me, "Would you like to go downtown at lunch time?" I said "yes' but was baffled because my idea of downtown was going from the Bronx to Manhattan via subway and I would not have ventured that far without my older sisters. Downtown Liberty meant walking a few blocks—a really tame outing. Another day an adult came to the classroom to tell us about the Catholic Youth Organization (CYO) that sponsored athletic events for young people. "Who wants to sign up for the fowl shooting contest in Callicoon?" I cringed as most of the students raised their hands and practically jumped out of their seats. "What kind of strange place is this?" I thought. "Do they really have guns? Why do they want to kill birds?" They would have laughed me out of town if they had known what I was thinking. We did go to Callicoon where there were competitions and yes, a foul shooting contest using basketballs.

At home there were many happy moments—when Joe and my mother would fool around. They were like newly-weds with their lives ahead of them. He loved puns and I soon became an avid punster. Once that skill is acquired, it is difficult to turn off. I find it a fun way to use words and a clever way to speak. For some people though, it can be annoying.

My stepfather's way to relax when he came home from work was to sit in his chair in the living room and read the newspaper while my mother got dinner and I set the table. Joe Brady loved to watch the evening news on television and often we would be seated at the kitchen table eating supper. That was a new experience for me: this table was really a dining room table in the middle of our large kitchen. Formal dinner, formal news on WCBS. We talked during commercials and when the news broadcast was over. That was the beginning of my needing to know what was happening in the world. What started out as strange would eventually grow on me and ultimately lead to my becoming a news junkie.

My stepfather insisted on formal dinner with serving bowls and platters, something that I found strange because we had eaten more informally in our apartment. That first year I had no idea how to serve myself because in the Bronx Aunt Nellie or my mother had dished out my food. In the country my mother was often at the stove attending to last minute details so I imitated what my stepfather did. He was a civil engineer and working hard; I definitely did not need such large portions. Before long I had gained so much weight that my parents had a doctor test me for worms. That was not the case, thank God. It resolved itself when summer came and I learned to ride a bicycle. I was also growing so I returned to my svelte self.

Another ritual was saying good night. This involved going over to my stepfather seated in his wing back chair, leaning down, and kissing him good night. He was a heavy smoker and I instinctively wiped my lips to remove the taste of tobacco. He made a comment to my mother so after that I had to pretend that all was well. Basically it was a case of cease and desist. I was smart enough to know that Joe Brady was the boss so I had better conform to his ideas. He could be funny and a good conversationalist, but I learned quickly that crossing him or even questioning him never went well.

My stepsister joined our family the summer before I began seventh grade. Her mother, Thelma, had died when Clare Anne was five. I remember her mother as a warm, loving woman. When I visited them one summer, I was playing with a kitten that ungraciously threw up all over me. I was in the Bradys' bedroom searching for powder to hide the stain. Thelma came in and asked what I was doing. I was so scared that she would yell. But no, she kindly showed me how to minimize the stain. I was so relieved. She became one of my favorite adults that day.

In July 1954 our parents sent Clare Anne and me to Camp Broadlea in Goshen, NY. A flurry of activity getting all the clothing we needed and sewing on nametapes. We slept in dormitories so it resembled the boarding school that operated there ten months of the year. We were in different age groups so we seldom saw each other.

Four weeks away from home had its fun times: learning new activities like archery, canteen time after supper when we got mail and could buy candy; playing jacks or pickup sticks on the floor of the cabin during free time when rain prevented us from playing outdoors. I missed home so much that I spent part of each day writing to my parents. I did have one goal that summer: to learn how to swim. I managed to learn the arm and leg motions, but panic set in when I could not breathe in the water. At the end of the month our parents came to take us home. I had had swimming lessons but all I had to show them was the dead man's float. Something tells me that I probably could have done that naturally if I had been thrown overboard. When we lived in the Bronx we seldom went to a pool or the ocean. I associate that with the fact that polio was raging; everyone knew someone who was paralyzed because of it. Adults hinted that swimming in pools was a way to contract the disease so in my mind it was better to stay out of the pool. By the time the polio vaccine was available, I had moved to White Sulphur Springs, another place where access to a place to swim was severely limited. As an adult I have tried many times to learn how to swim: in college taking swimming lessons in freezing February at the YMCA in downtown Rochester; vacation time at Saugerties where we could swim in the Hudson River, and later when we had a pool. Despite the best of intentions I never overcame my fear. To this day I am a landlocked person unable to swim.

A strange thing happened while I was away at camp. I spent so much time in the outdoor latrine with symptoms that resembled diarrhea. I was too embarrassed to tell anyone. Three weeks later when it happened at home and I could talk with my mother I learned that I had my first period. I was ill prepared. Some months before there had been much discussion when we visited my grandmother. Unknown to me my mother asked my grandmother to tell me about menstruation. So one day Nana said, "The Blessed Mother will give you a special gift in the near future." Whatever else she may have said after that never registered because I took her literally and was imagining the gift. The problem was that my idea of a gift was so different from hers. Never in a million years would I have considered what happened---my spending time in the latrine many times a day and putting wads of tissue paper in my panties so it would not come through on my clothes—a gift. I hated that I was sick and trying to deal with the symptoms. Sometimes it is better to speak plainly and not set a child up for disappointment. I could not wait to feel normal again. As I soon discovered there were other physical changes that I would experience. Some were welcome—developing breasts; others were confusing—the growth of body hair and pimples. All this was baffling. I wondered if these were changes or if I had just not noticed these things before. My body seemed to have a will of its own. How often I wished as a teenager for a book(s) that could explain all these things that were happening. There had to be others like me who wondered about changes. I did not have a close friend with whom to discuss these puzzling issues and often felt uncomfortable in my own skin.

When my stepsister, Clare Anne joined our family, I automatically became a big sister. I was in seventh grade; Clare Anne was in the third grade. She was cute but terribly annoying. She was probably a typical eight year old, but she had been the center of attention after her mother died and she went to live with her maternal aunt and uncle in Oswego. I had spent a year alone with my newly remarried mother and step father so I no doubt resented sharing the limelight. I soon discovered that it was easier to be the youngest, rather than the older sister.

Clare Anne was the apple of her father's eye. She had one serious defect. Every day we carried a lunch box with a thermos. Inevitably Clare Anne would manage to break her thermos once or twice a week. My mother was so exasperated that she put me in charge of seeing that Clare Anne would come home with her thermos intact. That did little to improve the situation. In fact, all it did was spread the blame. Then there were two children dreading the return of our parents. Too bad we didn't have stock in thermos companies; we could have been rich.

When my mother corrected Clare Anne for failing to do something, it frequently escalated from speaking to a screaming match. My mother's voice rose to a pitch that I seldom heard and it sent shivers down my spine. Inevitably my stepfather would intervene and he always took the part of Clare Anne. Perhaps he wanted peace and quiet; I surely did, but not at my mother's expense. In his eyes his daughter could do no wrong, but that made my mother the wicked step mother. There was even an occasion when I sided with my step sister. My mother's attention shifted and she began to correct me. To make her point she slapped me across the face. I was stunned. Why would my mother do that? I did not deserve such treatment. It was the first and only time that my mother hit me and I can still feel the sting. Perhaps she wanted her husband to know that she did not play favorites, that both of us had to be reprimanded to keep us in line. It would not stop me from intervening when I thought that something needed to be said.

When we arrived home from school, we'd have a snack and then retire to separate rooms to do homework. I set up a card table in my parents' bedroom; it was closer to the one and only kerosene heater in the living room. When Clare Anne arrived, she worked in our bedroom. Before long our parents would arrive home. If they were late, I immediately thought that they were in an accident. My heart raced. "What would I do if my mother died? Even worse what would happen if they both died?" There were many days that I mulled over those possibilities.

In the spring of 1954 Clare Anne got really sick with whooping cough. She was wracked by paroxysms of coughing. As she struggled to breathe wheezing sounds began. Every breath was difficult. We shared a bedroom with twin beds. She coughed almost constantly all night long. It was impossible to escape the whining sound and the wheezing. For once in my life, I did not catch this disease but the doctor said that I could have transmitted the disease if I went to school so I had to stay home with Clare Anne. As the days rolled by, I could not wait for her to get better so we could return to school.

My stepfather could be a vindictive man. After my mother returned home from a Christmas party at her job, he inferred that my mother was flirting with co-workers at the party. He wasn't even there, but he was so jealous that he accused her of that. The recriminations went well into the wee hours of the morning. Such nights when they would drink and talk were rather common. As my mother got quieter, Joe Brady would berate her. I was in the next room wide awake listening. He was so angry and combative that I felt for sure that my mother would leave him. I thought of the library books that I had to return to the public library in Liberty and how happy I would be to return to the Bronx. The next day came and nothing happened, nothing except a pall of silence thick as a

London fog. Neither spoke. I became the one trying to bridge the gap between two adults. Those were such painful nights and days. I was my mother's defender: I could not understand her taking such abuse and not standing up to him. He was formidable—charming, witty, and logical. For reasons I could not fathom, my mother stayed with him even when he verbally cut her to pieces. It warned me never to cross him and also told me that my mother's love for Joe Brady was far greater than her love for me or any of her children. I felt even more isolated in this house in the country far from friends and relatives in the city. Marriage may have joined them together, but it made me feel so alone.

It was at times like these that I prayed. "Jesus, please stop my stepfather from attacking my mother." My stepfather used words like weapons; I knew how hurtful they could be. I prayed the Rosary in an attempt to block out all that was being said in the kitchen just steps away from my bedroom. The repetition of Hail Mary's had a soothing effect. Other times I simply asked God to stop the terrible things being said to/about my mother. I prayed for her to be strong so she could stand up to him. That prayer was never answered, but at least I felt less alone. Over the weeks and years my experience of being a child in this new family made me question how happy any marriage could be. What if I married a man who turned out to be angry and caustic? If my mother was the example, then I would be in for a lifetime of sorrow. There had to be a better way.

Meanwhile I applied myself with renewed vigor to study. It had one good effect. In June the highest ranking student received a General Excellence medal. A beautiful girl in my class had been the undisputed champ for many a year. Then I came along, a city kid, an interloper who studied like crazy and received the medal in seventh grade and again, in eighth grade. Oh, happy day! I still remember the joy of receiving each medal and looking at it in its special box lined with satin. Those medals validated all those days and weeks of concentrated study. *Vale la pena.*

Chapter 3

I HAVE CALLED YOU FRIENDS

Friends are our companions, the persons with whom we share life. We connect with others in a world that is constantly changing. As youngsters we adapted as if we had a sixth sense about when to go downstairs and out to play in front of the apartment building or to meet up at the reservoir/park. Before cell phones, pagers, and electronic devices we managed to find playmates. A process of natural selection occurred when we got together with those who liked playing ball, jumping rope, or using the play areas in the park (seesaws, monkey bars, swings, and sliding ponds). We also had friends at school with whom we played at lunchtime when we could go outdoors or later we chatted while walking home from school together. Making friends was easy.

As a child I lived near a reservoir/park uphill and behind our apartment house, a favorite destination. We could wander through the bushes pretending we were in the wilds, play on the swings, and roller skate. Oh, how I loved to roller skate! The skates were worn over one's shoes and one always needed a skate key to tighten them. Since we lived on a hill with a wide sidewalk, I had learned to skate by heading downhill alternating holding/not holding onto the buildings. That way I could stop and not go flying out into traffic on Gun Hill Road. Skating on a flat surface in the park/reservoir was better, though smooth black top was the preferred surface. Sometimes we walked a few blocks to the newly paved play street in front of St. Brendan's School. Skating was mostly a communal sport so we had company. Of course there were sports- related injuries, primarily scraped knees, but these never hampered our desire to move quickly. It was such great fun.

When we moved upstate to a small village it was a challenge to find, let alone make friends. Distance was a major factor. I got to know the Hills brothers who lived in the house near Route 52, the main highway. Unlike the city boys I knew, they made potholders, a skill that I thought was reserved for girls. They were country kids who brought me cat fish that they caught in the brook; I laughed at the whiskers but our cats loved eating those fish. They dug clay from the brook—this fascinated me for I thought that clay only came in packages from Woolworth's. The one draw-back was that you had to work with that clay right away; when it dried out, it was as hard as a rock.

At St. Peter's School in Liberty I made friends with Maureen, also a sixth grader. She seemed different from the other girls in our class who had lived there all their lives. Perhaps she was a recent arrival like me? I remember going to her house in the town of Liberty to visit. We both liked to read and we shared stories. There was an openness about her so we could talk freely. This was my first country friendship and I was so happy. I couldn't wait to get together again, but then her family moved farther upstate rather suddenly and I lost my new best friend.

Joyce was a friend who lived nearby. We were classmates so we had that in common. The difficulty was that her father had remarried and she had to help her stepmother care for her younger siblings. Those duties kept her busy and we had fewer opportunities to get together.

My classmates moved on to Liberty High School, but my parents placed a premium on Catholic education. First they investigated the possibility of my attending St. Helena Girls High School in the Bronx. They considered my living with my grandmother, but she had a one bedroom apartment in Parkchester and her son, my Uncle Howard had the bedroom while Nana slept on the couch in the living room. There would be no privacy and no place to study. After much discussion my parents decided that I would attend the one and only Catholic High School for girls in Sullivan County. St. Joseph's was located in the rustic, remote town of Forestburgh, N.Y., a few miles outside Monticello. Our freshman class of twelve consisted of three day hops who lived nearby and nine boarders most of whom came from New York City. I had to board because at thirty miles from home this school was beyond the legal distance to be transported by school bus. Boarding at school would be a respite from home life that had gotten to be on the wild and wooly side.

Meanwhile back in the forest, I arrived with great trepidation. The first hurdle was meeting my roommate. Each of us had a roommate with whom we shared a room for the next ten months. As a result of all that time together talking about life, it was natural for our roommate to become friend for the year. My roommate in freshman year was Marie Connerty from Astoria, Queens. She seemed normal at first sight—dark brown, shoulder length hair, about my height, with a pretty face. The first night she wanted to keep the window opened wide to get all the good country air. "Marie," I said, "It gets really cool at night up here in the mountains." Marie was not convinced; in fact she made a point of showing me a knife with a 10" blade that she had brought with her. No doubt she would have no qualms using it. So we shivered through that first night. The next day she finally agreed to close the window. Once we got that out of the way it was much calmer until one day she discovered large, black ants. Teenagers with enormous appetites, we usually had food in our rooms. Apparently the ants were voracious eaters too. Marie went crazy. She insisted that we move all the furniture into the hall, then clean and spray everywhere ants might go. After we fumigated the room, it was a relatively peaceful year. Marie worked hard so her grades would improve. She must have been successful because Marie did not return to St. Joseph's the following September. I think she convinced her parents that she would follow their rules and they allowed her to live at home. As a sophomore I roomed with Mary Lee Hasselbach, a senior and a blonde beauty from Long Island who seemed to know more about make-up than the models for Cover Girl. We had interesting conversations; it was like having an amiable older sister. My last roommate was Lynn White from Dobbs Ferry. She was friendly, outgoing, and really interested in learning about the lives of the sisters. After high school she entered the convent in Amityville, NY, the motherhouse for the Dominican sisters.

A typical day in our mountain retreat included: Mass for those who wanted to go (I did), breakfast followed by assigned chores; classes all day with a break for lunch; after school sports or choir (Gregorian chant and hymns); study period; chapel where we prayed the Rosary; supper followed by study period and then free time before bed. Boarding school offered a variety of experiences. I finally got to take piano lessons. My sister, Joan had tried to teach me piano when I was around seven, but that did not go well. But now in high school I wanted to try again. My best time to practice was after breakfast, but there was a problem: I had to play a silent piano lest I disturb the sisters who were eating in their refectory across the hall. Imagine how strange it was never hearing what I was playing. How could I know if I were doing it right? It was like being Beethoven, only I was a teenager with none of his musical abilities. When class assignments increased in January, I stopped taking lessons.

Like most teenagers we were always hungry. Dinner began with soup. Over the course of the week the basic chicken soup added one new element each day: celery, carrots, barley. When they served hamburgers, I would run out and around to the front entrance of the convent, go to the basement and bring back a large, fresh onion. It tasted better because it involved a bit of intrigue.

On Fridays the chaplain would speak to us during religion class. With a larger world view, he would talk about workers' rights and world issues which at that time I found profoundly boring. At his instigation we became part of his project to plant new trees. Our biology teacher had us go out and plant the seedlings. We started with spades and planted a few only to learn that he had a thousand seedlings. We would still be there like fossilized Johnny Appleseed if we hadn't thought of a quick fix. I used the cross bar of a wooden hanger; pounded it into the soil and then twisted and squeezed the roots into the hole. It was probably only one step better than letting them dry up in the air, but it did do the job. The more we planted, the more there were. Besides this was Foresthurgh: we lived in a clearing surrounded by tall trees. Did it make any sense to plant baby trees when the forest seemed to be doing quite well, thank you?

The school frowned upon going home on weekends. They had a No Departure Rule because almost all the boarders were from New York City and could not go home; therefore everyone who boarded had to do the same. Even at thirteen, I knew that reasoning was flawed. The school would however permit me to leave if there were a medical necessity so my family and I devised a plan: once a month I needed to go home for a dental appointment. That way I was with my family before returning to our spartan living conditions Sunday afternoon. Weekends at school began with cleaning our rooms on Saturday, sports or long walks in the afternoon—the property included many acres and an array of buildings: a guest house up the hill and on a side road, a grotto with a statue of the Blessed Mother, like Lourdes; the school, chapel, convent, and post office clustered together as well as a large lake around which there were both a boys' and a girls' summer camp. When the lake froze over we could ice skate. There were competitions to see who could skate more quickly. Since this was a skill I never really mastered, I just wanted to stay upright and not fall, and I definitely thought speed a hazard to any sane person's health. Sleigh riding was different. We sledded down the hill outside the Cardinal's house where Cardinal Hayes had stayed and when monster snow storms came, on the paved road down from the guest house toward the small bridge. We did our level best to distract our Spanish teacher, Sr. Mary Owen when conditions warranted outdoor activities. Since it was last period, any distraction was fun, except when she screamed at me, "Stop twirling your hair!" The tone of her voice was so angry you would have thought that I had committed a felony, but no, all I did was run my fingers through my hair. It was a habit that really annoyed this teacher.

    Our first resident counselor showed us how to make wreaths using princess pine. It was fun walking across the frozen lake to pick the low lying pine, but when we were safely indoors bending a wire hanger to form the frame and then working with the pine branches soaked in water was much more difficult than I had bargained for. The good cause for which we raised money from the sale of our wreaths has faded from memory but I cannot forget how my chapped hands ached for days. There had to be a better way.

    One day a few of us were complaining about how rough the toilet tissue was. I suggested that we write to the company so they could correct this problem. When I got the address from the carton in which the rolls were stored we were off and running. Even if those in charge had ordered this product to save money, surely the company would change its ways. I helped write the letter and came up with how to sign off: Your Sincere Wipers. We never got an answer—I am not sure that we put our return address—and we were not called out for our funny/serious prank, but we enjoyed our first foray into the world of advocacy.

The sister in charge of the boarders was our surrogate mother; she had a room on our floor and kept a watchful eye over us. She was a friendly adult presence in our lives. Sr. Mary Victor stands out for her warmth and understanding. She hailed from Brooklyn and that fact proved very helpful. In senior year I wanted to take the scholarship exam for St. John's University in Queens. Sr. Mary Victor's parents offered me a place to stay overnight in Brooklyn. The plan was for her father to drive me to the campus the day of the test. When I arrived from Sullivan County by way of bus and train, there were two distractions that night: their pet bird that flew all over the apartment and landed on their shoulders to take seeds that the mother held between her teeth; from where I was sitting, it looked like a vulture that swished around at will. Late that night the father was taken sick with a bleeding ulcer, an ambulance came, and by morning I had to get to St. John's by myself. I got on the bus, spotted teenagers who looked as if they might be going my way, and followed them onto the campus. That worked fine, but returning to their house was tricky. I had timed how long the bus took on my way to the university; so I got off the bus after the exact same time. I managed to find their street but the houses were all attached and looked alike. Without their address I was close to panic in a borough about which I knew nothing when a neighbor called to me and directed me to their house. Somehow I got back to Port Authority to take the Short Line bus home. I was totally relieved to be back at St. Joseph's on familiar turf.

During the summers I was home in White Sulphur Springs, a small village on Route 52 outside Liberty on the way to Callicoon. With both parents working in Liberty, a town five miles east, I cleaned house, tried to tame the bucking-horse washing machine, pinned the wet clothes outside on the clothes line, ironed (my mother liked ironed sheets), and helped prepare supper. By day I also listened to music on the radio, read *Newsweek* and many library books (historical fiction and love stories were my favorites), wrote letters, and sometimes baked cookies and tomato soup cake for my sister, Joan in the convent. Country living could be dangerous. My first solo attempt lighting the gas oven resulted in a minor explosion. It caught me off guard as I jumped up and away, with newly singed eyebrows. Undaunted I planned to bake Snickerdoodles, I placed the margarine perpendicular to the cardboard measure as if it were a bar graph. After 15-20 minutes I checked the oven; no, they were not done. In fact, even after 45 minutes they were bubbling away and looked nothing like the picture in the cookbook. Sensing something wrong, I needed to know if they tasted better than they looked. Our gray tiger cat would eat sweets even climbing the back of my leg to get melon rinds. "Here, Dusty. I have something special for you." Dusty dashed over, sniffed, and then retreated. Even the cat would not eat them. Those cookies were a greasy mess fit only for disposal, but by default I did learn how to measure shortening properly.

I wanted a bike. At Christmas I received a toy cash register which only opened after ten dollars in quarters were deposited. Every time a quarter went in it chimed like a real cash register. Over the next six months I saved $17 (some larger currencies had been inserted). That summer my stepfather added to my down payment and bought me a new blue bike, a 26" Schwinn. I was miffed because he also bought Clare Anne a bicycle without any contribution from her. It made me question being so disciplined even as I began to understand that, "Blood is thicker than water."

The bicycle would become my most precious possession, but first I had to learn to ride. It was a challenge but I got the hang of balancing with some help as I practiced on the flat dirt road in front of our house. Proud as could be I went over to the Hills, Kate and Phil, who were rocking in their favorite chairs on the wide expanse of their porch observing who came and went from the post office/general store. We had a nice chat and they admired my new bike. When I turned to leave, I had to ride downhill over grass. As the bike gained momentum it dawned on me, "I don't know how to stop." My steering skill was not well developed either. Within seconds I rode straight into a huge maple tree. Humiliated and in pain, I felt as if I had cut myself in half in seriously private parts. That night I could barely sleep; my legs felt as if they were going round and round in perpetual motion. By the next day I was up and at it again. Before long my blue bike was like a sleek car that I drove with graceful skill to the post office for mail, to the chicken farm to get eggs, and along country roads where traffic was almost nil. Not far from the house, I discovered the perfect place if I ever decided to run away. The bushes would hide me and my bike and I thought that I could stay there and no one would know where I was. It was my secret place if and when I needed it.

Summer evenings were special. After supper Clare Anne and I would play Parcheesi on our front porch with the boys who lived next door. As day turned into night we were a grand feast for mosquitoes. The boys were immature and laughed at weird things like the time they made fun of an old couple in a nearby house whose silhouettes were visible on the window shade as they undressed. The games came to an abrupt halt when Clare Anne had a disagreement with the boys. Ever after my stepfather would not allow us to play with those boys again. It was no great loss.

In the heat of summer when Clare Anne was upstate, I would often ride my bike after supper when it was cooler. My favorite destination took me a short way west on Route 52, left at the gas station and up the side road. Usually I walked the bike the last bit to the top of the hill where I caught my breath and looked out over the countryside. The sun's rays would soon recede and darkness would claim the fields, but in those moments the balance of light and dark was exquisitely beautiful. I loved the trip downhill— with the wind whizzing through my hair as the fields and houses flew by in rapid fire succession. At that moment I could not imagine anything more thrilling than riding downhill on my bike.

Life in the country was both lonely and lovely; the latter because nature was hauntingly beautiful in summertime when the countryside was lush and green and crickets performed a musical concert every evening. At night there were birds swooping down from the giant maple trees on our front lawn. Only later did I learn that they were bats scooping up mosquitoes. Had I known they were bats, I would have panicked. I tried my hand at gardening: digging and loosening the soil, placing the seeds, then watering and waiting. To my surprise lettuce was a group of leaves, not at all like the head of lettuce that we bought at the supermarket. Radishes and carrots were fun, but it was hard to judge when to pick them since they grew underground. Morning glories bloomed by day. I felt so sad when the flowers closed and was so surprised when they opened as the sun's rays reached them again. I had a lot to learn about nature.

What I really enjoyed was observing and playing with our cats. Their coats gleamed in the sun as they moved stealthily through the grass. Beautiful to behold they were even more fun to pet. My stepfather ruled that we could only have a cat if it went out at night. By day the cat hunted for birds and came home for rest and food. One cat came four days in a row with her "kill" of the night: a bird. I tried to tell her that it was wrong, but some instincts are hard-wired. One afternoon I saw birds swooping down upon her in our front yard. Apparently birds could retaliate when their families were in danger. By night our cats had howling trysts with willing suitors. Litters of kittens were born on a regular basis. Disposing of them presented problems. My stepfather disposed of one litter and I watched the grieving mother searching in vain for her kittens. When the next litter was born, he took me along as he drove down the country road into the woods near the place where we dumped garbage. The kittens were in a cardboard box, squealing for their mother. He attached the box to the car's exhaust pipe and let the car's engine idle. Before long there was silence. It was an efficient and brutal way to dispose of the kittens. Why didn't we try to get the kittens adopted or even better, neuter the females? This was a tragedy that no child should have witnessed. Another time he sent me out with the kittens in a brown paper bag to the nearby brook. I had no idea how to avoid what I was told to do. I had no desire to do this, but I was more afraid of what my stepfather would do if I returned with the kittens. It probably would have cost the mother cat her life. Even though their eyes were not yet open, the kittens escaped from the bag and struggled to swim in a desperate attempt to live. Before long they were carried away by the swift current never to be with or ever get to see their mother again.

Some summers my stepsister, Clare Anne was around except for the times we drove to Cortland, the half way point to meet her Aunt Clare and Uncle George with whom she stayed for the summer. Later Clare Anne also went to Catholic high school in Oswego. Our parents worked so we were left to our own devices. We followed the brook upstream one day and felt like explorers. Berry picking was a rewarding activity. Blueberries were best; the bushes were my height and the berries within reach. Raspberries grew by the roadside on the way to the chicken farm. I loved the taste but it was a challenge to pick the succulent berries for they were protected by thorns. In late August we could pick blackberries that grew just over the barbed wire fence behind our house. Once again thorns made picking difficult, but I discovered that overcoming adversity made the berries even sweeter. Isn't this true of so many things in life?

The summer that I turned seventeen, my stepfather taught me how to drive. On the date I had requested for my driver's test, he drove me to Monticello. I was so nervous. As I was beginning the written exam, the examiner told me, "Stop. You reported on the wrong date. Your appointment is one week from today." My stepfather intervened; he had taken off from work; could he not let me be tested? The examiner walked away from us. There would be no test that day. I dreaded getting into the car for the trip home. But then something surprising happened. As I tried to apologize for mixing up the date, my stepfather was so angry at the examiner that he fumed all the way home about the man's stubbornness and stupidity. He ignored the fact that I had caused the mix-up, not the examiner. After dropping me home he went to work. A week later we returned to Monticello. By then I was calm and had no problem with the written and road tests. When I got my driver's license that August, I felt so proud. Joe Brady had purposely not taught me how to change a tire. As he said, "You are a woman. Someone will always stop and help you." His optimism was put to the test on my first ever solo drive to Forestburgh. I was so happy to be driving but then I heard a thumping sound. Sure enough when I pulled over to check, the car had a flat tire. There I was on Rte. 42 surrounded by trees, with no car in sight. There was a house up the hill from the road. I went there, knocked on the door, and explained my predicament to the woman who answered. She said, "My husband will be home for lunch soon and he will help you." It worked out as she said, but I realized that help does not always come as quickly as we like and it would be better if I learned more than how to drive along winding country roads.

I loved senior year of high school. For once I got mail from all over the state: colleges responding to my letters requesting catalogs. There were applications to complete and entrance exams to take. The day of the SAT we went to Monticello High School. Somehow I forgot my glasses; after six hours bending over to read the questions, I was bleary eyed. As a senior I remembered how Sr. Francis Jerome, my teacher, had told me in freshman year about a recent graduate who was attending Nazareth College. We relied on brochures to learn about the colleges. There was no thought of visiting those distant places. When I received acceptance letters, Nazareth offered me a partial scholarship with the possibility of also working on campus. That fact made my decision easy.

September 1959 my parents drove me to Nazareth College in Rochester. It was a long ride passing through towns with strange names; I remember trying to sound out Ska-ne-a-te-les. (It would not be long before I spent a weekend with Ellen Kuhl and went Trick or Treating in her hometown, but that day Skaneateles was an unknown commodity and very difficult to pronounce.) At Nazareth I met girls from Geneva, Rome, Syracuse, Greece, Jamestown, Utica, et al—all these faraway places. I was delighted to be among world travelers. Only later did I discover that these were cities in New York State. Founded by the Sisters of St. Joseph of Rochester in 1924, Nazareth was a Catholic liberal arts college for women. At that time almost all our teachers were sisters. My first year I lived at St. Joseph's, a small house located near the edge of the campus reserved for freshmen. It was there that I met my roommate, Mary Hanlon who hailed from Weedsport, a town near Syracuse. As the oldest of three sisters, she was a natural big sister. I often asked her, "Mary, how does this outfit look?" After all the years of wearing school uniforms I had very little fashion sense. In those days the college had rules mandating attire for class, formal dinner in the dining room, and chapel. At the Investiture ceremony in early fall we received our black cap and gown which we wore for assemblies each Thursday and every Sunday when we walked through the tunnel across the campus to the Sisters' motherhouse chapel for Mass. At mixers on the weekends we met boys from St. John Fischer and other area colleges. Many of the girls were actively pursuing an MRS even as they worked on a BA or BS degree. This was really evident when we gathered in the kitchen and heard the girls' discussing their dates and also when they made or received phone calls on the hall pay phone. We could have written soap operas based on those conversations.

Making friends was easy. We spent many hours working in the campus kitchen and dining room and afterwards we ate together. We worked hard, but had many laughs and really enjoyed each other's company. Friday nights we often gathered in Sully's room for an impromptu soirée where we listened to records both classical and popular (Johnny Matthis was a favorite), read poetry, caught up on gossip, and relaxed. Those were fun times. We would go off campus to a college hangout where we could get a pizza and beer/soda. It was in their company that I experimented with various drinks, but had no desire to drink heavily after having seen at home how alcohol can lead to saying hurtful things that linger long after the pleasure of drinking.

We were not allowed to have cars on campus at Nazareth so public transportation was the order of the day. When Mary Sullivan told me, "We can get tickets for the Rochester Philharmonic at a reduced rate for students," I responded, "Count me in." Classical music a la radio was a family favorite, but a live performance would be a first for me and the thought of season tickets was almost too good to be true. Those evenings were the beginning of a lifelong affair with Philharmonic Orchestras that performed in Rochester, then New York City and beyond. Besides attending concerts, we worked as ushers for theater productions and got to see plays like "The Princess and the Pea" starring Sid Caesar and Imogene Coca. With a music department and Glee Club, Nazareth had a variety of cultural events. As much as I loved singing, I was scared to sing before an audience. Instead I joined the Schola so I could sing at Mass as part of a choir. It would be years before I felt enough at ease to sing with the Bronx Choral Society. Nazareth's glee club performed their Christmas concert after which I wondered aloud, "Those live Christmas trees will go to waste with the college closing for Christmas recess." A few of us took one of the trees back to St. Joseph's. Within minutes we decorated it with all sorts of impromptu ornaments made of paper, plastic, aluminum foil, and who knows what else. My housemates gathered around and we had a great time talking and relating to our very own Christmas tree. Our bubble burst when a typed message appeared on the college bulletin board the next day requesting that the tree be returned. Unknown to us the trees were destined for the motherhouse. So we undecorated our lovely tree and moved stealthily behind the dorms to return it to the auditorium. Our happiness was short lived, but I am sure the tree enjoyed its little detour before gracing the Sisters' chapel.

I remember attending a semi-formal dance at St. John Fischer College. I met Joe the Wednesday before the dance; we went out to our local hangout in Pittsford to get acquainted. We had quite a bit in common: he was a classics major and I was majoring in Latin. Getting ready was the most fun: Jean Wallen lent me a pale green dress, a girl on our dorm floor, a beaded bag, and Mary Hanlon a pair of low healed dress shoes. After the flourish of dressing and applying make-up, out came a camera to take pictures of me and my date before we left for the dance. With an extended curfew (2:00 AM) we had time to go downtown with my senior sister, Joyce, and her date to a hotel for drinks. It was a really wonderful evening.

My final semester at Nazareth I had a more challenging experience. One Saturday evening we were at a restaurant waiting to be served. It was one of those maddening super slow service situations. Part of me wanted to leave, but then I decided to stay, be served, and return late to campus. Perhaps we would not be that late. I did ask someone to leave a side door open so I would not be locked out. Sad to say, the Sister awaiting our return was well aware of this tactic and knew that we had not signed in. So there I was a month before final exams, caught red-handed breaking curfew. I was afraid that they would make an example of us. The next day we met with the Sister in charge of residents. The glow of the evening before had faded and now we, yes there were a few of us, would learn our punishment for breaking curfew. Would they suspend me? I hoped not, but honestly did not know. I was a first-time offender; that should count for something. I did not know if my being a member of the Sodality of Our Lady would help or just make my act more reprehensible. Would there be repercussions if the Dominicans learned that I had been in serious trouble? Would this jeopardize my entering the convent? After what seemed like an eternity, we learned that we would have a week of internal suspension. That meant signing in every hour on the hour at the dorm from 8:00 AM until 10:00 PM.

We also could not go off campus for a week. With a huge sigh of relief I realized that I had dodged the bullet. I would still be allowed to take final exams. Not many years later they discontinued the curfew; the college went co-ed and there were coed dorms. We were actors in a play whose script would soon be revised, with a story that would soon be outdated.

One evening in January, 1961 Pat Kulaga and I went for a walk on the Nazareth campus. Heading toward Old Country Road, we were leaning into the darkness as the wind howled and snow smudged our faces with frigid lace. I was struggling to tell her why I wanted to enter the convent. It seemed so real to me, and yet when I spoke of it to others it was hard to explain. Strange but true when I was away from home and among the best of friends, I felt called to a vocation as a Dominican sister. My cousin, Barbara and my sister, Joan had entered the convent when I was a girl. At age ten, I sat sewing nametapes on the cotton handkerchiefs Joan needed to bring with her on Entrance Day. I had thought, "Some day I want to do the same as Joan. I want to be a nun." It was not that easy. We learned that a vocation is a calling from God. I was too young to make that decision, and yet the thought lingered as I grew.

How does God make this known? I went to daily Mass, received Communion, and God was central to my life. I went to confession on a regular basis. At the end of confession the college chaplain, Rev. William Shannon, asked me, "Have you thought of religious life?" His words caught me off guard. "Yes, but I don't know if this is for me," I responded. There were no visions or fireworks, simply the deeply felt sense that God wanted me to follow him in a special way. I also spoke with Sr. Mary Lourdes, my theology professor and someone with whom I shared my inner life. I respected her and for me she was truly a wisdom figure who listened with an open heart. With her I raised my fear that, "I don't want to do this simply because my sister Joan did it. Wouldn't that alone be enough to say I should not do this?" She patiently listened to my objections, but as she said, "God works through those we know. This may be the way God showed you how you could do this too." I let it rest for a while. After all, a vocation did not have an expiration date. I prayed and let life take its normal course. When it became clear that entering the convent would be a good choice for me, I had to decide where and with whom I would spend my life. I spoke with Fr. Shannon when it felt that this decision was just too complicated. As he said, "You are choosing between two goods like choosing an apple or an orange. The Dominicans and the Sisters of St. Joseph are both good. There is no bad choice." Somehow that calmed me and I was able to see that I could not lose: either congregation would be good for me.

The summer after freshman year back in White Sulphur Springs my parents were relaxing over drinks one evening when my mother asked, "Judy, what do you hope to do with your life?" I had not planned on saying anything just yet, but here they were waiting for me to answer this all-important question. It seemed silly and downright dishonest to invent an answer so I said, "I want to enter the convent." They were not surprised. In fact they wanted to know if it would be Sparkill. After all my sister, Joan and my cousin, Barbara were both Dominican sisters of Sparkill. I knew this group of sisters from my earliest years as a student at St. Ann's in the Bronx. By now my mother was really warming to the topic and asked shrewdly and sweetly, "Why don't you wait until you graduate?" They both knew how I loved being at college. What they didn't know was how strongly I felt about offering myself to God in my youth much like relishing a plant with buds that will open and bloom. Not willing to concede, my mother said, "But Judy, won't you miss having your own home? You are such a homebody." She had me there; I did enjoy making our house a home and there was little hope of that happening in the convent. I told them honestly, "Nothing is final. I hope to decide when I return to Nazareth in the fall." End of discussion and on to supper. I was really hungry so that suited me fine.

At first I set November 15 as the date by which I would make my decision, but then realized that it was the feast of St. Albert the Great, a Dominican saint. I laughed thinking how that favored the Dominicans. Instead I chose December 8, the feast of the Immaculate Conception, patron of the United States as the date by which I would decide. Life continued apace with the normally hectic first semester of sophomore year: classes, work, schola, Mass, private prayer. Suddenly it was December. Near midnight on the evening of Dec. 7th I set pen to paper and wrote to Joan, "This is a day early but I know that you are eager to know my decision. I want to enter the Dominican Sisters of

Sparkill." When my letter reached Joan she went to Mother Kevin to share the good news with her insuring that I was the second postulant desiring entrance for the following fall. It meant nothing to me at the time, but in practice it meant I would be #2 in a group of 57 postulants; it determined where we sat in chapel and refectory, as well as where we slept in the dorm.

Not long after I left Nazareth to join the Dominican sisters in Sparkill, I concocted ways to communicate with my friends. It was a challenge initially because I was not allowed to receive or send mail from/to them directly lest they tempt me to leave the convent. We devised a plan to circumvent the novitiate rule. My friends maintained a running correspondence with my mother. My mother shared my letters with them and one would write back. So Mary Sullivan McCarthy, Mary Hanlon, Pat Kulaga, Ellen Kuhl, and Jean Klier remained my friends. I even managed to attend class reunions that were held every five years. In 1968 when I returned from our class' fifth year reunion, my sister friends in Middletown had placed a hand printed sign at the convent door, "Can anything good come from Nazareth?" (John 1:46). I laughed out loud. "You bet there is!" I said to the nuns when I went inside. For most of the college reunions I enjoyed staying with my friends, Pat Kulaga and Mary Sullivan McCarthy. We had time to share at a deeper level and to be joyously honest with each other about life and all that we were up to. At some point as our friends married and had children, I envied them; I even felt as if I had nothing to offer. Of course there were academic achievements and positions in schools, but celibacy made me feel so alone. At one point I could not wait to return for a reunion: I had defended my dissertation and earned a PhD and even had a book published the year of the 2008 reunion. But I was stopped in my tracks with severe back pain and sciatica that forced me to cancel at the last moment. Pride takes a fall!

Over the years a strange thing happened as I attended the Nazareth reunions. I found myself getting to know women other than my close friends; these women might have been my friends if I had been at Nazareth four years and not just two and had gotten to know them in the normal course of events. In truth I think that we had an exceptional class: we were certainly intelligent women of our time, but more importantly we had heart, that undeniable ability to coalesce as a group that cared about/for each other, our loved ones, and the wider world. We attended college in the early '60s and experienced upheavals when we went forth to work and live. But through it all we were comfortable in our own skin and knew that we had that most precious of all gifts, loving friendships.

June 2013, the fiftieth reunion of the Class of 1963, was exceptional: many more of our classmates came to celebrate our days of youthful exuberance as well as the years of our maturity. When we arrived on campus the years melted away and we were once again young women with the hopes and dreams of long ago. My roommate, Mary Hanlon Fegraus had come from California, Ellen Kuhl, SSJ arrived from Brazil where she has been a missionary for many years, and Jean Klier, also a sister, came from Michigan. There was the usual getting caught up on spouses, families, careers, and in some instances health issues. Many are now retired or in some cases, devoting time and energy to projects of choice, enjoying grandchildren, volunteering, reading and travel. I knew I was in a good place when dinner conversation turned to books that we were reading. The truth was that the liberal arts, a love of literature, art, and music, are still dear to our hearts. I have come to appreciate how the Nazareth experience was a time for meeting and making friends and how formative that was for my future relationships.

Chapter 4

HERE I AM, LORD

Dominic walked into our yard and acted as if he had come home. He was fun to watch—playful and friendly to all. It was a mystery whose dog he was. Had summer vacationers left him when they returned to the city and smaller quarters? And why would he choose us, a cat-centric family? Who could resist his big, brown eyes and loving temperament? He adopted us. All we had to do was choose a name and that was easy. Both his coloring, black and white like the Dominican habit, and when he came, just before I would leave home to enter the convent, led us to call him Dominic. Statues of St. Dominic show the saint standing holding the Scripture with a dog at his side carrying a lit torch. This refers to a dream that his mother, Blessed Jane of Aza, had before she gave birth to a son. When she prayed and consulted a priest about this strange dream, the priest told her that her son would be a preacher who would share the flame of truth with the world.

My sister, Joan and cousin, Barbara, both Dominican Sisters, had come for a visit before I left home. Although born in the same year and both graduates of Aquinas High School, Joan and Barbara were two distinct individuals. Joan was serious, a woman who relished learning, who must have been a delight to have as a student. She excelled in all subjects, but chose Chemistry as her major. In fact she was the first woman to be awarded a full scholarship in 1950 to study Chemistry at Fordham University. She pursued her dream for two years before she followed her calling to be a Dominican sister. Her scholarship had to wait until Joan was a professed sister in 1954 and by then she was teaching full time and studying part time. She accepted this as God's will and worked as hard at teaching as she did at her own course work. Barbara was a more joyous type. She too waited—working a year before entering the convent. Barbara's gift was to regale us with funny stories of all she had done during her two years in the novitiate. These stories kept us laughing. They seemed a perfect pair: Barbara outgoing and gregarious and Joan reserved and happy to yield the floor to Barbara. They visited us by day, but had to stay overnight at a local convent which in our case was an eight mile car ride to Livingston Manor where there was a convent large enough to offer them hospitality. My stepfather would pick them up after Mass in the morning and they would spend the day with us in White Sulphur Springs. Because it was summer they could visit until 7:00 pm when they had to be back at the convent. Even though they visited us in the country, they wore the long white Dominican habit and stiff black veil. It would be a number of years before they could wear secular clothes.

We spent many hours chatting over meals. Barbara entertained us with stories and Joan would share some of her exploits working at St. Thomas Aquinas College. Joan was assigned to the college the same year I went to Rochester to attend Nazareth College. She was part of the original cohort of sisters who would do tasks that a college professor of our time could not imagine doing. There were postulants assigned to work at the college, but the Sister professors would also clean or do anything that was necessary. These were the years when our postulants and professed sisters attended the college and there were no funds to hire lay people. My parents admired the work Joan did and my stepfather would have liked for her to speak more, but Barbara was center stage.

It was still quite hot in early September so we went outdoors to play with our dog and relax on the front porch. This would be our last chance to socialize for quite a while. Those who entered could not speak with professed sisters lest they exert undue influence over the younger sister. There was a concern that a charismatic, more mature sister could be such a strong influence on the younger sister that she would stay not because she had a vocation, but because she admired the older sister so much. Joan was quiet and far from exerting undue sway over me so that was not a problem, but for those in authority there was always the fear that my older, super intelligent sister cast a powerful shadow in which

I might enjoy basking. They would severely limit our interactions to ensure that I was entering on my own accord.

Friday, September 8, 1961 dawned sunny, warm and humid. An ordinary day, but not quite. This was the day I would leave my parents, friends, and home and begin a new life. Hopefully, a good and perhaps, a perfect life. In homes across New York other young women were doing much the same as I for this was Entrance Day for the Dominican Sisters of Sparkill. We left behind closets filled with used clothing and worn shoes, boxes with school books and mementos of school events. What we had achieved was of little concern; we were beginning anew with Sisters with whom we would share our lives. We arrived much like our dog, Dominic— full of joy and hoping to be adopted by a new family of religious women. God was calling each of us from families far and wide to become part of the community in the small village of Sparkill in Rockland County, NY.

The sisters and novices at the Motherhouse were awaiting our arrival. Fifty-seven young women were traveling from New York City, St. Louis, Missouri, and points north and east. Friday, September 8, the feast of the birth of Mary, "the day that the Lord has made" (Ps 118:24). We carried with us the hopes and dreams of families who loved us dearly and valued the choice that we had made. Entering the convent in 1961 was a challenging venture just as it had been for hundreds of women who preceded us. Some would call us brave; others would wish we had waited or chosen differently. Expectations were high as we walked into the novitiate, a relatively new building that housed the postulants and novices. It was a short walk from the Motherhouse and provided space for sleeping quarters, a chapel, rooms for classes on the religious life, a recreation room, storage space for our trunks and suitcases, and a laundry room. Entrance day I wore a floral print skirt and blouse that my sister, Joan had sewed for me. That in itself was a minor miracle for Joan had the domestic skills of a mouse. I had no idea that she could sew. When we arrived, we exchanged the clothing we wore for a simple black dress with white cuffs, a stiff white collar, and a short cape that fell gracefully over our shoulders and arms. The postulant dress covered us from neck to ankle. With black lisle stockings and low heeled oxford shoes, we looked like actors auditioning to play Maria in "The Sound of Music." The final touch was a soft black veil with a band of white above our forehead. Simple, strange, stark— a sign that we were leaving our secular life to embrace the life of a religious sister in the Order of Preachers, more commonly known as Dominican Sisters.

My friends from Nazareth College met us outside the novitiate: my roommate, Mary Hanlon; Pat Kulaga, Mary Sullivan, and Ellen Kuhl, the friends I made while studying, living, and working in the kitchen and serving in the dining room; and Alice Malinkowski, who lived in the New York area and wanted to share this special day. Leaving my friends was the hardest part; something I did not say aloud for my parents would have been hurt. They had raised me and sacrificed to send me to college; surely they ranked higher than anyone else in my affections. I loved my two years at Nazareth. It was a fun time and a place where I got to study with young women who equaled and surpassed my love of learning; with professors who challenged me to think, speak, and write better than I had ever done. College by its very nature is a temporary venture. Had not the Dean of Students, Sr. Josephine Louise told us at our class' first assembly in September 1959, "Look to your right and to your left. One of you will leave and not be here by the time you graduate." At the time, I thought her words were overly dramatic, but here I was leaving the best friends I ever made to become a religious Sister. A year ago my mother proposed, "Judy, why don't you wait until you finish college?" Those words had a certain wisdom, but I thought, "Why wait when I know what I want to do?" After fourteen years of Catholic education I wanted to put my faith into action, and with all my heart to give myself to God. We would become the brides of Christ, an image I found strange. How could so many women all be his bride? I welcomed the words of St. Paul, "I have given you in marriage to one husband, presenting you as a chaste virgin to Christ" (2 Cor 11:2). I wanted to give myself when I was young, beautiful, and full of promise to the God who made me. I felt like the first, fresh crop of vegetables: glowing with the freshness of spring and oh, so sweet to the taste.

We walked over the asphalt path from the novitiate to the Motherhouse. We were excited, but nervous. It was a moment of beauty captured in pictures: standing with my parents on the stumps of what had been gigantic willow trees. Behind us was a small lake with an island, home to a life-sized white statue of Mary holding the infant Jesus. Surrounded by friends and family we laughed and talked. One picture shows me with a copy of *Winnie the Pooh* tucked under my arm; it was in Latin, a nod to my then favorite language, a gift from one of my friends. When the bell tolled, we kissed our parents and friends good-bye and moved toward Sacred Heart Chapel. This chapel was the size of a church with columns supporting the tall ceiling, stained glass windows depicting scenes from the life of Jesus, and two larger windows on either side of the choir benches: one of Mary bestowing the Rosary on St. Dominic and directly opposite, Jesus seated surrounded by children; behind us up beyond the organ a stained glass window of Jesus revealing his Sacred Heart on fire with love for all. Ahead of us there was a gigantic mural of Jesus crucified with Mary, his mother, John the Apostle, and Mary Magdalene standing below the cross. After the second tolling of the bell, afternoon prayer, Vespers began. The sisters and novices chanted psalms from the Little Office of Mary. I had no idea what they were singing. They alternated sides chanting the Psalms in Latin. It sounded eerie, other-worldly. It was unlike Gregorian chant or antiphonal singing that I knew. I felt like a lost soul caught in a whirlwind of indecipherable sounds. My heart pounded. How could I not understand any of the words/phrases that they sang? After all I had studied Latin and sung with a choir for two years. The chanting was followed by recitation of the Rosary. I breathed deeply; finally prayer that was familiar. We answered each Our Father and Hail Mary in English.

After Vespers we walked through the enclosed cloister to the Motherhouse, across front hall and downstairs to our refectory. There were chairs on both sides of a long U shaped table. The first women to apply to be postulants were on either side of Sr. Mary Clare, the postulant mistress, at the head of the table, alternating sides and continuing down and around in the order of each sister's acceptance into the community. We stood in silence until a prayer of blessing was said. Ordinarily we observed silence and listened to readings while we ate, but this was a special occasion so we had "recreation." Sr. Mary Clare rang a bell to signal that we could speak: recreation was the order of the day for it was Entrance Day. It was also Friday and the smell of fish filled the air.

The room rang out with enthusiastic conversation as we met the women near us and shared our religious names. We had the same sense of wanting to be here and yet not knowing what to expect. They served food family style, in large bowls and on platters. Like a celebration at a restaurant, we shared pitchers of water. We had cloth napkins to minimize use of paper (that's why we brought a napkin holder with our new names!). At the meal's beginning we had to turn over the plates at our place and reverse the process at the end. Toward the end of the meal servers brought in dishpans half-filled with soapy water and a small dish mop. This brought a howl from a postulant from St. Louis seated across from me. She found many things strange, but for her the dishpans were the strangest. I was thinking that washing and drying dishes at our place would save time. For best use of the soapy water we soon learned to put silverware in the bottom, wash glasses, cups and saucers first, and scrape dishes well before washing. I would have preferred rinsing the dishes so they would be free of soap residue, but that was minor in the list of inconveniences. The sister who found everything so weird returned to her home in St. Louis after a few days. She had been great comic relief because she reacted so naturally, voicing her opinion that what we were doing was weird. In many ways she said what we may have thought but were careful not to say. It was evident from the start that every postulant had the power to say that she wanted to return home and the congregation had the right to ask any sister to leave when/if it was apparent that this young woman was ill suited for religious life.

That first evening we had some free time and could walk out by the lake. I remember speaking with our sisters from St. Louis. I marveled that they had traveled so far. I wondered if I would have done the same for they would seldom get to see their families. Our parents would be able to visit us once a month except during Advent and Lent, but the St. Louisans would not see their families until Reception Day in May. They would be with us when we had visiting days so they got to know our families. They were friendly and easy to get to know. I had not yet traveled west of Rochester, NY so they came from places I did not know. They used expressions that were different from our New York English, e.g., pop instead of soda. Over the next few months and years as we got to know them individually, there was no doubt that they were a wonderful addition to our congregation. They had some faults like rooting for the St. Louis Cardinals when most of us were New York Yankee fans, but then we can't all be perfect.

There were so many details to learn: lining up two-by-two so we could enter chapel as a group, walk down the center aisle stopping to genuflect all at the same time, and going to our assigned seats. This system also helped us to take count before we left the Motherhouse after Compline (Night Prayer) to return to the novitiate. The women who had applied for admission last were in the front; those who applied first were toward the back. Our senior postulant, Sr. Regina Edward was the official counter; as #2 I would then recount. I learned how hard it is to count 56 women all dressed in black; getting an accurate count was not one of my strengths. Someone could have been detained so if our counts differed we would count again. All this was to ensure that no one would be left behind to walk the path alone in the dark. It meant standing patiently for everyone to return from their charges with the boys or other places like the kitchen. As the days advanced I would read sections from a miniature New Testament; I hated standing there in silence with nothing to do.

Ground floor of the novitiate there were storage rooms for our trunks, a laundry room with bins for each of the novices and postulants, a large room with wooden chairs where we would have recreation each evening for an hour. That first evening the novices, forty in number, greeted us with songs and much talk. The novices who had entered a year before us had received the habit in May 1961 and to us newcomers they appeared as confident, capable veterans of religious life. We met our mothers, a novice who took one or two of us under her wing. We would get to know her and we could ask questions about matters that puzzled us. Sr. Agnes Joseph was my novice mother; she was a genuinely good person, someone that I grew to admire. She was tall and carried herself like a queen. She could be serious but also had a great sense of humor. In my eyes she was a perfect novice who modeled what I hoped to be. My twin was Sr. Francis Christine from St. Louis, a vivacious, funny young woman. My fondest memory of her was after we were professed when she introduced us to the Beatles. She played the record in Little Side, the boys' refectory when we were waiting for the other sisters to come down from Night Prayer. It was love at first hearing. We felt happy dancing to their music. Thanks to her we got to know and love the Beatles.

When we went upstairs to the dormitory, there were five rooms on each floor, each large room with ten cubicles separated by a curtain similar to what hospitals use to separate patients. They showed each of us our cell that had a bed, chair, attached bureau and closet around which there was a curtain that we could close for privacy. Some of us postulants were in the upstairs dormitory with the novices. It was strange seeing them out of habit; they were young women like us except that they knew exactly what to do. It was time to undress, shower, slip into bed; lights out at 9:30. The hot, humid day turned into a torridly hot, humid night. No breeze. No fans. A really uncomfortable night. I had left our home in the mountains where nightfall brought cool air; in this valley of Sparkill only warm air surrounded us. Getting to sleep was a long process; surrounded by new people, each of us in a strange bed, longing for a breeze. When sleep finally came, I had all sorts of dreams. I was asking, "Why am I here among strangers? I could be heading back to college with my friends. Surely this is a big mistake." Images clouded my mind and I felt that I would never adapt to this way of life. Sleep was fitful. By the time a bell rang in the morning, I was glad to get up and move. I calmed myself by saying, "Observe everything that happens. If this continues to be dreadful, I'll leave and start my own community." I had no real idea how I could do that, but it was important to know that I had an alternate plan in case this did not work out. My doubts took backstage as I concentrated on dressing, making my bed, sliding the curtain back, and walking over to the Motherhouse. In Sacred Heart chapel we had Morning Prayer (Matins and Lauds), a half hour meditation, and Mass. Even Mass was different. Just when I thought something would be familiar, it too turned out to be strange. Unknown to me there was a Dominican rite whose prayers differed slightly from the Roman rite. It was easier to adjust to commemorating Dominican saints and blesseds because my Dominican Sister teachers in high school had introduced me to many of the well knowns: Dominic, Thomas Aquinas, Albert the Great, Catherine of Siena. I just never knew there were so many more saints and blesseds! Where had they all come from? It was an invasion of unknown, holy Dominicans like a never-ending parade of ants. It would take a lifetime to learn who they were and why they were considered holy.

When the Sisters chanted the Little Office of Mary in Latin it sounded so bizarre. The mystery of the eerie sound came down to using what many consider a universal key that all could sing —F#. To ensure that we sang on key, a sister sat at a manually pumped organ to sound the note before each Psalm. We each had an Office Book with the Latin text on one side and the English translation next to it. Like European cathedrals, Sacred Heart Chapel had a cluster of rows divided into individual stalls that faced each other. This facilitated chanting the Office. We learned the rubrics: alternating sides for sitting and standing for each Psalm, chanting one verse on one side while the other was quiet, all standing and bowing for the first part of the Gloria Patri (*Gloria Patri et Filio, et Spiritu Sancto*). A wooden plaque with the word, *Chorus* indicated which side began; this was moved from one side to the other each Saturday afternoon. There was an assortment of singers: a leader, the Hebdomedarian (a professed sister), two Versicularians, novices who sat in end seats so they could come out to the middle of the choir to chant certain prayers. At first it sounded and looked like a closed circuit marvel, but over time we were able to become active participants in this prayer of the Church. There is something awe inspiring praying together and realizing that other sisters/brothers are praying throughout the day. It's a way of encircling the earth with prayers of praise. Our years at the motherhouse proved to be the most fruitful for chanting the Office. With large numbers there were bound to be good voices. The setting captured the beauty of chant within the architectural beauty of Sacred Heart Chapel. There were other chapels in convents throughout the world, but Sacred Heart was special. It was the place where we learned to pray as one community. It embraced us in times of sorrow after the death of a sister as well as when we celebrated Entrance Day, Reception Day, Profession Day, the day of our final vows, and commemorations of Silver Jubilee and Golden Jubilee. If walls could speak, Sacred Heart Chapel would reveal the depth of human emotion and divine love. The best days of our lives would be celebrated within its embrace.

Prayer was the primary activity of our first weekend. We were like homing pigeons returning to Sacred Heart Chapel for morning prayer and Mass; at noon the Angelus, Rosary, and examination of conscience; afternoon prayer, Vespers; and after supper Night Prayer, Compline. When we arrived early we could take a seat in the rear of the chapel; before formal prayer we would line up, walk down the center aisle as a group, genuflect and proceed to our assigned seats. Assigned seats allowed us to store our missal and Office books within easy reach. We also had access to a small chapel on the second floor of the novitiate. We would pray there in the evening before retiring. In that setting I first heard and learned to sing, "Good Night, Sweet Jesus." In the dark with only the glow of a candle near the tabernacle that hymn sung *a capella* touched our hearts for it asked Jesus to guard over us. By the time the hymn ended our voices were as soft as a lullaby. It was a tender moment.

> Goodnight, Sweet Jesus,
> Guard us in sleep,
> Our souls and bodies,
> In thy love keep . . .
>
> Waking or sleeping,
> Keep us in sight,
> Dear gentle saviour,
> Goodnight, goodnight . . .
>
> Goodnight, Dear Jesus,
> Goodnight, goodnight . . .
>
> Rev. James Curry, words and music

Years later when this hymn was almost forgotten, I asked Sr. Eileen Donovan, a sister who was particularly kind to me when I was sick and we were assigned to the same high school in the Bronx, how it came about that she had entered the convent. I knew that she was a proud graduate of Walton High School in the Bronx so she did not have our sisters in high school. She told me that during World War II she had gone to St. Helena Church on Sunday afternoons to pray for the safety of the troops. The church was so crowded that it was standing room only as young and old alike fervently prayed the Rosary, had Benediction of the

Blessed Sacrament, after which they sang "Goodnight, Sweet Jesus" in the darkened church. Eileen was deeply moved by that experience. She felt God's love and believed that God would protect her and her loved ones in every special way. She always remembered that moment and felt that it was a major factor in her entering the convent.

When I entered the convent I really did not know the history of the Dominican Sisters. That summer I had read a book about the Order of St. Dominic and was impressed by St. Dominic. I knew the Dominican Sisters of Sparkill by their works: I had attended one of their schools, St. Ann's and my older sisters had also gone to Aquinas High School in the Bronx. I knew that there was a home for boys at Sparkill but did not know particulars. Like my sisters, I would learn that Alice Madeline Thorpe, born in England, had come to New York City and converted from Anglicanism, was moved by the poverty of women and children in the city. In 1876 she founded a group of Third Order Dominican Sisters under the auspices of the Archbishop of New York to respond to the needs of women and children living in poverty. The Sisters soon looked for a place to care for the children where they would have fresh air and space to play. They came to be called the Dominican Sisters of Sparkill when they acquired property and a large house in that tiny village in 1884. Over the years the sisters cared for boys and girls in the city, and in large houses in Westchester County and Rockland County.

St. Agnes was both a home and a school (grades one through eight) for boys. When we entered the novitiate some boys were orphans, but many had only one parent who was not able to work and care for their children. In some cases there were siblings who came to St. Agnes. Monday, September 11 we learned what our "charge" would be. I was first assigned to be an assistant group mother for Rosary Group, seventeen boys ages 4-6. My partner was Sr. Cecilia Therese, a fellow postulant with a quiet sense of humor. (I remember her another time when we cleaned the tables in the upstairs refectory after meals, measuring the distance between dishes so all was the same distance, saying, "We could get a job catering after all this experience." She was none too thrilled, but I think that she was right. We would acquire skills that seemed silly at the time and she was trying to put a humorous spin on them. A sense of humor helped when we were told to do things that we thought were a waste of time.) We helped feed the boys, got them ready for school, and supervised them on Sunday afternoons. Rosary Group had the cutest, most lovable little boys. In October after some postulants went home and it was necessary to change charges, Sr. Mary Clare assigned me to Little Side Refectory where the younger boys had their meals. I was part of the "after dinner act" whose duties included clearing off and washing the tables, sweeping and mopping the floor, setting up dishes for the next meal. I still was with the children, but more active physically. An unforeseen benefit of that charge was the immense pot of cherry Jell-o for the boys' dessert. I love red Jell-o and before washing the pot, could scoop out a serving. It was so refreshing!

In mid-October Sister Mary Clare posted a list of the Sisters who would take turns supervising the boys so the group mothers could be with the community for prayer. I remember checking the list and noting the days, times, and the name of the group. Once that was known I thought it was just a case of doing what we were required to do. But no, we had to ask permission to take a turn out. That had me baffled. I was ready and willing to do what was assigned. "Here I am Lord; I come to do your will" (Ps 40:7). It did not dawn on me that prayer was our primary obligation. I had to be excused from being at prayer with the community; then I could relieve the other Sister so she could pray with the community. On October 22nd I wrote to my parents, "One afternoon I was out (watching the boys on the field) it was positively gorgeous—Indian summerish." The field was grassy, perfect for running and playing, and in the distance were the tree-covered hills bathed in all shades of autumnal colors.

We would also take turns on switchboard, a small console in a tiny room off the Prioress' office. It was similar to ones I had seen on television, but it took some practice to connect the caller with the person requested; disconnect when someone hung up; get the sister if she were nearby and take messages for those not available. I arrived for my first turns on switchboard with a small paper with my notes for addressing each situation. In addition I had to answer the front door, quite a long walk through the corridor and front hall to the entrance. One afternoon Sr. Regina Rosaire came to the switchboard. "What a pleasant surprise," I thought, "this is my first grade teacher whom I loved." It was fourteen years since I had her as my first grade teacher at St. Ann's and here she was in Sparkill. I was smiling, hoping she remembered me, but she said, "I was on an important call and you disconnected me." I apologized, but it was evident that my incompetence had really upset her. In her position as Secretary to the Mother General my fumbling efforts were not appreciated. On another day with that reprimand still ringing in my ears, a call came in for the Sister during Night Prayer. I was determined that I would get her if I had to walk to the end of the earth. So I left the switchboard, walked rapidly through the cloister to Sacred Heart Chapel, up the center aisle to get the sister. Everyone was kneeling for Exposition of the Blessed Sacrament. I genuflected on both knees and got the sister. It never occurred to me that I could have taken a message, in fact I should have taken a message rather than drag her out at that solemn moment. Years later I saw the movie, "Auntie Mame" starring Rosalind Russell. When she was impoverished by the Stock Market Crash of 1929 she had to work at a variety of jobs, one of which was a switchboard operator. After a formal greeting, "Widdicome, Gutterman, Applewhite, Bibberman, and Black" spoken at breakneck speed, she proceeded to tangle wire after wire. The switchboard lit up with incoming calls and mixed connections: the chaos was hilarious. With my brief experience at switchboard, no wonder I laughed. I knew only too well the desire to connect caller and the absolute panic of crossing wires and disconnecting those who were speaking. Rosalind Russell showed me how comical it could be.

The fall semester began Monday, September 11 at St. Thomas Aquinas College. Founded in 1955 to prepare our sisters for teaching, STAC was staffed by our sisters and at that time served only our sisters. We could walk the path from the novitiate to the college in a few minutes. As a junior I had fulfilled course requirements like science and mathematics. That meant that I would not have my sister, Joan as a teacher. Part of me wanted to see how it would be to have Joan as a teacher, but it would have been awkward for both of us. Instead I had Advanced Spanish Language, Spanish Literature, Shakespeare, Current History, and Principles of Education. That semester I took 14 credits and 16 credits the spring semester.

We had access to the college library, a large space where we could do research and study. Silence was strictly enforced by the head librarian, Sr. Alfred. Another trait that puzzled us was her covering the table tops with stiff plastic. At the time we thought she was a fanatic, but years later when I returned to use the library I marveled that the tables still looked so good. By that time I had studied in other libraries and knew that tables took a beating. The library tables at STAC were in fact a monument to Sr. Alfred who protected the wood from scratches. Because of her we also viewed table tops in a whole new light.

Of the many professors who taught me at STAC, one woman stands out: Sr. Catherine Anthony Maher who taught Spanish and Philosophy of Education. She was a preeminently gracious person with an ability to draw students into whatever subject matter she taught. This made a huge difference in my life. Because I majored in Spanish I had her for many courses. In Spanish literature courses she opined that those who suffer great trials are often those who experience great joy. She pointed to the lives and works of Santa Teresa de Jesús and San Juan de la Cruz both of whom wrote of their deeply contemplative lives during which they suffered greatly but also enjoyed visions of God that far surpassed any human joy. Sr. Catherine's insight has stayed with me all these years. It has applied to so many situations in which I had the courage and patience to wait for good fortune when I encountered seemingly insurmountable problems. The words of P.B. Shelley, "If winter comes, can spring be far behind?" were invigorating, but it took the wisdom of Sr. Catherine to realize the reassuring rhythm of life and love.

There was no Latin major at STAC so it was logical to study another language. While not my first choice, Spanish was a close second. Thanks to Sr. Catherine Anthony's positive, upbeat attitude I grew to love the language. At that time I spoke Spanish with a Bronx accent. I listened to countless tapes and recordings applying myself to imitate Spanish speakers. I wanted to give it my best just as Sr. Catherine gave us her best. Yes, she was knowledgeable but more importantly she made us feel competent when we were struggling to balance study, prayer, and charges. I knew how to balance college courses with work and how sometimes it felt overwhelming. At Nazareth we would stay up well into the night, but in the novitiate we had a tight schedule and only limited time for study. Before exams a few of us found a way to review after lights out; we used the large storage room at the end of the dormitory; it had an overhead light, but no tables or chairs, so we sat on the floor. That extra time to review made all the difference.

Study was/is important, but they did not let us see our grades until we were professed in May 1963. I really wanted to know soon after we completed the course. It seemed so natural: one takes a course, fulfills the requirements, and gets a grade. Why would they not tell us? Did they think that someone with good grades would lord it over someone who did poorly? There was no time to bask in the sunshine of success. It was always on to the next task. There was little incentive to excel. Were they worried that a poor grade would discourage a postulant and lead to her leaving the convent? If postulants were going to be teachers, they would have to satisfy the requirements for a BS in Education. By the time we saw our grades, I was nearing graduation. Grades almost seemed irrelevant, except of course if/when we were sent on to study for a Masters degree.

A few of us had gone to college and others had worked for a year or two. Those of us who had studied advanced mathematics tutored those who came from schools where they had not taken courses to prepare them for the course they were taking at STAC. In a letter home I asked my parents to bring study aides to help me with my courses and for tutoring, and to have my subscription to "Time" magazine forwarded to me at Sparkill. So much for leaving our past behind: in learning there will always be a connection between what was learned in the past and the desire to learn in the present and going forward to the future.

In the midst of courses and charges there were still practical concerns. One morning I had washed my postulant dress and had it in the dryer. This task took more time than I had anticipated. It made no sense to abandon the dress; it would have gotten wrinkled. This was a balancing act between getting to use the machines in the novitiate laundry and getting to Spanish class on time. I waited as the dryer droned on and on; finally it stopped and I was able to hang up the dress. I headed for the exit and raced over to the college. I arrived late, apologized to Sr. Catherine Anthony, explaining how I wanted to take my dress from the dryer. She remained calm. The difficulty arose when

Catherine shared this story with her friend, none other than my sister, Joan. Sure enough the next time we could speak, Joan asked, "I heard that you arrived late for Spanish class. What makes you so special that you can arrive whenever you like?" She could not imagine my putting my needs ahead of what I was obliged to do. I wanted to say, "Don't take my actions so seriously. I was only a few minutes late. And when are you going to stop minding me?" In reality I did not talk back to her. She would always be my big sister and this was the price I paid for being born ten years and a generation after her.

Sunday afternoons found us in our conference room to write a letter to our parents. Some found this a grueling task. How could we be expected to write a letter to our parents when we did basically the same things every day? I had to think a bit, but then I wrote about special events: celebrations of feast days, changes in liturgy, upcoming events like the Bazaar, the major fundraiser at the beginning of October, dates and times for visiting days with our parents and family. Writing home came more naturally to me for I had written to my parents on a regular basis when I had boarded in high school and college. This time 'round, there was even more at stake. I knew that my parents would first read and my mother would pass on what I wrote to my friends at Nazareth. My mother became my private Associated Press acting as intermediary between me and my college friends, so I would learn what they were doing and they would know how I was faring. At Thanksgiving Sr. Mary Clare even allowed me to receive cards from my friends. The give and take of correspondence sustained me that year; my letters had a larger audience and strengthened the friendships formed at Nazareth. This would have been harder if they had graduated and were spread all over the country. We could not write or receive mail during Advent, but how wonderful it was to open a mountain of mail—cards, letters, and in some cases small gifts (holy cards) and books. We were not home for Christmas, but we were finding a new home among the Dominican Sisters.

Communication given the limitations of distance was a more intentional act. It was a time when long distance phone calls were reserved for emergencies or special events and we relied on handwritten letters. Compared with internet and social media, written communication seems outdated, but for those who relied on the US Postal Service, sending and receiving letters was an honored tradition. There was nothing better than reading a letter from a friend or relative, rereading certain sections, and sharing parts with others. A letter united writer and reader and provided a chronology of events. Letters were for savoring like sipping a deliciously rich cordial.

Convent life had its diversions. In October we walked up the mountain to a place where we could picnic. It gave us a whole new vantage point from which to see our property on one side and on the other, the majestic Hudson River. In January we went sleigh riding outside the novitiate. Throwing oneself down on a sleigh while wearing an ankle-length dress and long coat was a bit of a handicap, but it added to the fun and excitement. The aches and pains the next day were well worth the effort. One afternoon in January the lights went out when we were praying Vespers. We made our way to the refectory, ate supper by candlelight with recreation, and then washed dishes and cleaned tables. Life must go on. Over to Sacred Heart Chapel where there were large candles lighting the way to our stalls. Praying by candlelight was difficult, but it felt as if we were in a medieval cathedral with light and shadows both showing and concealing statues, altars, and the Sisters in their long habits. Black postulant dresses were a liability, but how beautiful were the novices and professed in their white habits. We sang the Salve Regina *a capella* sans organ. My friend, Mary Sullivan had told me that there is no instrument as beautiful as the sound of the human voice. That night proved her point. As I wrote to my parents, "The Salve is beautiful in itself, but it was extra-special that night with the candlelight and clear, light voices."

In second semester I added new courses, namely English and American Poetry, Cosmology, and Geography. I also had many classes with professed Sisters, a few years my senior who returned to Sparkill to complete their course work on Friday evenings and all day Saturday. They traveled from the Bronx, Manhattan, Brooklyn, and Queens after having taught all week. I braced myself for Geography, because I remembered how I struggled to learn that subject in sixth and seventh grades. The professor's lectures were particularly dry and dreary. As I scrambled to take notes and capture "the facts, just the facts," in the words of Sgt. Joe Friday (Jack Webb) on "Dragnet," I saw the professed sisters seated near me correcting spelling tests. I was upset. Did the professor not see them or realize that many students were doing something else? How could they expect to learn what the professor was presenting? There were major differences between me, a postulant and the professed sisters. They were responsible for teaching large classes with well over fifty students and had the same prayer obligations as we had at the Motherhouse. Under those conditions they needed to use every precious moment to keep their heads above water. Perhaps they were ahead of their time, pioneers perfecting multi-tasking before it became popular?

As the semester progressed I sorely missed the camaraderie with my college friends. There was almost no opportunity to speak with others about the great ideas raised in our classes. At Nazareth we had soirees on Friday evenings to share poetry and ideas raised in our favorite and not so favorite classes, listen to music that we loved, especially Broadway shows and singers like Johnny Mathis. The arts played a prominent role in our personal development as well as across all disciplines. If Nazareth was like running a marathon, STAC resembled a relay. There was a race to be sure, but we were sprinters putting in time and earning credits so we could teach. There did not seem to be a grander scheme beyond earning a degree and being accredited to teach.

When we returned to the novitiate after night prayer we had recreation each evening. We would chat and get caught up with our novice mother and other postulants and novices. A special treat was listening to recorded music. The problem was that it was always Irish music; most sisters sang along and jumped up to dance. Although I have an Irish surname, I had never heard, let alone learned the lyrics, nor how to dance the jigs and reels. Many of the postulants had taken Irish dance lessons so they loved dancing. The music was loud; anyone trying to have a conversation could not be heard. The lyrics of Irish songs were so sad. For me there was a huge disconnect between the music and the lyrics. I found myself thinking, "How can they be so happy dancing to this noisy music?"

When I was a child living in our Bronx apartment both my mother and sister, Joan played the piano; one would accompany my sister, Geri who sang show tunes or family favorites like, "Glow Worm," a song that my mother played at ever faster tempos while I laughed and clapped with excitement. Even our cat, Smokey Stover got into the act when he ran across the piano keys when someone forgot to cover the keys. Upstate my family listened to classical music on WQXR radio and watched shows on television like Lawrence Welk who featured various soloists and Victor Borge who combined classical piano playing with comedy. I listened to popular music when I was home alone doing mindless tasks like dusting furniture or using the carpet sweeper to clean the rug. At Nazareth I had season tickets for the Rochester Philharmonic that performed at the Eastman Theatre. Mary Sullivan, one of my kitchen worker friends, and I would take the bus that ran along East Avenue into downtown Rochester and enjoy the concert, leaving early to run like fools so we could catch the last bus so we would be back on campus by the 11:00 pm curfew. I remember my sister, Joan telling me, "You will do better as Brady in a community that loves all things Irish." I just wish she had warned me about Irish music.

Producing shows was an important part of novitiate life. When we had to do a show for the novices, we worked on a spoof of "The Honeymooners," a popular television series showing the hare-brained schemes of a bus driver and his friend, a sewer worker. The main characters, Ralph Cramden (Jackie Gleason) and Ed Norton (Art Carney) provided more than enough material for great hilarity. After a few practices, we were all set. As the name Norton was bandied about, we were doubled over laughing. One major problem: Sr. Cecilia, the novice mistress, and Sr. Mary Clare, the postulant mistress, were sitting there with straight faces. Later we learned that they had no idea what the show was about because they had never seen it. To make matters worse, the last name of the former novice mistress was Naughton, something we did not know. In those days we commonly used our religious names and only used last names for legal purposes such as when we voted. After all that preparation, our skit was a both a success for those our age and a flop for the leaders who felt that we had disrespected Sr. Evangelist Marie Naughton.

In a letter home I mentioned that I was elected to the planning committee for the Christmas pageant. Every Christmas pageant would culminate with the Nativity scene. I suggested getting some props. Every day as we walked the path we passed statues of Mary with sheep grazing nearby. Wouldn't our play benefit if we "borrowed" some sheep? When no one else was in sight, I walked through the grass to check the sheep. Those statues were firmly secured to the earth. Only a natural disaster or construction equipment could have moved them. Another brilliant idea bit the dust. Despite my disappointment our play went on as planned. I even read a selection from John W. Lynch's epic poem, "A Woman Wrapped in Silence," whose words and cadence moved my heart and I hoped the hearts of all present. Poetry preempted props that night.

> ...*a moment paused*
> *Above a quiet place, and found, just this,*
> *A woman wrapped in silence, and the seed*
> *Of silence was her heart that tried to give*
> *All that it held to give, and ever more. (p. 6)*

> ...*This is God's chosen way with men,*
> *To take men's way: and so the streets she walks*
> *And all the roads, the shepherds and the shepherds'*
> *Sheep, the winds, the firelight, Israel's hills,*
> *Will find just this, no more, a woman plain*
> *Upon the earth, and in her arms, a Child. (p.9)*

> *And then*
> *she knelt and held Him close against her heart,*
> *and in the midnight, adoration fused*
> *with human love, and was not separate. (p. 45)*

(John W. Lynch. *A Woman Wrapped in Silence*. Mahweh, NJ: Paulist Press, 1968)

Our eight months as postulants (September to May) gained momentum. During that time some postulants decided to return home. We seldom knew why they left because their departure was clothed in secrecy; it happened at a time when we would not see them. It was odd: this young woman was with you eating in the refectory, sleeping in the same dorm, praying with the community, studying at the college, and suddenly she was no longer there. I did not know any of the postulants before I entered because I had lived upstate so my sadness at their leaving was much less than those who were friends over many years as classmates, neighbors, and fellow parishioners. The longer we knew the other postulants the more difficult it was. Missing each other was an endearing human trait I would not trade. Who would want to share her life only to discover that her absence meant nothing when she was no longer with the community? Each of us is unique; no one departs without making an impression on the minds and hearts of those with whom she lived.

As the time approached when we would receive the habit, the novices began to train us to do specific tasks. An avid reader for as long as I could remember, I was hoping to be assigned to read in the refectory. Sr. John Ann, a spirited novice had the task of mentoring me to become a reader for the upstairs refectory where the professed sisters and novices took their meals. Sister taught me the order and timing of readings for each meal: fifteen minutes of serious reading at breakfast; for dinner a brief reading from the Gospels followed by a spiritual book selected by the Novice Mistress; at supper readings that included: "Saints and Saintly Dominicans," selections from the Rule of St. Augustine, our Constitutions, and the Directory. The reader's chair was high above the tables at one end of a long, narrow refectory. It gave me the willies because it looked like the electric chair used in NYS for executions and I feared what might happen when I sat on it. Once I calmed myself and managed to climb up and take my seat, I had to arrange the various books for that meal. My main concern was projecting my voice so I would be heard by those at "top table," where the Mother General who was in charge of the whole congregation, the Prioress who was in charge of the Motherhouse and those highest in rank sat. The length of the room and the fact that some sisters were hard of hearing were other factors to be considered when reading.

I enjoyed the preparation to read in the refectory: previewing the texts to acquaint myself with unusual words or phrasing. I wanted my reading to be smooth so those listening would understand. My first day, the breakfast reading, fifteen minutes of straight, serious reading went well. Sr. John Ann had warned me not to look up or hesitate because there would be many professed Sisters ready to bolt out the door. These Sisters worked at our college and others lived at the Motherhouse while their convents were under construction at newly opened Catholic schools in Rockland County. They needed to make a hasty exit to gather their books and mantles to drive to their missions so teachers, parents and students would not be kept waiting at the doorstep or out in the cold.

At the main meal, no problem with the Gospel verses, but the book selected was the history of the evangelization of the Midwest by Dominican priests. There were so many characters: a bishop, a priest, a backwoodsman, and a Native American. I wondered, "How will they ever understand who is who and what each one is saying?" It became crystal clear to me that I would have to use my voice to differentiate the characters. The narrative part was fine, but then came the dialogs. As I changed my voice to imitate what I thought would be an appropriate accent, it became a challenge: so many characters and so much dialog. At one point I looked up to see if they could hear me at top table. The prioress was looking straight ahead and her face was red; she seemed to hear me. I continued on until a bell signaled the end of reading. I was relieved and somewhat elated. I had survived the main event. What I had not noticed as I projected my heart out was that the novices seated near the reader's chair were looking at each other as if to say, "This is hilarious. We have never heard anyone read like this." Later that day Sr. Cecilia told me, "Mother Kevin has said that you are never again to read in the upstairs refectory." I was crushed. Had they thought that I was mocking the characters or trying to get a laugh? Nothing was farther from the truth. I was applying the skills I had gleaned from my Speech course as a sophomore at Nazareth College. My dream of reading in the refectory was dashed. It felt like the end of the world.

Each evening we heard about another saint's life. We often wondered if the stories in "Saints and Saintly Dominicans" were true. Who would espouse themselves to God when they were young children? The stories were just too fantastical for us twentieth century women. Despite that, the readers faithfully read the texts that we learned to take with a grain of salt. I heard that a Sister a few years ahead of us with a brilliant mind and a ready wit took it upon herself when she read to introduce or expand verbal flourishes. No one noticed. How could that be? The Sisters were so inured to strange stories that no one questioned when they heard that a three year old had espoused herself to God. How I wish I had been there to hear her revisions.

As winter yielded to spring, our thoughts turned to new life. There was an air of expectancy: who would be approved to advance and receive the habit? March 6 we got word that the Council had approved forty-eight postulants to receive the habit. Only then could we write home to share the good news and ask for simple things: white headed straight pins, #8 white thread, safety pins, white blotters, a white sweater, and two skirt hangers. We were measured for the black mantle that we would wear over the habit. Finally on April 7th we received the dazzling white habit parts. Our task? to sew nametapes on the tunic that was the main part of the habit and would be attached to a yoke; the big and little sleeves, the former sewed into the tunic and yoke and the latter worn over our lower arms and held in place by an elasticized arm band; the scapular that we wore over the tunic to show that we were bound to God; and the guimp, the rounded cape, and collar that were put on last. We had to learn how to assemble and sew the various parts together. With the help of the novices for whom this was second nature we learned how to position the tunic, arrange two pleats at the outer edges, and finally sew the yoke to the tunic using #8 white thread. We would then attach the big sleeves to the yoke and tunic.

We also had to learn how to pin a veil and how to attach it to a white cap that would cover our head. We worked in groups of two to practice positioning the straight pin. Sr. Eileen Sullivan volunteered to go first as I watched. "Oh, no," I cried as blood trickled down her face. We laughed nervously as she wiped the blood from her forehead. She was not mortally wounded, but it was a vivid reminder that we had to move in at an angle and after contact with the cap adjust the angle away from the scalp. We cheered each other on until everyone learned the rudiments of attaching a veil. Our habits were in our closet quietly waiting for Reception Day. No item of clothing would ever be so special as the Dominican habit, not even the doctoral cap and gown I wore many years later. We were advancing from aspirant to novice and would have time to delve more deeply into the spiritual life of a Dominican sister.

Reception Day, May 7, 1962 dawned bright and beautiful. Dogwood trees along the path were in bloom, spring flowers were taking their bows, and the aromas of an awakening earth beckoned us outdoors. The afternoon ceremony in Sacred Heart Chapel began with the procession of forty-eight young women each wearing a full length white wedding gown and veil and carrying a lighted candle. Bishop Griffiths greeted us and asked what we desired. We responded, "The mercy of God and your mercy and the holy habit of St. Dominic." The brides of Christ disappeared into the sacristy where a bevy of activity would produce a monumental change. Our sponsors, the Sister who had sponsored each of us when we entered religious life, were in the sacristy to assist. In my case my sister, Joan was in the choir loft helping with music and singing so another sister took her place.[1] It was quite a scene as each of us discarded the wedding gown—no small feat when there seemed to be hundreds of small buttonholes to open— to put on the Dominican habit. We needed help with each part: the tunic attached to the yoke and long sleeves, the cap to cover our hair, scapular, little sleeves, guimp, and collar were in place followed by the veil. A quick check by the professed Sisters and we were ready to return. While we were busy being habited, the choir sang Solemn Compline. We could hear the chanting from our vantage point behind the main altar. Finally the sacristy door opened and forty-eight novices of the Dominican Congregation of Our Lady of the Rosary walked into the chapel. We were nervous, appearing for the first time in the Dominican habit, trying to adjust our inner selves to the outward appearance of novices for the completion of the ceremony. Each sister officially received her religious name; the bishop moved along the line of novices kneeling at the altar rail saying to each, "Daughter, in the world you were known as (Judith Brady). Henceforth you will be known as (Sister Judith Mary)." We had used our religious name since we entered, but hearing the bishop say these words in sonorous tones, sent shivers down my spine. Throughout the ceremony there was glorious choral music that reached its apex with the "Te Deum," a hymn that praises God, arranged for soprano and

---

[1] See Appendix for Letter from Sr. Joan Dolores to Sr. Judith Mary written May 6, 1962.

alto voices with organ accompaniment. It would remain our all-time, favorite hymn.

> *You are God: we praise you;*
> *You are the Lord: we acclaim you;*
> *You are the eternal Father:*
> *All creation worships you.*
> *To you all angels, all the powers of heaven,*
> *Cherubim and Seraphim, sing in endless praise:*
> *Holy, holy, holy, Lord, God of*
> *power and might,*
> *heaven and earth are full of your glory.*
> *The glorious company of apostles praises you.*
> *The noble fellowship of prophets praises you.*
> *The white-robed army of martyrs praises you.*
> *Throughout the world the holy Church*
> *acclaims you:*
> *Father, of majesty unbounded,*
> *your true and only Son, worthy*
> *of all worship,*
> *and the Holy Spirit, advocate and guide.*
> *You, Christ, are the king of glory,*
> *the eternal Son of the Father.*
> *When you became man to set us free*
> *you did not spurn the Virgin's womb.*
> *You overcame the sting of death,*
> *and opened the kingdom of heaven*
> *to all believers.*
> *You are seated at God's right hand in glory.*
> *We believe that you will come, and*
> *be our judge.*
> *Come then, Lord, and help your people,*
> *bought with the price of your own blood,*
> *and bring us with your saints*
> *to glory everlasting.*
> *Save your people, Lord, and bless*

your inheritance.
Govern and uphold them now and always.
Day by day we bless you.
We praise your name for ever.
Keep us today, Lord, from all sin.
Have mercy on us, Lord, have mercy.
Lord, show us your love and mercy;
for we put our trust in you.
In you, Lord, is our hope:
and we shall never hope in vain.

The *Te Deum* echoed throughout the vast reaches of the chapel. Afterwards we processed down the aisle and went outside where our parents and family members soon joined us. It was wonderful to see the white, the glorious white after months of wearing black. Smiles, hugs, and words of congratulations accompanied by pictures to capture the thrill of being a novice and a bride of Christ.

When we entered the refectory to eat supper that evening, I could not imagine how I would eat. The cap was pulled so tightly over my hair and around my face that opening my mouth was painful. I ate so little that I wondered if I would lose weight or starve to death. Even going to Communion would be a challenge. As we knelt at the altar rail to receive Communion the next morning, I prayed, "Please, God, help me to open my mouth." Simple physical concerns replaced grander prayers the first few days. Everything was so new and so strange. I just hoped I would adjust and feel comfortable being a novice.

For three full days there were eighty-nine novices, a fact captured on video as we walked the path to the novitiate and posed on the outside stairs. There has not been such a large group since those days in May 1962 between our Reception of the Habit on May 7th and the senior novices' Profession when they made their vows of poverty, chastity, and obedience and received the black veil on May 10. We were giddy with joy and excitement. Once the band of Sisters ahead of us was professed, we became the official novices, but for a few days we all blended in: veterans and neophytes alike.

After May 10 we felt the loss of the novices once they professed their vows. As much as we had come to know and value the band ahead of us, when they were professed we could no longer engage them in conversation. Keeping one's distance after getting to know Sisters was a huge change. We and they were the same flesh and blood people who had shared recreation in the novitiate for eight months. They had started as mentors but then became friends. It was hard putting the brakes on relationships that had begun to flourish, but it was the reality that we had to accept. It was a mini version of what would happen when we would be professed the following year. In one mission we could become friends with other sisters and before we knew it, they or we could be reassigned. On the flip side, if we did not like someone there was the chance that reassignment could resolve the daily discomfort of living and working in close proximity. I must say that I missed sisters more often than I breathed a sigh of relief. These rules were meant to teach us detachment, but growing in trust and confidence is more important than snipping off the buds of friendship. We learned that we were meant to direct our affections to God and so we did, but how can we love the God we do not see unless and until we love the person/neighbor that we do see (1John 4:20)? I know that they did not want us to become so attached to one sister that we would ignore the community. In Thérèse of Lisieux's autobiography, *The Story of a Soul*, she wrote of seeking out a Sister that she did not like when they had recreation and befriending her. That is heroic and something to be imitated. I am not sure that I could be so heroic or saintly as she. When I read that I wondered how the sister reacted to her attention. There are loners, people who keep their own company. Are they loners because no one is attracted to them or do they simply prefer to be alone? I for one would never choose to be a loner, though there would be times in life when responsibilities demanded discipline and solitude such as the year that I wrote my dissertation. But in the normal course of events and certainly in the novitiate I was happy to be among equals. We were all new to what we had chosen and needed the comfort and support of our Sisters in training.

As novices we concentrated on learning the formal rituals of the sisters. We practiced a variety of inclinations: an inclination of the head when passing the statue of the Blessed Virgin Mary; a medium inclination; and a profound inclination. We learned the practice of the *venia*, first kissing the scapular and extending one's body straight out on the floor resting on the right side with the left leg on top of the right as a symbol of humility and obedience. It was easier for us to do since we were young and physically able, but it would never be my favorite move.

Novice year is meant to provide time to pray and discern what a vocation to the Dominican sisters involves and if one is suited for it. As postulants we had attended college but as novices we had to forego secular studies. We also would not work with the boys in St. Agnes. We did have courses in music and art and delved more deeply into all that consecrated religious life entails. Our primary concern was to develop a rich, deep life of prayer. This was a wonderful time to become better acquainted with God and with oneself. Developing and deepening an inner life was more than wearing a habit. Surely we had to respect the habit, but religious life was never just skin deep. As novices we became more deeply involved in the Liturgy of the Hours fulfilling the duties of Versicularian. We assumed the duty of praying in community and by ourselves. The rhythm of communal prayer included the Hours of the Little Office of Our Lady throughout the day, meditation, Mass, personal examen, and reciting fifteen decades of the Rosary. Our private prayer included time spent before the Blessed Sacrament--praying silently, doing spiritual reading, and just being with Jesus, our companion and friend. We could make the Stations of the Cross—genuflecting at each Station, kissing our scapular, and silently praying, "We adore thee, O Christ and we bless thee because by thy holy cross thou hast redeemed the world," reflecting on all that Jesus lovingly suffered to redeem all people.

I remember thinking that I might be bored not being able to read a novel or delve into secular reading. So I developed a plan: the Bible would be my salvation. I knew from an introductory course to the Old Testament how exciting the Hebrew Scriptures could be. So I read other books of the Bible (the Song of Songs, Psalms, Ruth, Judith, Tobit, the Epistles, and Acts of the Apostles). I also studied the Introduction, footnotes, and cross references for each book. One such search led me to read all of Psalm 22 that begins with the words that Jesus uttered on the cross,

> My God, my God, why have you forsaken me,
> far from my prayer, from the words of my cry? (v. 2)

I was haunted by these words. Somehow I thought that being the Son of God would protect him from the anguish a crucified man would experience. Was Jesus totally distraught? How could he not be in distress? Yet I read,

> You have been my guide since I was first formed,
> my security at my mother's breast.
> To you I was committed at birth,
> From my mother's womb you are my God. (v. 10)

With these words Jesus reviewed how God is present at each stage of human life. Jesus has every right to implore God,

> But you, O Lord, be not far from me:
> O my help, hasten to aid me. (v. 20)

The images—being a worm, not a man; mocked by onlookers; like water poured out; while evildoers pierced his hands and feet, even dividing his garments among themselves— led me to ask, "Who would not weep when beholding this Man of Sorrows?" Yet Psalm 22 continues by encouraging all to give glory to God for it is this God who heard his prayer.

> For he has not spurned nor disdained the wretched man in his misery,
> Nor did he turn his face away from him, but when
> he cried out to him, he heard him. (v.25)

Somehow Jesus in the depth of human suffering cried out using a psalm whose text he no doubt knew by heart. Those who torture and kill do not, however, have the final word. No, God rules the world:

> To him alone shall bow down all who sleep in the earth;
> Before him shall bend all who go down into the dust.
> And to him my soul shall live;

> My descendants shall serve him.
>
> Let the coming generation be told of the Lord
> that they may proclaim to a people
> yet to be born the justice he has shown. (v. 30-32)

It was this careful reading of Scripture that gave me a deeper appreciation for Jesus who is both human and divine. He was not play-acting in his passion and death. Jesus showed us both the depth of his love and his intimate connection to his Father. Only a belief in the mercy of God could begin to explain why Jesus suffered and died for us.

Every Sister is required to make a yearly retreat. A Dominican priest came to the Motherhouse for a week to offer Mass, preach three conferences a day, and hear confessions. There were many retreats at the Motherhouse throughout the year so every Sister could make a retreat. Retreats were scheduled during Easter week, at the end of June, and twice in the month of August. Novices also made a ten day retreat before Profession of Vows. As novices we were present for at least one of the conferences so these provided opportunities to hear inspiring talks by different Dominican retreat masters. When so many Sisters arrived for retreat, their presence enhanced the chanting of the Little Office and singing at Mass and Benediction of the Blessed Sacrament. These retreats brought not just an influx of Sisters from the missions but also a greater awareness of the larger community/congregation. Silence was observed throughout the day to encourage discourse with God. Weekly confession was the practice, but on retreat there was also the opportunity to go to confession to a different confessor. That was a comfort for anyone who needed a fresh look at one's spiritual life. (On mission there was an ordinary confessor and an extraordinary confessor to provide access to a different priest.)

Meditation, the half hour between chanting the Office and Mass, was a time of quiet that we observed together in Sacred Heart Chapel. There were simple prompts read at intervals if we wanted to concentrate on devout reading. We could also read Scripture or an inspirational book. I did my level best to stay awake and like others, had moments when I felt like dozing. Since we were all together and seated, it was embarrassing to sleep especially if one's head fell forward. Generally I could stay awake, but as the days wore on, I questioned if I were really meditating. Why didn't they give us more guidance on how to meditate? Perhaps I thought that I should be making more progress in prayer. After all, there was no one levitating or experiencing visions, at least not in my stall. Gradually I realized that there are many ways of approaching meditation. Dominican spirituality allowed us the freedom to find what worked well for each one. What I do to this day is read the Epistle and Gospel for the feast of the day and then reread it slowly stopping at a certain verse if it captures my attention. Some days nothing attracts me and I have to admit, "Dear God, I need your help to clear my mind of distractions. Please show me the way to use this time wisely, to love you and know your love for me." If I have no sense of God's presence, I wait and am still. I trust God and know that God will show me what is good, perhaps not during meditation, and maybe not when I am praying for God is present in our lives and in the words and actions of other people. Sometimes it is maddening to think that I am ready, but nothing happens. Where is this great God of love and mercy? Why do you not speak to me? If lovers and friends have their difficulties communicating, surely my relating to God will have speed bumps along the way. It may even mean going off road over unfamiliar terrain, scary for me who likes to plan ahead. I often lack the words to express what I feel much like when I was learning Spanish and not understanding what was being said or not getting the joke that had my native speaker classmates doubled over laughing. I was new to the spiritual life and was humbled by all that I could not do. God's time is definitely not my time.

We also did spiritual reading. Scripture was my first place to explore, but writings by religious writers also instructed and inspired. Like many others I read and pondered *The Imitation of Christ* by Thomas á Kempis. First written in Latin in the XV century, this book offers a wealth of advice for developing an interior life. All was good until one day I read, "As often as I have been amongst men," said Seneca, "I have returned less a man." While I was living a cloistered life at the Motherhouse, before I entered the convent I had gone out among people and shared good times and uplifting conversation. If this author meant that we must limit ourselves, refrain from human discourse, and observe silence all our days, then he lost credibility. Did not Jesus live among men, women, and children as he shared the message of joy, the good news that God's kin(g)dom is among us? He spent nights praying to his Father but by day returned to heal illnesses and forgive sins. We could not be sponges absorbing everything; rather we had to be critical readers, building on what we knew to be true and questioning what needed to be disregarded for a greater good.

Each weekday we devoted our energies to charges to which we were assigned. A group of us novices reported to the Sewing Room in a separate building near the Boys' Infirmary, outside Sacred Heart Chapel. Called the Bake House, it had originally been used to store bread. It was a large room with two rows of Singer Sewing machines along the outer walls and a large table in the middle for cutting. There were ceiling-high closets to the left side of the entrance to store bolts of white fabric, mohair, black, and material to make aprons. Those of us new to sewing by machine had to begin sewing apron strings. Once that was mastered I could sew the gusset and cap worn under the veil. Sewing the tunic, large sleeves, and small sleeves came next. Only when I could sew a half inch border with precision could I sew the scapular. We needed to know how to thread the machine and how to thread a bobbin. Finally we could sew the guimp, attaching the collar and then sewing the uniform ½" hem on the rounded border of the guimp. If the bobbin thread needed to be rethreaded in mid-stream, it was important to match the stitch so it could not be noticed. A young professed Sister was in charge of cutting out the habit parts and other items such as aprons. Sr. Constantia was the senior Sister who sat in her rocking chair encouraging us to work and occasionally praying the Rosary aloud. Sr. Constantia suffered from neuralgia, and covered her face with her shawl when nerve pain attacked. Despite her infirmity she was with us every day to encourage and exhort us to pray. Over time I became friends with her and her dear friend, Sr. Cornelia. They were a great example of friendship that sustained and supported each one in her loving relationship with God and each other. As the years advanced I realized how precious these two sisters were. When I went to Sparkill, I would visit with them. Wherever Sr. Constantia was there too was Sr. Cornelia. After their passing I would visit our cemetery and plant bulbs in the fall so there would be spring flowers on each of their graves. There was also a cat in the Sewing Room who kept the premises free from critters. He merited extra attention and special food brought from the Motherhouse kitchen. (When Sr. Constantia was away on vacation in Saugerties, my responsibility as the senior novice was to go to the kitchen to get milk and an egg for the cat. The Sister in charge kept me waiting and made me feel like a beggar. I had not invented this routine; I was doing what Sr. Constantia thought the cat deserved. It was a relief when I could return to the Sewing Room and give the cat its special treat for the day.)

Some days we had more leeway. Another novice, Sr. Maureen Francis would sometimes retell the Gospel of the day in her New York Jewish accent. It gave us a laugh and helped us to complete our tasks. We sewed the habits for the Sisters living at the Motherhouse and for the new novices, as well as for ourselves as we approached first profession of vows. There was a great sense of satisfaction seeing material cut into proper parts, stitched and finally all ready for the Sister. One of the perks for the Dominican retreat master was our sewing a new habit complete with the capuche (hood). That required a special pattern. Eventually as a professed Sister I used that pattern to cut out a terry cloth capuche from a large mint green towel to use at Saugerties, our vacation home on the Hudson River. It was great protection from the sun especially after swimming when it also absorbed water. The one drawback was its weight so over time it was replaced by lighter items of clothing.

We always stopped sewing, straightened our work area, and closed the machine so we would be on time for prayer in the chapel shortly before noon. After prayer we went to the refectory for dinner. Some of us served in the refectory, others worked in the pantry serving the food, and after the meal loading the platters and serving bowls in the commercial dish washer, drying them and returning them to the designated closet. Since I had been removed from the list to read, I was front and center for serving. Before dinner the professed sisters lined up according to rank on either side of the hall outside the refectory. The sisters recited the *De Profundis* (Psalm 130) remembering in prayer deceased Dominican sisters as two novices moved along each line with a small dish with water; the sisters dipped their fingers in the water and dried them with the white cloth. Praying for deceased sisters, parents, relatives, and benefactors is a hallowed tradition of the Dominican Order. At the time this was just one more custom, but viewed from maturity I will welcome all the prayers that come my way.

As a novice I served top table where the Mother General and Prioress sat, then down one side. Walking the length of the refectory with platters and bowls of food was our responsibility. Serving the sisters silently and smoothly to assure that each sister had all she needed was our aim. As the readers filled the minds of the diners, we moved quickly and purposefully to serve the food, pour coffee and tea, remove the platters and bowls, and bring in dishpans full of hot, sudsy water. We of course carried these pans back to the pantry, emptied the water, and other novices washed, dried, and stacked the empty pans. All was done efficiently and quietly. It demanded concentration and discipline. Gradually we got the rhythm and became better servers. Once in a while something happened that was unexpected like the day a fellow novice slipped as she walked into the dining room, lost her balance and the contents of the dishpan splashed all over the floor. That stopped everything as we helped her up and mopped the soapy water so no one else would go flying. One morning when I was serving the former Novice Mistress, I was about to pour coffee into her extended cup. There was a small plastic bottle in the cup so I motioned toward it; she looked and just motioned for me to pour. So in went the hot coffee as her medicine bottle bobbed around merrily. Was this to test my obedience and ability to follow directions? I thought she was crazy. No normal person I knew would want the bottle to be submerged in hot coffee.

At the end of dinner and supper, a bell signaled the reader to stop, the Sisters rose and prayed. All servers and the reader made the *venia* in the space between the sisters as they stood to pray. Only then could we relax and in a few minutes have our meal with the other worker bees.

Over the summer of 1962 I had visits that sustained me and reinforced bonds of friendship. Sr. Helen Daniel, the President, and Sr. Eva Marie from Nazareth College visited me on May 22. They had a meeting in New York City and were able to squeeze in a visit to Sparkill. I was thrilled to see them and they were equally happy to see me. It was such a treat to see those whom I had grown to love and appreciate at Nazareth now at Sparkill to see me newly dressed as a Dominican novice. We were a contrast: they in the black habit and stiff, white guimp of the Sisters of St. Joseph and I in the white habit and veil of the Dominican Sisters. The Dominican habit is always impressive with its flowing lines and white color. Sr. Helen Daniel was the college president and more importantly, a gracious, graceful lady who inspired us to be loving women in our own right. Sr. Eva Marie was a very sensible woman in charge of scholarships so we knew her well and appreciated the scholarships that she channeled to us as well as her sincere interest in our welfare. On that bright, sunny day we walked up to the cemetery, a quiet place to be sure with its large bronze crucifix overlooking the graves, each bearing a cross with the name of the sister and the date of her death. We rested on benches in the shade of tall trees after which I showed them Sacred Heart Chapel. I had many questions about my friends and teachers, but the most rewarding was just being with them. I was so happy to unite Sparkill and Nazareth, intertwining the places and people I loved most. Shortly before I left college to enter the convent, Sr. Helen Daniel had given me a Jerusalem Bible with an inscription citing the primacy of love. Years later she left the Sisters of St. Joseph and her position as college president to marry a former Dominican priest. She followed her heart to be sure. We loved her and hoped all would go well. We were saddened to learn that she developed breast cancer and died shortly after. Dr. Jeanne Malone Loughery's memory will always glow in our hearts for she was a gracious, loving woman.

In early June my friends, Ellen Kuhl, Kathy Scheg, and Jean Klier came for a visit bringing news of my friends and all their activities. Ellen was part of the "furniture swap" my second year at Nazareth. Four of us with two rooms opposite each other decided to move our beds to one room and our desks to the other. That way anyone who wanted to sleep early or late would have peace and quiet and those of us who needed/wanted to stay up to study or write could do so without disturbing her roommate. Our grand plan lasted only a few days. When the Sister in charge of our floor discovered our arrangement, she informed us that we had to return beds and desks to their rightful places. We had no idea that would be a problem; in fact we thought we were enlightened and wondered why no one else had thought of doing this. 'So much for originality.

Both Kathy and Jean were dayhops and we were in the same mathematics class freshman year. Jean had invited me to visit her and her family in their suburban home in Chili. We passed hours in her beautiful bedroom with the plush white carpet listening to music. We also attended Mass at St. Pius X, their parish church. I can still remember the spring sunlight filtering through the church's windows. Her father even "adopted" me so I could attend the Father/Daughter Dinner with Jean and Mr. Klier. Once again it was a sunny day in Sparkill so we went outside to take pictures on the little island with the life-size statue of the Blessed Mother. They brought simple gifts: writing paper with stamps and a medal of St. Dominic, but best of all were home-made chocolate chip cookies that Ellen's brother had baked. I had thought I would never taste them again but here they were. Surprises like that are too wonderful for words.

The first week of August Rev. William Shannon, the chaplain at Nazareth College and my professor for Old Testament Theology, came to visit. He stayed overnight in the priests' quarters. When he stepped outside his room he was surprised by a young boy's voice saying "hello." It was the first thing he asked, "How did the boy get into the convent?" The following day, Monday I was able to attend his Mass at 7:30 am. After breakfast we had time to chat and we went out along the lake, up to the cemetery. On the way down we saw the St. Agnes boys playing on the field. He was amazed at the number of boys, something we took for granted. In the course of our visit Fr. Shannon recommended a book, "The Council, Reform and Reunion" by Han Küng. This Swiss theologian hoped that the Church would focus on the Gospels as the basis for reuniting Christian churches. Vatican Council II would meet that October and bring renewed life to our concepts of Church and mission. His suggestion pointed to the changes about to occur in the Church and the world. I was ever so glad that he visited me at Sparkill.

Sr. Cecilia, our Novice Mistress, was practical but sometimes inscrutable. Her practical side was evident when she invited us to be part of a planting project. Spring 1962 we planted eighty tomato plants on the east side of the novitiate. We pinned up our habits and wore aprons to try not to turn our white habits into the brown habits of the Franciscans. Getting the soil ready and then placing the plants in rows took time and concerted effort. This was one group endeavor that was fun because we were outdoors and doing something different. Most of us, new to tomato planting learned as we went along. This was the perfect outdoor activity after Night Prayer at the Motherhouse when we returned to the novitiate. It took time to water the plants, but it was wonderful being outdoors while the sun was still shining. Over many weeks of weeding, watering, and watching we discovered visitors that also welcomed the addition to their diets: squirrels, ground hogs, and Japanese beetles. When our families came to visit, our parents had advice about dealing with pests and any unwelcome critters. I minded three plants which allowed me to monitor the growth and travails of those plants. We also planted flowers in the circle in front of the novitiate. At first we did not know a weed from a flower, but gradually we caught on and were able to weed and not pull the flowers. This was an amazing project that gave us a sense of ownership and stewardship. Who knew we would have that opportunity? We were invested in our small corner of the earth. As the summer progressed there were enough tomatoes to be served in the refectory. The first day we passed the bowl around, each took a whole tomato. I could not wait to taste it. I was about to bite into the ripe tomato when Sr. Cecilia caught my eye; she motioned for me to cut it into sections. We were eating in silence as was the custom, but I wished that we could have cheered for the fruit of all our labors and yes, eat it whole like an apple.

    Sr. Mary Clare's feast day was August 12. To my great delight Sr. Cecilia asked me to bake a cake for the occasion. It was rather simple: a yellow cake with chocolate icing. All went well greasing the cake pans, beating the batter, and baking the cake in the novitiate kitchen oven. The two layers had to cool so I placed them on a wire rack on the kitchen table. After lunch I returned to ice the cake. "Oh, no," I cried, "How did they get up here?" There were tiny black ants on the table and on one of the layers. I wanted to cry. Ants were a perennial problem in the basement of the novitiate, invading our bins and the table in the laundry on a regular basis, but I had not thought they had made it upstairs. With no time to bake another cake I needed an alternate plan. The ants were only on the outer circle of one layer. Rather than throw out the layer I decided to create a smaller layer by trimming away the ants and cutting it in a circular shape. I iced the larger layer, placed the two layers together, iced the sides, and finally the top. It looked like a wedding cake by the time I finished and best of all, Sr. Mary Clare would have a cake for her feast day.

On Tuesday, September 18 our band of novices went to Saugerties for a day of sun and fun. The leaves on the trees were beginning to turn so we saw colorful sights throughout our bus ride. Mother Kevin and Mother Beatrice welcomed us when we arrived. The view of the Hudson through the trees and bushes was beautiful. We followed a dirt path walking about ¼ mile down through the woods and voilá, there was the Hudson River at our feet. We changed from habits and veils into bathing suits, sweatshirts, and sneakers. The dock was the place to sun bathe and there was a ladder so we could climb down into the water. Underfoot the river was squishy so those who could swam away where the water was clearer. Meanwhile at the outdoor grille near the path Mother Kevin, Sr. Cecilia, and some professed Sisters cooked and served hot dogs with all the trimmings. There was lemonade, watermelon, and a variety of donuts. When the tide came in we alternated swimming and sunning. The dock was large enough for all forty-five of us novices when we placed our towels side by side like canned sardines. We sang, ate, talked and had a really relaxing day. It felt good to be in the sun and get our suits to dry when the sun shone. Banks of billowy clouds moved in and provided shade. More grilling—hamburgers this time, followed by Napoleons, "long johns" (a long, skinny donut with apple filling), oranges, along with coffee, tea, and milk. It got chilly so we did square dances and played games on the dock, dashing over to the fire to warm ourselves. We wound up smelling like charcoal, but it felt good to be warm. When there was a brief sun shower, we ran into the dock house and each tried finding her habit, the difficulty being that all forty-five habits looked alike. Somehow we managed to change into our habits after a little "Hide 'n Seek" and even put on our veils without a mirror. We wended our way back up the hill to the main house. I was glad to have the habit on again for it warmed me, something all of us appreciated for the rays of the afternoon sun were shining on the other side of the Hudson. In habits we once again looked like ourselves. A Dominican priest was visiting Saugerties so we became the first group of novices to have Benediction of the Blessed Sacrament in the new chapel with its blonde wood pews and windows that afforded so much light. After Benediction we sang "O God of Loveliness," one of our favorite hymns. I especially liked the line, "Thou art the one alone whose love my heart can fill." On such a wonderful day it was natural for us to think of God and all the gifts God had given us.

We learned that Mother Benigna had purchased this property in 1932. I wondered to myself, "How was she able to purchase the Spalding estate during the Great Depression?" Thanks to Mother Benigna we had a place to vacation. It allowed us to get away to the Hudson Valley, be with our Sisters in a relaxed setting, and share our experiences of the past year. Even the thought of going to Saugerties was therapeutic let alone the actual experience. It was an opportunity to meet and get to know other Sisters in an informal setting. We wore our habits to Mass each day, but then changed into "play clothes" after breakfast and went down to the river. There were rowboats that we put to good use and a sand bar within rowing distance of the dock. At low tide it was a beautiful beach; at high tide it almost disappeared from sight. Saugerties was a fun place that benefited body and soul. We read books and magazines just for fun, talked with friends and others whom we met through Sisters we knew, swam near the dock or even better at the sand bar, sunbathed, rowed downstream to Glasco and occasionally across to an island on the far side of the Hudson (This was expressly forbidden but I couldn't resist; when I went I wore a life jacket and went with Sisters who were strong swimmers for I could not swim. We went down immediately after morning Mass so we could row across the Hudson, get out and explore the island a bit, then row back—all before anyone arrived at the dock!), walked the dirt road, and after supper walked to an ice cream shop on Spalding Lane. Since our dormitory was down the hill from the main house, at night we moved beds to create a space where we could dance to recorded music. Who could ask for more?

I still remember the ride back to the Motherhouse. The yellow school bus was so crowded that seats made for two had to be shared by three. Sometimes it was just easier to stand holding onto the seat. Most of that time I was talking with Sr. Joachim (Ann Bartley). We had not worked together or attended the same schools so Saugerties was our ticket to friendship. Ann and I learned that day that we both appreciated humor and enjoyed each other's company. Many years would pass and we would teach in different schools, but that thread of friendship would grow stronger. We remained in touch after Ann left the convent, worked in politics, married, and returned to teaching and counseling students in the NYC Public School System. She had an enormous talent for relating to people and children especially those who lived in situations that were less than ideal. She earned a second Master's degree while juggling working full time, leading a group for parents of addicted teens, caring for her husband and mother, and sustaining two households: an apartment in the Bronx and a new home in the Poconos. By some quirk of fortune we reconnected the fall of 1992 when I was undergoing treatment for breast cancer and she was breaking out from a marriage with an abusive husband. Every Wednesday Ann would pick me up at the convent to go to Memorial Sloan Kettering Cancer Center in Manhattan where I had blood work done and saw a nurse for counseling. On the way we compared notes. We both had tales of sorrow and could empathize with the other. In addition we managed to laugh over situations once we had squeezed out all the sorrow and moved on to see the irony of life. I was working a new job and could not wait to get home to take off the wig, remove the saddle bags (breast prosthesis), and take an anti-nausea drug. Most days I went to bed because that was all I could do at that point in the day. Once I took the pill I could not drive so Ann was my savior. I looked forward to seeing Ann each Wednesday. She helped me get through really tough times.

The new postulants had arrived on September 8th and now we were the ones to whom they looked up. Their band was smaller than ours so it must have been a challenge for the Postulant Mistress to cover charges. Like us some postulants had attended college and waited two or three years. Most postulants in those days entered after high school so they made this major life decision at age 18. The way religious life was structured there were many opportunities for growth and time to discern if the life of the Dominican Sisters of Sparkill were indeed a right fit. The postulants followed in our footsteps and tested the waters. Months rolled by quickly for them and even more quickly for us. We were acclimated to being novices: assuming roles of Versicularian for chanting the Little Office of the Blessed Virgin, devoting time and energy to learning basic concepts of being a vowed woman religious, and serving the community in the chapel, refectory, throughout the Motherhouse and the novitiate.

In the evening we had to ask the Novice Mistress for a penance if we had failed to follow the Rule. It engendered humility and honesty: as we admitted our faults, each Sister then made the *venia* at the feet of the Novice Mistress. A communal version of this practice was Chapter of Faults.

St. Dominic never wanted the Rule to be binding under pain of sin; rather it was a fault not to follow the Rule and Constitutions. As novices we had Chapter of Faults in the novitiate conference room. We sat in straight backed chairs in two rows facing each other. Each of us would approach the Novice Mistress at the head of the chairs to name publicly our offenses. After receiving a penance, usually prayers to be recited later, each Sister made the *venia* and returned to her seat. It was such a relief to get that over. The following year as young professed, our band had Chapter of Faults with the Prioress in the Motherhouse. We were so nervous. When a Sister confessed to dropping many platters and bowls, we could picture the whole event. She had been running down the ramp and lost her footing. Humpty Dumpty had a great fall. Unlike Humpty Sister was fine, but all the things she was carrying broke and scattered. With that image in our minds, the grandfather clock began to chime. One-two-three-four… we could not contain ourselves. First a few, then all burst out laughing. It was so contagious that the Prioress called an end to that Chapter. What a huge relief to be saved by the bell. This practice would soon be discontinued when we revised the Constitutions. I was ever so grateful not to have to go through that ordeal ever again.

Letters home and visiting days were weekly and monthly events respectively. I was writing longer letters and my mother was the intermediary between me and my friends in their senior year at Nazareth. They were facing many challenges: living off campus, student teaching, writing a thesis, comprehensives, as well as all the social events throughout the academic year. My friend, Sully (Mary Sullivan) was editor of *Sigillum*, the yearbook. She was perfect for that job. There was talk of her going to graduate school while other friends were applying for teaching and nursing jobs. Some of my friends were already members of the Sisters of St. Joseph choosing to enter before they graduated. It was harder to keep in touch due to the many changes in their lives. What became obvious was that I was more heavily invested in the Dominican Sisters once I became a novice. I had friends among the novices and postulants. Prayer was a meaningful endeavor. I liked my work in the Sewing Room. Where else could I learn a new skill that gave me a sense of satisfaction because it provided habits and other sundries for the professed Sisters and the novices-to-be? It was truly holy work. Who knew all the good that those who would wear those habits would do? My prayerful wishes went with the habits I sewed. As a teenager I had embroidered pillowcases and I loved creating something beautiful, but sewing habits was a far richer experience.

Christmas was extra special because as novices we had the opportunity to create a festive atmosphere for the postulants, but even more so for the whole community. Novices would decorate Sacred Heart Chapel, the refectory, and later the novitiate. Christmas Eve morning we decorated the Sewing Room with a fireplace using red construction paper and mortar from a sticky flow pen. We made an angel for Sr. Constantia that rested on the table where she sat. As I wrote home, "we needed ingenuity and so does the viewer seeing as the angel is wearing a flowing gown of mohair trimmed with green rickrack; a body made of spools of thread; a head of white darning thread with buttons for eyes, a pin for a nose, a trimmed straw for a mouth. Handles from a shopping bag were the base for her glistening wings." The upstairs refectory was tastefully decorated with linen tablecloths and lacy green and red placemats. The centerpiece at the head of the table was a crib set made the past summer in ceramics class. That afternoon we novices got to decorate the novitiate recreation room. Just like at home, the biggest challenge was getting the lights to work. It was easy to assemble, mount and center the six foot tree, but finding two circuits of lights that worked was a matter of trial and error. After what seemed like an eternity, we got the blue lights lit and the Christmas tree was a beauty. That evening first the boys from St. Agnes, then a group of professed Sisters came to the novitiate to sing carols. That set the mood for us to go into the recreation room where we sang a few more carols and opened our presents. The celebration continued Christmas morning. We awoke to find new habits and mantles that we wore for the special feast. We looked so clean and felt so dressed up as we made our way to Sacred Heart Chapel! We attended six Masses, the last one a Solemn High Mass with three priests officiating. Led by Sr. Ann Catherine, the Sisters and the boys sang a new setting for the Mass as well as hymns in harmony (alto and soprano). All these celebrations helped us to focus on Christ's coming as a babe to Mary and Joseph. As I recall Christmas of 1962 as a novice, the words of a hymn that I would sing many years later come to mind, "What wondrous love is this, o my soul, o my soul!" Like its composer, William Walker (1809-1875)), I hope that when I am freed by death, I too will sing on to praise the wondrous love of God who became man and chose to be with us.

Winter passed quickly as did the solemn season of Lent. March 17th, St. Patrick's Day, was the patron saint of the New York Archdiocese and a time to celebrate. We watched the New York City parade on the television in the Motherhouse community room. I remembered how Joan and Geri had marched every year, but this year we were looking for our boys from St. Agnes who marched in front of Aquinas High School. We were so excited and proud to see our boys wearing their new uniforms and carrying their shiny new drums… We were praying with all the Church throughout Holy Week. Holy Saturday at the Vigil Mass was very special. A dramatic moment I will always remember occurred when the organ sounded and the *Gloria* was proclaimed in song. At that exact moment we removed our choir mantles and a sea of black changed instantaneously to white, the white of our Dominican habits. It was thrilling.

April 14, 1963 we celebrated Easter Sunday. That evening many Sisters began their annual retreat. For us novices it would be our ten day retreat prior to Profession. The retreat master was Rev. Aedan McKeon, OP who had given the retreat at Nazareth College when I was a freshman. The Easter week liturgies have wonderful Scripture readings that lift the heart and soul. Father McKeon's conferences added to the power of those readings for he showed how we fit into the glorious scheme of things. We met Father when he came to the Sewing Room to be measured for his habit. He was tall and handsome, "easy on the eyes" as some would say, and had a wonderful personality. (We could not have known then, but Fr. Aedan would preside at our Golden Jubilee Mass many years later.) I took notes after each conference for future reflection. When Joan learned about this, she asked to see them. I was more than happy to share my notes with her. We were blessed to have time to pray and be with God for soon we would be pledging our lives to Jesus. It probably resembled the precious moments loved ones have before their marriage ceremony. We were young but so eager to give ourselves completely to God. As I wrote to my parents, "What I'll be doing that day (May 8th) by way of giving up will be small, ever so small, compared to what I'll be receiving. God is good!" Who could ask for more?

The grounds of the Motherhouse were bursting with new growth: pear and dogwood trees in bloom along with tulips and other spring flowers proclaiming the triumph of life over death. Daylight Saving Time on April 28th had added light to each day so I was in a happy mood anticipating May 8th. I wanted my parents to understand the ceremony on Profession Day so I wrote telling them that I would be the second Sister to kneel before Mother Kevin to say my vows:

> *To the honor of Almighty God, and under the protection of the Blessed Virgin Mary and of our holy father, Saint Dominic, I, <u>Sister Judith Mary</u>, make to God in your hands the simple vows of poverty, chastity and obedience for one year according to the Rule of Saint Augustine and the Constitutions of the Dominican Congregation of Our Lady of the Rosary.*

The Bishop would then bless our scapulars praying that "we may be worthy to put on Christ our Lord." The choir intones *Veni, Sponsa Christi* inviting us to receive the crown which Christ has prepared for us. Various prayers are recited in Latin: "Hearken, O daughter…Forget also thine own people and thy father's house. And the King shall greatly desire thy beauty." The Bishop prays that we may be given time to do penance for sin praying that the Lord Jesus Christ "be behind thee to guard thee, within thee to direct thee, above thee to bless thee." He also prays, "May God the Father bless thee, God the Son heal thee, the Holy

Spirit enlighten thee. And may He watch over thy body, save thy soul, enlighten thy heart, and direct and draw thy mind to heavenly truth." The Bishop blesses the black veil after which the choir sings, *Posuit signum*, "He has placed a seal upon my countenance that I may accept no other lover." When the choir intones *Amo Christum* we make our prostration and the choir sings,"

> *I love Christ, into whose bridal chamber I shall enter, Whose Mother is a Virgin,*
>
> *Whose Father knows not woman...When I love Him, I am chaste; when I touch Him,*
>
> *I am clean; when I receive Him I am a virgin.*

As we made the prostration, I so wanted to pray for everyone that I had written on a piece of paper and pinned to the yoke of my habit: "I pray for my parents, (George and Margaret and step father, Joseph) and relatives living (Nana, Joan, Geri and Mike and my nieces and nephew, Tom and Ann and their children, my aunts, uncles, and cousins) and deceased (dear Aunt Nellie, my father George), friends, and all those whom I will serve or get to know in the future." We had learned that St. Thomas Aquinas called Profession a second Baptism, a total consecration of our bodies, minds and hearts to God so I wanted to share this special moment with everyone I knew or would ever know. As I wrote to my parents, "As I lie prostrate at Christ's feet, I know I'll rise to be His ever so specially—who can describe the wonder of this?"

> The Bishop then blesses our rings and places it on our third finger.
> *Receive then the ring of fidelity, the mark of spiritual nuptials, the seal of the Holy Spirit that you may be, and may be called, the Spouse of Christ.*

During the Kiss of Peace that followed the blessing of rings, the *Te Deum*, a hymn of praise and thanksgiving to the Trinity, was sung by the choir. Solemn Benediction of the Blessed Sacrament concludes the ceremony. After all those wonderful prayers and blessings we would process outside where our families would meet us, embrace us, and take pictures. It was a perfect day for pledging my love and I was thrilled to have my parents and relatives with me. Alleluia!

After Profession I had a strange reaction: I felt anonymous. Wearing the black veil helped us to blend in with all the professed Sisters. Like the days after Reception of the Habit, we needed time to adjust to our new status. We would be in Sparkill for another year of Formation. This allowed us more time for formal and personal prayer in Sacred Heart Chapel. This was especially important in terms of remembering why we had entered and what we had professed. I was assigned to teach fourth grade in St. Agnes School replacing a postulant who would be receiving the habit. I was happy to get experience teaching though it is difficult to substitute for a teacher so late in the school year. Sr. Ann Bernadette, the principal, had said, "You have a strong voice and you will do fine." I tried to recall her comment in the days ahead. That first day as the door to the high-ceilinged classroom closed, I felt like a prisoner locked in with my class. When it was time for recess, I had no idea where the bathrooms were, but the boys knew and led the way. For the most part the boys were good and cooperated even though it was the end of the school year when most children cannot wait to be out of school. They were a credit to Sr. Patricia's many months of dedicated teaching.

We continued with classes at STAC. Over the summer I remember sneaking off to the cemetery to read *Wuthering Heights* for the Novel course; other courses followed in more traditional settings in the fall and spring semesters. I was able to complete courses and graduated *summa cum laude* from St. Thomas Aquinas College on June 6, 1964. It was the last commencement held in Sacred Heart Chapel. The following year commencement was held in the college gymnasium or outdoors on the STAC campus. By that time the college enrollment had soared with a great number of lay persons in addition to the Sisters enrolled at STAC.

When I first professed my vows in 1963 I meant them for all my life. The truth is that we made our vows for one year and renewed our vows in 1964, 1965, and 1966. We would make Final Vows in 1968. It was better to make temporary vows in those in-between years for we had not yet been out on mission and had not lived the active/contemplative life that included prayer, teaching, and living in community with the Sisters in that local community. At the Motherhouse there was space and many Sisters; in the local community there was a smaller group of Sisters among whom we lived, worked, and prayed in close proximity. If a Sister sang off key or had annoying habits, these things could be maddening. If the superior had favorites or refused permissions to do things that were ordinarily permitted like taking a walk or accompanying a Sister when she went home to visit her family that could result in resentment. My first superior on mission was a good school woman but in the convent she tried to pit us one against another. That infuriated me. How could we call ourselves Christians let alone consecrated religious if we did not come to the aid of those with whom we lived? That was only one superior, thank God. In all the houses to which I was assigned, the Sisters supported one another. If there were groups, there was always a group with whom I indentified. I also met and came to love Sisters quite a bit older than I. Age was not a barrier for they were women of wisdom whose opinions and sense of humor I came to cherish. All of which is to say that I was a more seasoned, mature woman when I made Final Vows on August 15, 1968. By age twenty-six I was better able to say, "Here I am, Lord. I come to do your will."

Chapter 5

CHANGE AHEAD

I entered the convent to respond to a call to follow Christ. I chose the Congregation of the Dominican Sisters in Sparkill, New York because I knew that this was a life that I could live. It was a decision made after months of prayer. I knew many Dominican Sisters and had observed how my sister, Sr. Joan Dolores and my cousin, Sr. Barbara Ann were flourishing as Dominican Sisters and teachers. Many of my fellow postulants knew each other because they attended the same school or lived in the same neighborhood and were members of the same parish. That was not my experience because we lived upstate and I had attended college in Rochester, NY for two years. You might say that I was new to the scene.

We heard warnings against "particular friendships." I did not comprehend that concept until many years later. In the novitiate I was glad to meet other young women motivated to love God and serve God's people. Their enthusiasm and dedication would lift me up when I felt less than highly motivated. Once again we met while learning how to be consecrated women religious. Each of us entered with preconceived ideas of what it meant to be a Dominican Sister but these would be refined and often, replaced by the reality of religious life. First and foremost was our life of prayer. We prayed as a community with all the professed sisters of St. Agnes Convent in Sacred Heart Chapel. We were young and our voices were a welcome addition to chanting the Little Office of Our Lady. My band (the sisters who entered with me, were postulants and novices, and finally professed vows together) loved choir practice on Sunday afternoons. We were learning new music and relished singing in parts (alto and soprano). It was also an opportunity for me to see my sister, Sr. Joan Dolores for she accompanied Sr. Ann Catherine, the director; we could not speak but at least I saw her.

In addition to customs we had to learn the meaning of the Rule of St. Augustine and the Directory. First the novices and later professed sisters were models for us: how to conduct ourselves in daily life. We met sisters as we worked on charges to which we were assigned: in my case working with young boys in Rosary group, then Little Side Refectory; taking turns supervising the boys so the group mother could be at communal prayers; learning skills in the Sewing Room as a novice, and after profession, teaching in St. Agnes School. There were professed sisters who were senior to us who showed us what to do and whose good example encouraged us to do our best.

We learned the art of networking: connecting with someone whose skill or work proved helpful. It always helped to know someone who worked in the boys' sewing room. With so many active, young boys their clothing was always in need of repair. When we stopped by to collect clothing for the boys in our group, we could also get something personal sewed or pressed. We took turns working in the kitchen when the Sisters were at morning prayer: setting up pitchers of milk and juice, baskets with rolls and butter, and breakfast cereal for the Sisters and the boys. It was an enormous endeavor preparing three meals a day for 300 boys and 200 Sisters. Some chores required two of us working together: lifting the commercial sized cans to pour milk into pitchers. Besides those who worked in the kitchen, there were Sisters who served the food and still others busy in the pantry washing and drying pitchers, bowls and platters. The novices silently and devotedly performed services so the Sisters at the Motherhouse and St. Agnes could serve in their ministries of teaching, child care, and administration.

On visiting days when our parents and siblings came, the Sisters from St. Louis would serve refreshments and chat with our families. These conversations eased the fact that they would only see their own families at Reception of the Habit and Profession of Vows in May. My mother and other Sisters' relatives baked cakes and cookies that we would enjoy that day and for days afterward. I made sure that my sister, Joan would have baked goods even if she did not get to visit my parents that day. On Fridays, "fish day," the dinner menu included a variety of succulent pies for dessert. One of the Sisters remembered that my stepfather liked lemon meringue pie so the next visiting day she presented him with his very own pie. He was so pleased. It pays to have friends in the right places.

Little Side was in the basement near the postulants' refectory and cloak room. One evening we finished mopping the floor and were standing around talking. Someone mentioned the fact that, "Centrifugal force allows you to swing a pail full of water and not spill anything." "No," said Sr. Assumpta. "Yes, yes," we cried. "Get a pail and see for yourself." She proceeded to get a pail and filled it with water. She chose a spot where she would not hit the fluorescent ceiling lights, and then quickly swung it up and around. All was fine for a second or two, but then we heard the metal clank and the sound of water gushing over the tables, dishes, and floor! We had failed to take into account Assumpta's height— she was nearly six feet tall, and the ceiling was quite low. The refectory had to be clean before the other sisters came from evening prayer. We were laughing so hard that it was difficult to pull ourselves together to get the mops and rags to wipe up the water. Science was not advanced, but we had more laughs than if the experiment had gone perfectly.

On another occasion Sr. Francis Christine, my "twin," (we had the same novice Mother) had a surprise for us. We followed her into Little Side and she proceeded to play a record. "Why such a fuss?" I thought. For the first time we heard the Beetles, whose music had taken our country by storm. We loved it and began to dance on the spot.

August 1964 I reported to Our Lady of Grace Convent in the Bronx. It was my first mission and I was excited and scared. Before long I was amazed how friendships formed even though we had so little time for socializing. Truth be told, I met some women who were not just great teachers but also really fine persons. I taught third grade. With fifty-four students maintaining order was an absolute prerequisite for teaching. In addition I had to plan activities to reinforce what the students learned. With no access to a mimeograph or printer, I had to be creative when teaching reading. Each day I hand printed reading exercises on white shelving paper for each of the three reading groups so they could work while I taught each group in turn. I spent the school year preparing materials to teach different reading levels only to be assigned to another school and parish. I left behind decorations and rolls of white shelving paper filled with exercises from the Teacher's manual hoping that my successor would benefit from those resources. In fact years later when I met and became friends with the sister who taught in that classroom after I left, she told me there was nothing in the closet when she first arrived. Did someone throw out all that I had done and used that year or did someone else appropriate the materials? If they were used to help the students, wonderful; if they were tossed out, shame.

Shortly after I arrived at this convent I volunteered to make rice pudding. My grandmother's recipe began, "Nine tablespoons of rice to make it nice." The trouble was I did not know the rest of it so I read other recipes and chose ingredients accordingly. After an hour and a half I opened the oven door— the fragrance of cinnamon and vanilla was throughout the convent but the pudding was not done. It cooked away for the better part of that afternoon. It never did become pudding; it began and remained sweet milk with undercooked rice. To this day a good recipe for rice pudding has eluded me. If only Nana were here to tell me the rest of her recipe.

We were allowed to go to the wake of a sister's parents. One afternoon Sr. Stephen Ann and I were returning from a wake for the father of one of our sisters. As we walked along, I asked, "Stephen, does it matter that the street names have a W before the number?" It certainly did. Here we were on the west side of the Bronx when we needed to be on the east. As we pondered what to do, an older man in a black car pulled up and asked if we needed a ride. "Yes. Could you take us to Our Lady of Grace Convent on East 226th Street?" We threw caution to the winds and rode with a complete stranger hoping against hope that we would get home on time. You would think that a dragon awaited us that would sweep us into a fiery pit if we arrived late. As we thanked the gentleman, we raced inside to hear the clock chime: one, two, three, …six o'clock. We had made it home in time! *Deo gratias.*

After two years in the Bronx I was missioned to Our Lady of Perpetual Help School in South Ozone Park, Queens in 1966. It took so long to drive there, and later when we used public transportation, it was a forever trip: walk to the bus, take the bus to the subway, then take the subway into the city. For many it seemed like the foreign missions. Sr. Assumpta was trying to give her father directions to drive out from the Bronx for a visit shortly after arriving at Our Lady of Perpetual Help. Exasperated, he shouted, "How could you not know how to get there? Did they blindfold you and throw you in the trunk when you went there last week?"

I was assigned to teach the fourth grade. It was a delightful age group; I liked the course work for that year just as I had enjoyed my own fourth grade experience with Sr. Margaret Francis (Adelaide Harmon) years before. Each morning my students would meet me at the gate when I was going over to school. The classroom was wall to wall students, but we were a good match: their eagerness to learn fed my youthful enthusiasm for teaching. How I would love to see them again to find out how their lives have unfolded and to compare notes about their memories of fourth grade experience!

I also taught sixth grade for a few months at Our Lady of Perpetual Help. When Sr. Brendan Mary (Lillian McNamara) had to remain absolutely quiet to heal nodules on her vocal cords, they needed a substitute teacher for three months. The principal had me teach my 4th grade in the morning and Brendan's sixth grade in the afternoon. This meant preparing lessons in Bible history and geography; the material involved pronouncing many difficult names and places. I was determined that they would learn it correctly to avoid their having to relearn or worse, not ever knowing the correct pronunciation. My 4th grade class was fun; the 6th grade class was a challenge. At our first Parents' Conference in November I was so nervous that I prepared a little speech. In effect I told each parent, "Your son/daughter will be a future leader of our country. I think that he/she will do great things." All this led up to the real reason they had come: to receive their child's report card and to see how their child was doing/behaving in class. Parent/teacher conferences were agonizing for parents with a child who did not do well in school. At least that year they got a boost; even if the marks were not so great, their child would be a future leader—wow! Who could ask for more?

We had fifteen sisters at Our Lady of Perpetual Help convent with a cross section of young and more mature sisters. The older sisters had rare talents like Sr. Denise who was a travel guru. Long before we could search the internet she could tell you how to travel by bus and train in every borough. This came in handy when we were going hither and yon. I remember standing on a subway platform not knowing how to get home; we called Sr. Denise to find out how to get back to the convent. We would have been lost many times except for her expertise. I was amazed by her skill because after years living upstate I had only a rudimentary knowledge of the MTA in New York City.

Our superior/principal was hospitalized five times over the course of that year. At Thanksgiving Sr. Rita Vincent (Jean Marshall) and I were chosen to visit Sister Superior in Boston. It was my first time going to Boston so I was excited. We stayed with the Sisters of St. Joseph whose convent was in a poor neighborhood. We arrived after dark and could see their dining room, each sister's place set with china and cutlery—such a contrast with the homes of those around them. Saturday we went to the hospital where we visited with and cheered up our superior. Sr. Rita was a natural; she seemed to know just what to say and how to comfort the patient. She even washed sister's hair, no small feat in a hospital room. That was our one outing. After Mass on Sunday we returned to the Bronx. We visited the sick, but never got to sightsee. That would have to wait until I was assigned to high school. Our music teacher, Martha hailed from Boston, Massachusetts and she sponsored a trip to Boston. I was one of the chaperones. All good things come to those who wait. A major feature of that trip was a Boston Pops Concert. At the intermission I asked one of our students, "How do you like the concert?" "Fine," she said, "but I am surprised that the players look so young." "So young?" I asked. "Yes," she replied. "I thought we were going to see grandfathers (Pops)." That was a fun reaction.

The list of assignments for the following year always came out in August, but that year (1967) it came out on a weekday in May. I learned that I would be going to Our Lady of Mt. Carmel in Middletown, New York in the fall. I tried to eat dinner but had a hard time chewing let alone swallowing the roast chicken and vegetables. I was practically sobbing and could barely see straight to return to teach my class. I loved the children, the parish, and the sisters in the convent but obedience required me to go upstate. When I met Fr. Mendler outside school at dismissal, he knew that something was wrong. Indeed it was for I began to cry. As pastor he had no power to reverse the decision, but at least he understood how I felt and how much the people and children of our parish meant to me. When he had come as pastor, we heard that he was dearly loved by the parishioners in his former parish. He found it heartbreakingly difficult to leave a parish where he had so many friends and begin again in a different parish where he knew no one. The pastor of Our Lady of Perpetual Help, Fr. Mendler was a gentle man who loved to garden and who took an interest in the sisters as persons, not just as teachers for the parish school. He was one of the few pastors I ever got to know personally. He made it a point to be outside school in the playground when the students were dismissed. That way we could exchange a few words.

In August 1967 I reported to Middletown, NY. When I had lived upstate we had occasionally gone to Middletown to shop for clothing. On one of those trips, my mother bought me a wine colored wool coat. I looked so small in the luxury of that winter coat. In fact I needed a few years before it fit properly. But now I was out in the country far from stores. Our Lady of Mt. Carmel was a beautiful convent—new, open, spacious, with abundant natural light. It had a recessed chapel, a refectory, kitchen, and community room on the main floor, and our rooms on the 2nd floor. I began to unpack my trunk and after supper went upstairs to complete the task. By then it was dark and I was slowly crawling upstairs, leaning on the wall, groping for the invisible light switch. I promised myself that if I did not trip and kill myself that night, I would always be aware of light switches in a new place so I wouldn't be creeping about like an intruder. We were so far away from New York City that the phone seldom rang. When the phone did ring, I jumped up and down, crying "Contact with the outside world!" as I ran to answer it.

The first day of school arrived and I went to meet my class. *The Times Herald Middletown Record* had sent a photographer to capture the moment when the students entered from the parking lot directly into the classroom. No sooner had he completed his task than a little boy named Daniel began to cry. Actually it was like the howl of a distraught animal.

What could I do? I also felt like crying for this was my first time teaching first grade; we were both afraid. Sr. Petronella, the principal, arrived on the scene and took Daniel to her office. It turned out that he was too young and not ready to begin first grade. Her action calmed the other students and after taking a deep breath, I began my first day teaching a new class. Her intervention was life-saving. My students that year had the most creative imaginations I had encountered; they were thinking outside the box even more than I. We had fun as we/they learned; I used different terms: word games and arithmetic games instead of tests. After lunch when they were tired, I taught them how to print the next letters by singing directions as I showed them how to form the letters. That perked them up and we bridged the energy gap.

My in-house consultant that year was Sr. Joan Beairsto, a dynamic person who had taught first grade for many years. Unknown to me she had requested not to teach first grade so I won the lottery. Each evening she would teach me how to print the next letters; I learned gradually like the students because in truth I would not remember how to print the entire alphabet. We made use of the Learning Center for teachers in Middletown from which we could borrow records, books, and filmstrips for our students' use. So it happened that I had Counting Man, a large metallic figure with hands reaching upward with removable digits; he was there by the window so students could learn about adding and subtracting. He inspired me to invent two imaginary figures: Herman the German, a hulk, and Skinny Minny, a slight figure. They joined our learning community and added humor to our classes. With songs that we learned from records each of the three reading groups moved to their group places. One of these was, "Tommy was a tiny turtle, a tiny turtle was he. Tom took a walk, a tiny, tiny walk and he never came back to me." The children loved their song so getting to their group was a pleasant experience.

The parents of one of my first graders invited me to see their dairy farm. Maureen was so excited to bring her teacher to meet her parents. It brought back memories of living in White Sulphur Springs where our property bordered a farm with its lone piebald horse and a few cows. The parents were working together on this joint venture. The father was using modern methods of milking cows, something I had never seen. They were a young couple; Maureen was their oldest child. It was wonderful to see this family who loved their children and were so close to the land. I wonder if they were able to maintain their farm and if any of their children now work the farm?

We benefited by being able to ask those who were more experienced teachers how to resolve simple and even complex problems. When I arrived at Our Lady of Mt. Carmel School in Middletown I was told that my first graders would receive their First Holy Communion in the spring and that these young children would make their first confession in fourth grade. The parents of my first graders requested a meeting to discuss the new policy. I sensed that this was a meeting for which I needed help so I contacted Sr. Ann Richard (Ursula Joyce), a psychologist who taught at our college. She provided articles about the psychological development of children. The night of the parents meeting the cafeteria was filled to overflowing. The principal had not come so I was on my own to face this audience. I delivered my comments based on the articles that Sr. Ursula had sent me. The parents could barely contain themselves until they could ask questions. "Why are you changing the order of things? We went to confession and only then received First Communion in the second grade." I explained how young children were not capable of committing a serious offense, but that did not convince the parents. Over and over they rose to challenge me. "I want my child to receive Communion at the same age that I did. If it was good enough for me, it is good enough for my child." I was in a bind because this change seemed fine to me but the parents' lived experience was blocking them from hearing or agreeing with any theologically/psychologically sound argument. The pastor, Father Reilly arrived, sensed what was happening, and managed to quiet them down. It was my first experience facing a challenging crowd. Somehow the meeting came to an end and I returned to the convent a wiser woman. My class did receive their First Holy Communion in May. The earth continued to turn; there were no cosmic consequences. In fact these young boys and girls had a real desire to welcome Jesus into their hearts. All of us, teachers and parents, were humbled and thrilled by this experience.

My first graders were on the front line of students who witnessed a change in our habit. For years our hair was hidden, covered by a white cap and black veil. First a few sisters throughout the congregation volunteered to model different styles. I think my sister, Joan was one of these. Then we could choose the style that we liked. Of course we had to make the veil and practice putting it on and pinning it in place. I enjoyed the flurry of activity in my convent. In March 1968 we wore the new veil to school. The students lined the path from the convent over to school. What had they thought? That we had no hair, that we were bald? It wouldn't be the first time that people had weird ideas about nuns—like the little girl in the supermarket who asked shyly, "Are you the Flying Nun?" That day in March we walked through an honor guard of excited children who were thrilled to see that like everyone else we had hair at the top of our head that now peeked through the new veil. It was like walking the runway at a fashion show.

My time in Middletown was brief. In 1968 I was assigned to teach at St. Helena Girls High School in the Bronx. Finally I would be able to use the Spanish I had learned in college. That summer I studied Spanish at Hunter College and lived at Thorpe Convent on East 63rd Street. It was a brutally hot summer and our rooms were on the 4th floor of a convent with no elevator or air conditioning. When I learned that Fordham University at Lincoln Center was air conditioned I went to their library in the evening to study. At 9 PM I returned to the convent to climb up to the hot house for the night.

St. Helena's had forty-five sisters who lived in the main convent, over the school, and in a separate brick building called the cottage. I was assigned to live on the 2nd floor of the convent, next to the community room. It had been a large bedroom that they subdivided: Sr. Joanne Therese lived in one half, I in the other. It was going to be a hectic year teaching high school Spanish and Religion. Graduate study added to the busy life of a teacher. There were other responsibilities: moderating the Photography Club and co-moderating Yearbook. Working on Yearbook and in the convent kitchen I met other sisters, shared tasks, had many laughs, and experienced community in our various endeavors. Every day began with prayer so that and our mission of teaching unified our efforts. It was a whirlwind of activity.

My knowledge of photography was severely limited: taking some pictures on a Brownie box camera. For Photography Club I had to learn how to load film in a single lens reflex camera, how to focus the camera, and later how to crop the pictures for use in the yearbook. The juniors who were members of the club taught me how to use a camera. Unlike digital cameras, I had to wait until the film was developed; it was not a matter of instant gratification. By trial and error I gradually learned what constituted a good picture, how to frame a shot, the intricacies of apertures, which type of film to use for indoors/outdoors, bright light/low light. It was science and art combined. What began as a task grew into a hobby. I also took a photography course at the New York Botanical Garden. That provided the opportunity to photograph autumnal scenes with trees whose russet/yellow leaves hovered over and were reflected by the Bronx River. Combined with travel, photography yielded a wonderful record of places I visited and the persons with whom I traveled. Brother Carlos, a Marist brother from Spain was my mentor. His advice, "Always look for and take a picture of the prettiest young lady." That seemed prejudicial, but it did ensure beauty would win the day. We tried to take pictures of many of the students, not just those who were pretty, but also the girls who were not posing or tying to be in every picture. The "hams" get enough attention; I wanted to capture those who were doing ordinary things. If beauty is in the eyes of the beholder, then surely I could reveal the natural beauty of these young ladies.

While Photography Club met once a week, Yearbook involved many afternoons per week. In the fall we had to supervise informal outdoor pictures for each senior. There were over 300 students in the graduating class so this was no small endeavor. There were also class pictures for all the undergraduate classes taken outdoors with different backgrounds. Each homeroom had over 30 students so it was a matter of scheduling, notifying students and faculty, and getting each homeroom to report and pose in smaller groups. Weather had a huge impact on outdoor pictures. We had heard that there was always good weather on Jewish high holy days so we scheduled class pictures on the religious holidays. That year it actively rained and we had to resort to holding an umbrella over the photographer as he took the pictures.

Sr. Eileen Gannon had majored in and taught English so she was the resident scholar for all things written. I was learning photography rapidly and would complement her language skills with my artistic eye. We had days when the yearbook photographer came to shoot informal pictures and other times to shoot events like Ring Night or honor assemblies. That first year was amazingly good fun. We were attempting to create a literary and artistic yearbook even while still learning the basics. We had to inspire the Yearbook staff: seniors and some juniors to brainstorm for themes that would unify all the sections of the whole book. My favorite theme in the six years we were moderators was "Man the Creator" against the backdrop of Michelangelo's Creation as depicted on the Sistine Chapel ceiling. This was before we were aware of sexist language, especially in an all girls' school. There was always much discussion about the person(s) to whom we would dedicate the yearbook. In 1969 when the New York Mets won the World Series for the first time, the girls from Queens stated emphatically, "We have to dedicate the book to the Mets!" We nudged them away from that idea, but knowing how that championship would elude the Mets for many years (1986), perhaps we should have seriously considered it.

Eileen Gannon came from the Bronx and attended St. Helena's straight through high school. Her parents still lived in Parkchester. She was bright, funny, and outgoing. Still wearing the long habit she was graceful even when overly burdened by responsibilities. We met the summer before I began to teach at Helena's when I delivered a notebook that my cousin, Barbara sent over to help Eileen study for a final at Hunter College. Apparently they both had the same professor at different times and he did not suffer fools lightly. Eileen looked exhausted like a balloon whose buoyancy had lapsed into a flat semblance of its former self. I would know by the following year how that felt for it was an intricate balancing act with morning prayer, meditation, and mass, community life, charges, preparing and teaching classes, supervising students for activities and clubs, taking graduate courses, traveling by public transportation to/from Hunter College (a bus and a train) two nights a week; and attending wakes of relatives of the sisters. It was like being on a carousel operating at maximum speed. In the midst of all these activities we managed to get to know the other sisters who were on similar schedules. It seemed impossible, but we formed friendships in the midst of busyness that made our heads spin.

I became friends with Eileen when we worked together at St. Helena Girls High School. In addition to co-moderating the yearbook we were assigned to work in the convent kitchen. Friendships often evolved when working on assigned tasks. There was little time to chit chat so friendship arose as sisters worked, cooperated, and relaxed together. The novice mistress had drilled into us a fear of particular friendships, but I for one did not grasp what that meant. Rather I valued the acceptance and recognition that could lead to true affection. There were real tasks to do, real challenges to tackle so it was a relief to find a kindred spirit with whom one could do the assigned task, work together to overcome obstacles, and share the joys and sorrows that are inherent in being human.

When someone as outgoing and likeable as Eileen is one's best friend, I knew instinctively that she was not my sole possession. That was never the nature of our relationship. Eileen was and would be friend to many. For me Eileen bridged a gap, helping me to understand situations and relationships. When we needed to work out details with authority figures, she was more diplomatic than I so she approached the principal or assistant principal. We both had minds in overdrive, but Eileen had a wonderful way of relating to others. In addition her joie de vivre was contagious.

The natural rhythm of teaching high school students, praying and living with our Sisters at St. Helena's was about to undergo many changes. Compared with the upheavals in American society in the mid-1960s to 1970's ours was an evolutionary process. Yes, there were times when it felt agonizingly slow, but overall we were a group of 800 sisters responding to the call to revisit the original charism of our founder, Mother Antoninus Thorpe.

Our habit underwent another change at Christmas 1968. At Midnight Mass we wore the short habit for the first time. The Marist brothers hosted a party that felt like a celebration; I remember being more conscious of how I sat for there was no longer a habit down to my ankles. It was so bitterly cold that the next day I bought black snow boots that came up to my knees so I would not freeze waiting at bus stops. When classes resumed the high school girls enjoyed our new look; they were busy checking out our shoes.

The summer of 1969 was important for me and for our congregation. I had the opportunity to go on a five week tour of Spain with stops in Estoril, Portugal, Lourdes, France, and Morocco. Our group included students from St. Helena Girls High School, St. Helena Boys High School, and St. Agnes High School in College Point, Queens. I was thrilled to be able to go to Spain. When I called my parents, my stepfather wanted to know, "Are they making you go on this trip?" "No," I replied, "No one is forcing me. This is a privilege and I want to go." He had biased views of anyone who spoke Spanish, let alone a whole country of Spanish speakers. Maria Formoso and I were the chaperons for the girls from St. Helena's. It was my first time flying and my first time going to Europe. This good fortune came my way because all the other teachers in the Foreign Language Department did not want to be away for five weeks; they knew the perils of chaperoning girls on a trip far from home. In my case ignorance was bliss. I learned early on that there was a fundamental difference between me and the girls. I was in Spain to soak up the culture, to visit art museums, cathedrals, and cities famous for artists, warriors, saints and so much more. My charges were there for a chance to interact with boys on the trip and Spanish boys/men where we visited. I remember being engrossed in a lecture the tour guide was giving and looking over to see the girls barely awake, leaning against the wall bored out of their minds. Our daily rhythms were also different. I was enthused and alive by day but they came alive at night. Brother Carlos, the Marist Brother in charge of the tour, channeled their energies into activities they liked: going to a carnival, the beach, and a disco, et al. One afternoon I was walking with a group of our girls when a few Spanish men followed us making lewd remarks about the girls. Apparently they thought American girls were an easy mark; I doubt that they would have done the same to their young women. It reached such a point that I turned around, slapped the man directly behind me, and told them to leave our girls alone. I was barely ten years older than the girls but I had to put an end to their harassment. Luckily the men laughed and they backed off so we could continue into the park and connect with the other members of our group.

Maria and I took turns checking rooms every night. Five weeks away was a long time. From the first dinner served in Portugal with a complete fish head in the soup and rolls so hard they could have been weapons, our girls could not wait to get home so they could go to McDonald's. We supervised the girls carefully, but they were experts at circumventing rules. I spoke with our girls as a group standing on the beach in Cádiz, "We have a short time until we return home. I want you to think carefully and not do something you will regret." They probably had no idea what I meant: I was really afraid that someone would return home pregnant. I was never invited to a christening, but one good offshoot was the fact that one of our girls fell in love with travel, so much so that she became a travel agent and guided many other travelers in their quest for adventure.

I was eager to learn what happened at the Chapter of Affairs that took place while I was in Spain. We were responding to the call from the leadership of the Roman Catholic Church to view our mission in light of the spirit of our founder, Mother Catharine M. Antoninus Thorpe. This process of *aggiornamento* arose when Pope John XXIII convened Vatican Council II in 1959. He would not live to see its completion, but Pope John inspired the bishops and cardinals to consider not only the inner workings of the church, but also how the church, the People of God, would relate to/with all those with whom they worked and lived. Vatican Council II (1962-1965) would open the windows and allow the Holy Spirit to breathe new life into the Catholic Church. The bishops with the help of theologians and the blessing of the pope had approved a number of documents and it was to these writings that we turned for our deliberations. Our delegates formed different committees/commissions to learn about and discuss issues pertinent to our congregation

The Pope had asked religious congregations to revisit the charism of their founder and to adapt their Constitutions to better serve the people of God. Prior to the Chapter our congregation engaged in a Self-Study Commission (1967-1968). All of the Sisters were invited to respond to questions about the Aims of the Congregation and the Spirit of its Founder and the Order; Interior Life and Religious Observances; the Vows; Religious Formation Program; the Apostolate; and the Purpose and Exercise of Authority. Our congregation of over 700 Sisters responded to questions that were then collated into a report that covered aspects of religious life as we knew it and how we hoped it to be in the future. The Sisters elected Chapter delegates who worked on Commissions. They used the results of the Self-Study when they met to consider propositions for change.

The first session of the Chapter of Affairs was held at Holy Trinity High School convent in Hicksville, NY for four weeks in the summer of 1969. My sister, Sr. Joan Dolores, was a delegate and had worked with the Government Commission. We knew that our governance needed revision. For many years our government structure resembled a pyramid with the Mother General assisted by the General Council at the top, superiors below them, and all the Sisters at the bottom. At that time the Sisters with final vows would gather in groups of twelve to select a delegate to the Chapter. Those delegates would convene in Chapter and vote for the Sister who would be the Mother General for six years with the possibility of serving a second six year term. The Mother General with the advice of her Council would appoint Sisters to serve as Principals of the schools and superiors in the local community; they also determined when and where the Sisters would be missioned. Like Musical Chairs the superiors would move from one convent to another with little influx of new blood. Principals of elementary schools usually served for six years, though principals of high schools stayed longer.

There were many issues that demanded attention but every time the Sisters had a chance to express their concerns governance topped the list. Changes in the government structure were based on two principles, collegiality and subsidiarity. Collegiality is the complete sharing of responsibility; each person in the community contributes her talents and gifts to achieve a living, harmonious, personal, and loving community. Subsidiarity is based on trust and love that the superior has for each member of the community. It means that decisions are made by the people whom they affect, at the level of those affected by the decisions. Both these principles assume that all members have the right and responsibility to dialog toward consensus and that corporate decisions are made for the common good ever mindful of the needs of all. Authority in religious life is a union of "like" minds; a ministry of service and friendship. These concepts infused vitality into religious life that had often been held captive by hierarchical structures.

My educated guess was that the Chapter would make wearing the Dominican habit optional. With this in mind I borrowed some clothing, sewed new clothes, and bought a few things. I flew on Iberia Airlines wearing my habit and returned five weeks later doing the same. Once I arrived in Spain I wore secular clothes. It was not traumatic; in fact it made sense. I don't remember our girls or any of the adult chaperones making any comments. It was far easier to wear regular clothing as we traveled around. I was hoping that over the summer the Chapter would have approved the proposition that Sisters be allowed to wear secular clothing appropriate for their work. The Chapter did approve so by the time I returned, what I had done was legal.

The Chapter of Affairs approved many changes. After months of deliberation and countless meetings change came to our governance structure. We replaced archaic terminology with terms that we knew from our civil government. Our highest elected official was the President; she would work with members of the Executive Team. All professed sisters voted to select the leadership. Terms of office changed from six/twelve to four/eight years allowing for reelection and continuity. We enumerated and described the responsibilities of each office holder. The local superior would be called Coordinator, a term that indicated that she lived and worked with the local community in a spirit of service; she was not the principal so authority in living and working did not reside in the same sister. There were still assigned positions to ensure that our teaching ministries, social services, and nursing positions had competent sisters.

Later the concept of personal option was adopted. Principals advertised available positions and sisters applied and interviewed like their lay counterparts. Sisters could also choose where and with whom they wanted to live. There were many convents attached to schools, but over time these decreased as sisters changed ministries and/or pastors used the convents for other purposes. With fewer large residences/convents, sisters had to live in apartments. What sounded luxurious to outsiders involved trade-offs. Those living in apartments had no: chapel, laundry, hired cook to prepare lunch or dinner, storage space, nor spacious grounds. Security issues arose when sisters lived in changing neighborhoods. On balance sisters came to appreciate the challenges that people faced in their daily lives. As they related to sisters in less spacious quarters they had to work at maintaining the quality of community living.

We could wear secular clothes when appropriate. Changes in habit had evolved over time from stiff veil to soft veil, from ankle length to below the knee habits, and finally the option to wear secular clothes. Most important was the formation of a Community Council composed of sisters elected by all the sisters. The Council held three or four weekend meetings in Sparkill throughout the year and exercised an advisory role to the Executive Team. It would be a place for continued discussion on matters of concern. After meeting in Sparkill the delegates would visit local houses to share the proceedings with all the sisters. This insured greater transparency and involvement of the sisters. For us it was an invitation to be active agents of our lives. It inspired confidence and encouraged discussion of issues involving the community.

Another aspect of community living was the acceptance of group living within a larger setting. The first group was Antioch at the Motherhouse in Sparkill. Energized by their example we formed Emmaus group at St. Helena Girls High School Convent. We were already living in three distinct places, but working out the details of finances and where the group would live took skillful negotiating and help from a congregational committee that served as an arbitrator for individuals or groups to resolve conflicts. It was finally decided that the Boys' School Biology laboratory would be relocated so our group could live in the cottage and that the basement would be renovated to include a kitchen, pantry, dining area, living room, laundry, and phone room. This also provided another entrance at ground level. Initially we moved over to our rooms and used the kitchen in the high school to prepare and eat supper together. By Thanksgiving 1971 we were finally able to eat together in the newly renovated space and to call Emmaus home. We were officially a local community that welcomed guests as Jesus was welcomed by the disciples on the road to Emmaus (Luke 24: 13-35). In fact we chose the name Emmaus to identify our group for we hoped to be a community that welcomed and shared the good news of the Gospel with each other and all who would come into our home. We too wanted to have hearts on fire with love. Hospitality would be our calling card and we would welcome guests as if each were Jesus.

Over time there were changes not just in dress but also in ministry such as personal option whereby the individual sister shared responsibility to discern when and where to apply for a different position/job. Prayerful discernment gradually led to the sisters' moving into a wide array of ministries: building affordable housing and an assisted living facility with services for senior citizens and handicapped persons on our property near the Motherhouse in Sparkill; sponsoring and renovating abandoned buildings in the Bronx to provide housing with services for formerly homeless women and their children; serving as pastoral ministers and teachers with the Native Americans in Montana; opening, staffing, and training indigenous women to continue a Well Baby Clinic in Lima, Peru; sponsoring, building, and maintaining housing and services for low income senior citizens in Manhattan, NY; working with immigrants in the Bronx to teach ESL (English as a Second Language), help them to acquire skills needed for living and working in NYC, and apply for US citizenship; ministering to prisoners in St. Louis, MO.

Few could have imagined how many would be empowered by the goal approved by the Sister delegates at the Chapter of 1976: a commitment to the "proclamation of the kingdom of God through a ministry for justice" to focus on "the enablement of the poor, of the powerless, of the oppressed, and of the spiritually deprived people of our times." Embracing the congregational goal resulted in social justice becoming a way of life and the basis for advocating for those in need.

Those days were heady with change. St. Helena's hired more lay teachers, women and men, many of whom became our friends. Our principal, Sr. Kathleen Doherty, was open to new ideas such as experimenting with different time schedules and having the whole school go on field trips to expand their worldview. It required a concerted effort for all the students (almost 1200 girls plus faculty) to go out on the same day. I remember getting to the ferry to go to visit the Statue of Liberty. The students scheduled for the earlier ferry were still on the Manhattan side. A heavy fog had prevented the ferry from sailing. We waited. When the fog lifted and we could finally reach the island, Lady

Liberty was even more wonderful to behold. What a thrill to visit our national symbol of freedom!

On another occasion our students filled the theater for a special showing of Franco Zeffirelli's 1968 movie version of "Romeo and Juliet." As the narrative got progressively sadder a few girls began to sob; others reacted by laughing nervously until the whole theater was convulsed by laughing or crying. It was the most tragically comic version of that play/movie I have ever witnessed. At another movie viewing I overheard the girls telling each other excitedly, "You have to see the ladies room. It's so beautiful." The wall paper was a rich magenta color with a multi-textured velvet finish making it unique, unlike anything they had ever seen. They might forget the movie they saw, but not the walls of the lavatory. Who could predict the effect a field trip would have?

Convent life underwent so many changes after we were professed. We welcomed the changes in liturgy, government structure, and daily practices. As younger sisters we more easily adapted because we welcomed change. For some of our older Sisters it had to be difficult, a reality I only appreciate now that I am older. We had friends and companions who eased the discomfort of transitions in dress, living, and work. We also realized that God was with us so we were not alone. Sisters from the very beginning of our congregation had weathered so many storms: extreme poverty in the early years of our founding, a fire that destroyed St. Agnes Home for Boys and Girls, relocating to Troy, NY and rebuilding so the children could return to Sparkill, surging numbers of young women entering that permitted staffing new schools and founding a college to educate our Sisters, followed by diminishing numbers of vocations in the 1970's, et al. We were/are in a far better place than so many of the Sisters that preceded us. If they could prevail, of course we will too. God is with us in good times and bad. That is how it was and will be. As we often prayed, *Tu autem Domine miserere nobis.* **R.** *Deo gratias [Thou, o Lord, have mercy on us.* **R.** *Thanks be to God.]*

Sept. 1927 Uncle Neal, my grandfather Cornelius W. Willemse, and my father, George Willemse

Clare Brady and Judy Willemse in Neversink, NY summer, 1949

Uncle Howard Esch and Great Aunt Nellie McDowell

Sept. 21, 1952 **The Wedding Party:** Joseph and Margaret Brady, Mary Quinn, and Best Man

Joan's Profession Day May 1954 Geri Willemse, Dorothy Sorger, Margaret Brady, Sr. Joan Dolores, Joe Brady, Sr. Barbara Ann, Agnes Wienecke (Nanna); Front row: Clare Brady, Judy Brady, Howard Esch

Sr. Joan Dolores

May Crowning May 1959: Judy and Joe Brady at St. Joseph's. Forestburg, NY

Entrance Day Sept. 8, 1961 Judy with Dominic the dog at home in White Sulphur Springs, NY before leaving for Sparkill, NY

Friends from Nazareth College: Alice Malinkowski, Mary Hanlon, Judy in Postulant dress, Mary Sullivan, Patricia Kulaga, and Ellen Kuhl

Sr. Joan Dolores, Sr. Judith Mary, Sr. Barbara Ann

Reception of the Habit May 7, 1962 Sr. Joan Dolores, Margaret Brady, Sr. Judith Mary, Joe Brady

Graduation from STAC June 6, 1964 Sr. Judith Mary and mother, Margaret Brady

Bazaar at Sparkill 1968 Sr. Judith Mary and cousin, Evelyn Esch

Trip to Spain June 1969 Maria Formoso and Sr. Judith

Sr. Judith Brady teaching at St. Helena Girls High School (later renamed Msgr. Scanlan H.S.)

Emmaus Group at Christmas 1973 First row: Sisters Eileen Gannon, Mary Normile, Mary Dunning, Frances Dryden, Bridget O'Sullivan, Catherine Tahaney; Back row: Sisters Alice Madeline Smith, Jean Thomas McHenry, Eileen Donovan, Veronica Lanham, Judith Brady

Sr. Eileen Gannon and Margaret Brady at Carmel Richmond Nursing Home, 1984

Silver Jubilee at Sparkill June 1986. The Band of 1961: Front row: Sisters Patricia Broderick, Catherine Rose Quigley, Geraldine Bowes, Mary Jo Heman, Eileen Sullivan, Kathleen O'Connor, Margaret McGirl. Back row: Sisters Ann Gregory Bischoff, Judith Brady, Catherine McKillop, Mary Grey, Nora Doody, Rose Edwin Pfannebecker, Eileen Cunningham.

Sr. Judith Brady, Mary Ann Fallek, Sr. Eileen Gannon outside Sacred Heart Chapel

The Parable Tour of Central America **August 1991.** Santiago de Atitlán: site of massacre of civilians on Dec.1-2, 1990

Guatemala street market: Sr. Agnes (Caldwell Dominican) and Sr. Judith

Woman reverencing statue of St. Dominic in Coban, Guatemala

University of Central America chapel in San Salvador: mural depicting the six Jesuit priests and their housekeeper and daughter, martyred on Nov. 16, 1989.

June 1993 Anna Bartley and Sr. Judith

Sr. Judith and sister, Geri Toal in Salt Lake City June 1993

Emmaus Group 1994: Front row: Sisters Eileen Donovan, Mary Normile. Back row: Sisters Judith Brady, Ann Eigenbauer, Rose Marie Duchesne, Alice Madeline Smith, Eileen Gannon, Jean Thomas McHenry, Frances Dryden.

Chapter 6

PARTY, WHERE'S THE PARTY?

Voices floated through the apartment. It was quiet time when children are asleep and adults have a chance to relax. I was safely tucked in bed so I could listen in comfort. My mother and my great aunt each had a glass of wine and were sharing their views of life. This evening and many thereafter they were on opposite sides discussing Franklin Delano Roosevelt's legacy. Aunt Nellie thought he was terrific; my mother had her reservations. This was a dilemma—hearing women I loved who thought so differently about our president. Nellie waxed eloquently about all he had done for the common man: Social Security, Workmen's Compensation, Federal Deposit Insurance for banks, in effect, digging us out of the Great Depression, but my mother was critical of the government for interfering in the lives of ordinary people. How strange! Why were they so far apart?

Little did I know then that I was witnessing how politics is a visceral affair. Friends and family can agree on many things, but when it comes to politics they often get into heated discussions and can even come to blows. That particular evening they parted friends, but I realized that even family can heartily disagree. This was something that I would experience as a young adult. When I went home to visit my parents, my mother gave me strict instructions, "Do not speak about religion or politics. Don't upset your father." Yes, indeed, I knew that as I became an adult, my views differed drastically from my stepfather's. He became more conservative as he aged while I was more progressive. He mistrusted government especially when there was government funding. He claimed that money came with a long list of government mandates.

In other words, there was no such thing as a free lunch. (He was well versed in the power of funding. Ever since my mother remarried, she had turned over her salary check to him. He controlled finances and doled out money for food, clothing, whatever was needed. We only had money when my stepfather gave us money. Even when I went away to college, I would have to find clever ways to ask him for money to buy a winter jacket or pay class dues.) Inevitably talk would turn to one of the two taboo topics. How could it not especially when I was dressed in full habit and veil? I was a walking poster for religion and beliefs. I would try to maintain a calm demeanor, but some topics were too close to my heart for me to remain silent. Inevitably there were disagreements.

Not long after World War II ended, the radio carried news of armed conflict in Korea. I thought, "Oh, no. Not again. Our soldiers will be sent to fight in another country." Did that trigger memories of blackouts: having to pull the drapes so no light would escape? Our fifth floor apartment on East Gun Hill Road in the Bronx was high up in the sky so I sensed the urgency of blocking our lights from an invading enemy. While war was "over there," it soon came here when our teachers taught us to go under our desks and cover our heads so we could survive a bombing. We had no idea that if the enemy dropped an atomic bomb we would have sizzled and been doomed to agonizing pain from radiation sickness. Only years later did I realize that our country was the first to use the atomic bomb dropping it on Hiroshima and Nagasaki in Japan. These bombings hastened the end of the war in the Pacific, but learning what the civilian population suffered: death, searing pain, radiation sickness, and cancers alerted the world to the horrors of nuclear warfare. The fact that an atomic bomb would poison the air, water, and land seemed only to increase people's instincts to want to survive. Our government responded by founding the Civilian Defense Corps. Fear induced whole new industries to build air raid shelters capable of protecting one's family and friends from radioactive fallout. They would be stocked with canned food and water, bunks and blankets, and had a sanitation system. We trusted that our loved ones would survive—a plan but also a false hope.

"Why can we not have peace?" I prayed that somehow the conflict would end, but it didn't and to this day North Korea uses precious resources to expand its military at the expense of their own citizens many of whom are near starvation. A surge in military spending robbed men, women, and children of the basics needed to live a human life. How could leaders persist in buying and developing armaments while disregarding the lives of their citizens?

As a child living in the country neighbor boys and I would storm a hill pretending that we were soldiers running uphill to spot, aim at, and shoot the enemy. If we got shot, we had the pleasure of yelling, rolling down the grassy hill and playing dead. That soon bored us, but adult leaders never seemed to tire of their war games. When we hear "the glad tidings of great joy" each year at Christmas, the idea of "peace on earth" appears to be totally out of reach. Once again those who pray and sacrifice may well help to bring this to pass. I am often more inclined to say, "Don't hold your breath." Like doubting Thomas I question whether peace on earth is an attainable goal. If individuals find it difficult to be peaceful especially with those who annoy and aggravate, how can we expect nations or groups of nations to create and maintain peace? It's a lovely thought, but totally impractical and unattainable.

As nuns we were super pray-ers. Every day we prayed fifteen decades of the Rosary some said aloud in the chapel, others while walking to and from the novitiate. In addition to our Morning Prayer, meditation, celebration of Mass, prayers before and after meals, afternoon prayer and the procession singing the Salve Regina, at the end of Night Prayer we also prayed for the conversion of Russia. Each night my mind wandered and I questioned, "What good can come from this prayer?" Surely we could remember these intentions throughout the day especially at Mass that has infinite value? My criticisms did not reach the ears of those in authority. Even if they had, I doubt that it would have made a difference. Those prayers continued and so did the power of the USSR. One evening in late summer 1989 the newscaster spoke of the break-up of the USSR into smaller countries. I sat up straight, "O my God, could this be a result of all our prayers?" Finally the Communist superpower would become less powerful. It had seemed so wildly improbable. I never thought that it could happen. Thank goodness I was wrong.

My mother and stepfather voted on a regular basis. She, a registered Democrat, and he, a Republican, probably cancelled each other's vote.

When they would discuss politics, my stepfather was logical and my mother emotional and often, less informed. At age 21, the legal age when one could vote, I would go the way of reason. It was obvious that if you lived in an area where a particular party had a majority then it made sense to register for that party. It often comes down to the party in power determining who is on the ballot and who wins in November. Outside New York City the Republican Party had a majority of registered voters in local towns and upstate cities so it was that party to which I hitched my wagon. Even before I could vote I had attended meetings of the Young Republicans at Nazareth College. In 1960 both presidential candidates held rallies at the War Memorial in Rochester, NY. We were there surging forward, hoping for a glimpse and a hand shake, as if they were rock stars. We made posters and actively supported our candidates. Getting to see and hear the governor of New York State was an honor; Nelson Rockefeller was a moderate Republican in a time when moderates controlled the party.

We had a priest/chaplain, Rev. Frey, when I attended high school who visited our religion class every Friday. He spoke about workers' rights, unions, and other social justice topics. He was not a teacher as was evident by his rambling on in a low, monotonous voice. I listened and was respectful because that's what was expected, but I found it hard to concentrate and even stay awake. He was also interested in ecology as when he ordered seedlings from a state agency. We lived in Forestburgh named for the giant trees that surrounded the school, convent, and local residences. Somehow he roped our biology teacher into this project. One day we had to work in pairs digging, planting the seedlings, and tapping the soil around the stem of the seedling. We worked all of last period and even a bit beyond only to learn that there were a thousand seedlings! We could still have been planting like fossilized Johnny Appleseed except for a plan I devised: use the crossbar of a wooden hanger, pound it into the earth with a heavy object, insert the seedling sometimes twisting the roots to fit, and then tamping the soil in place. It was mass production at its worst. All the time I could imagine the forest saying, "We are a proud and mighty forest of old growth trees. We are doing quite well, thank you. Let nature take its course." Give Rev. Frey his due: he opened our minds to consider that we all needed to be involved in issues of social justice especially caring for the earth.

It was a luxury to live at St. Joseph's School where we had space to play outdoor sports: softball and volleyball in the fall and spring, ice-skating and sleigh riding during the cold winters. In addition to fields and private roadways there was a huge lake around which there were both boys' and girls' summer sleep away camps. Such a rustic setting could also be a hazardous area. Sister Immaculata, our resident counselor, spoke softly, "Each of you has to get a red hunting hat. Soon it will be hunting season and you will have to wear it going to and from the school to the cafeteria and chapel." I was mortified going into a men's store in Liberty to buy a man's red hunting cap. I had to admit that it was warm, but boy, was it ugly. The worst part was that wearing such a hat would seriously compromise our hair that we worked hard to curl. We were less worried about being targets than about how we looked. Hunting season came and went with no casualties so who's to say the hat trick saved us from serious harm?

As college students we had all sorts of opportunities to be involved. In sophomore year I returned to campus with a caged parakeet that my family had inherited by default when his keeper, our aunt, died. It did not fit in with our cat-centric culture; our cats killed birds the way people swat flies. I volunteered, "I'll take it back to college. There's lots of space up there." Unknown to me there were rules against having pets, birds included. Sr. Barbara allowed me to put Tweety in the lab prep room until a suitable home could be found. Meanwhile Pat Kulaga and I volunteered to help at a child care facility on Saturdays. Getting to the site was a major hassle. We had to take multiple buses operating on a weekend schedule; it took an hour and a half each way. Not knowing quite what to expect, we found the girls all talking and crying about their beloved bird that had just died. Suddenly we became grief counselors. "What did your bird look like?" I asked. It turned out that their description fit Tweety to a T. The following Saturday we brought Tweety. Transporting a bird on public buses was no easy matter. Our fellow travelers saw the empty cage that Pat had in hand and heard wild, screeching noises from a shoebox with holes that I held. Tweety probably would have benefited from taking Dramamine to calm him, but I had not really anticipated his getting so distressed. I was afraid he would have a heart attack before we arrived… The girls got so excited, "You brought Petey. Where did you find him? Oh, look, here's Petey!" I felt like Jesus having raised Lazarus from the dead. If only they knew, but this was one time the truth would not out. The important thing was that Tweety had found a home and the girls were once again happy. Pat and I did not return to that place because the commute was too long, and I certainly did not want to be there if/when they discovered our ruse.

Politics was in the air the fall of 1960 and Rochester was a destination for the major candidates. Even though not yet eligible to vote, we were quite involved in the campaign. I attended a meeting of the Young Republicans on campus in classically furnished Medaille Hall; they served delicious finger food and the Republicans won my heart, or at least my stomach. The fact that we had that meeting in Medaille was astounding. A few months later when we requested that our dorm floor, winners of the competition for collecting the most Mission funds, be allowed to hold the prize pizza party there, they flat out said no. I could not understand why they were so adamant until at a class reunion in 1968 when I looked at the furniture, lamps, and rugs and realized that room was never meant for pizza. The Republicans got that right.

Pat Kulaga and I felt duty bound to attend rallies to support Richard Nixon's campaign for President. The odds were against the college supporting Nixon; after all only thirty Young Republicans out of an enrollment of 800 students attended that meeting. On October 19 after class we rushed to St. John Fischer College to hear the Republican candidate for Vice President speak. I was so impressed by his stately good looks and how he fielded questions that I later wrote to my parents, "Henry Cabot Lodge is more of an ambassador than a politician—but oh, what a vice-president he'd make!" We were at the War Memorial on November 1st with over 14,000 supporters to cheer for Richard Nixon. That night we were behind a bank of cameras and reporters. "We formed a vanguard—a mob of yelling Nixon collegiates waving placards and pushing like maniacs." The next day the front page of the *Democrat and Chronicle*, Rochester's daily paper, had a picture of Pat holding a banner, "Nazareth Supports Nixon." As might be expected, there was quite a reaction on and off campus. "People kept hounding the college—'I thought you were Catholics—why aren't you for Kennedy?'" This was a more hospitable time for a Roman Catholic of Irish descent to be seeking the presidency. When John Fitzgerald Kennedy campaigned in Rochester we were there in the upper stratosphere listening with muted enthusiasm. On Election Day I wore Nixon clip-on earrings to Mass in the college chapel. They hurt so badly that I removed them as I walked to breakfast. The election was close—only 118,000 votes separated Kennedy and Nixon. By the next day, Nixon conceded defeat and we learned that Kennedy would be president. We took some comfort in the fact that while Rochester went for Kennedy, Monroe County went for Nixon by a slim majority. We were disappointed as we watched Kennedy supporters celebrate, but we knew that as Americans we would support the newly elected president. It was a wonderful campaign during which we saw and heard the Democratic and Republican presidential candidates, the Republican vice presidential candidate, and the Republican governor of New York State. Playing an active role in the American electoral process nudged us closer to the future when we would support and vote for the candidates we considered best suited for elected office.

Years later at Middlebury College where we were required to sign a pledge to speak only the language we studied, television was off limits. The summer of 1973 as the Watergate hearings continued, my friend, Eileen would call me after 11:00 PM a few nights a week to tell me what transpired. To this day I can hear Eileen's voice reporting the words and actions of those who testified. I felt like a conspirator as I whispered on the public phone in the hallway. What Eileen relayed to me sounded like fiction, but it was documented in fact. Only on the day that President Nixon left Washington, DC after he and many of his staff were found complicit in the Watergate affair were we allowed to watch television. On August 8, 1974 many of us squeezed into a common room to view Nixon's departure on television. Our professors from Spain and Latin America were amazed that the presidency could pass peacefully from Richard Nixon to Gerald Ford. Their experience of nations' solving conflict was often a coup, overthrowing an existing government by force. What we took for granted was really new for them. It was a sad day when a duly elected president resigned office, but the rule of law provided a peaceful transition. I was proud to be an American.

The Vietnam War was raging and the draft had been restored. Many young men fled to Canada to avoid fighting a war that they deemed unjust. One afternoon I was speaking with my sister, Sr. Joan Dolores, and my teacher, Sr. Catherine Anthony. We were walking in our cemetery in Sparkill. Amidst the sunlit granite crosses with names and dates engraved for each of our deceased sisters, we were discussing the Vietnam War. "How can we support a war that is killing so many civilians and making young Americans killers in a foreign land?" They listened and seemed to understand. Catherine asked, "Why are you thinking so much about this conflict?" I had been reading *Commonweal* and listening to my transistor radio for we could only watch TV between 7:30-8:30 pm and seldom saw the news. Under those circumstances it was difficult to know all that was happening, but there were more and more people taking a pacifist stand. "I can't be an anti-war protester; that's not feasible. Isn't there some way to express my opposition?" At that time we Sisters were living a strictly regulated life. While we could express private opinions, it was more prudent to maintain silence and not make oneself a target. At least these two women whom I loved and respected heard me out and were not shooting me down. This was many years before our congregation would develop a process whereby we could take a corporate stand on issues of social justice. During the Vietnam War we knew relatives and former students who were drafted and served in Vietnam. Patriotism could not justify the deaths and destruction that resulted from war. We Dominicans with our motto, *veritas* had pledged our lives to seeking truth in all areas of life. Seeking truth instilled a deep desire to study all aspects of issues that affected human life. Yes, we prayed as we had prayed all those many years for the conversion of Russia. As teachers we could also raise questions as we taught our respective classes. It was not so much a matter of keeping our young men and women safe as it was to realize that we are part of a larger family of humankind and questioning the US government's right to tell other people how to run their countries. The seemingly easy fix of war has far reaching consequences. Communism will wither in time but the memory of military atrocities will flare up like embers that reignite and consume the house while everyone is asleep.

When all those events had time to sink in, I realized that my party affiliation was not a good fit. It felt like wearing shoes that were too tight. Being a Republican in the mid-1970's was no longer a matter of pride. There was no way that I could remain a Republican after Watergate. Too much skullduggery and criminality had occurred. Politicians don't have the best reputations, but Nixon and pals went way beyond the pale. Reregistering as a Democrat was part protest and a major part truth. I had far more in common with the Democratic Party. They at least were mindful of the poor and all those not born with a silver spoon in their mouth. The Democratic party showed more compassion for the underdog, respected individuals, and believed that government had the potential to raise us up as a people who can work together to make the American Dream a reality. This action effectively moved me from my admiration for Joe Brady and all he believed to the views of Nellie McDowell who knew that government can remove obstacles and improve the lives of all people.

When Jimmy Carter was elected president in 1976 he was the first candidate for whom I voted that would become president. Watching Jimmy and Rosalind Carter walk down Pennsylvania Avenue on Inauguration Day made such an impression that I saved the front page of the *New York Times*. To be sure that it would survive paper purges, I put it under my mattress for safe keeping. I liked that his speeches used familiar language often including phrases from Scripture. He championed human rights and was a refreshing change after the devious ways of Nixon. Even as the highest elected executive, presidents are limited. When radical revolutionaries stormed the US embassy in Iran and imprisoned American diplomats, President Carter's inability to rescue the American hostages by force and by diplomacy was a severe disappointment. The hostages were finally released on the day that Ronald Reagan took office (Jan. 20, 1980). I had a visceral reaction to Reagan's voice —smooth as velvet. I was never sure if he were acting or speaking in earnest. The proposed tax reforms filled me with dread; so often the rich and politically connected profit from lower taxes while those who are poor have little relief. I resented how he could charm and cajole the American people. Years later when Ronald Reagan died (June 5, 2004) I watched his state funeral on television. Finally as the sun set on the west coast, his coffin was placed on high as if he were a god to be worshipped. The people attending that final commendation were seated below the coffin as if in adoration. No one spoke of this, but I shuddered. It was bad enough so many lauded him in life; now they placed him on such a pedestal that in death he appeared god-like.

June 12, 1982 New York City was the scene of one of the largest worldwide massive demonstrations against nuclear proliferation. Riding the subway downtown from the Bronx we had lots of company—hoards of people from the outer boroughs who came out that day to support peace and oppose the dangers posed by nuclear weapons and nuclear plants. Like many religious congregations, our sisters marched that day chanting phrases and carrying banners. Most of our Sisters wore secular clothes as we had since 1970 so the Dominican habit was not so evident. What impressed me the most was being with a million people marching across 42nd Street, then north into Central Park. It was my first experience walking on the actual roadway of 42nd Street surrounded by people as far as the eye could see. Up above staunch skyscrapers and a clear blue sky bore witness to our actions. It was a thrill to see how many were actively involved. We showed the world that leaders need to respect and respond to the will of the people. Memories of the meltdown of the Three Mile Island nuclear power plant in Pennsylvania (March 1979) flashed through my mind. It was spring 1979 and I was planting tomatoes in the garden outside our convent. I asked myself, "Is this a fool's errand? Will prevailing westerly's carry contamination our way? Will our land and crops be poisoned resulting in countless cancers?" That one event made me realize how fragile and interconnected our environment is. I could not act as if nuclear war and accidents in nuclear plants would not affect me. The day we marched in New York City turned my fears into meaningful action. It would take many more events before our leaders learned how these issues are affecting us now and could well limit the lives of our people, pollute the atmosphere, and destroy the earth. Nuclear proliferation is not just the domain of planners and executioners. No, we the people have to stand up and resist war in every possible way. We wanted more than the absence of war; we hungered for peace in a world where justice and love can flourish.

Central America was embroiled in civil wars on many fronts during the 1980's. As an assistant principal of a coed Catholic high school in the Bronx and member of its Social Concerns Committee, I/we helped raise student and faculty awareness by celebrating Central America Week usually the week closest to the anniversary of the assassination of Archbishop Oscar Romero, March 24. At St. Helena Commercial High School we had a prayer service to help us learn about and pray for the people of Central America who were suffering persecution and death at the hands of their military. We learned how crimes against civilians were perpetrated by members of their militias many of whom were trained by Americans at the School of the Americas (SOA) in Fort Benning, GA. Renamed the Western Hemisphere Institute for Security Cooperation (WHINSEC) in 2001 this facility continues to draw criticism. Every year congressional representatives introduce legislation to close the school/institute, and every year the bill meets defeat. But the ranks of those who wanted us to train soldiers to be super killers were met by hundreds who attended peace vigils outside the gates of the military installation in mid-November. Some may consider their efforts useless, but change can and often does come incrementally. *Poco a poco* minds and hearts can grow toward peace. It need not be a failure; it may well become a slow victory.

Central America was very much on my mind during the 1980's. Getting accurate information about conflicts/civil wars was nearly impossible. One way of course was through missionaries, but there were few missionaries compared to the conflicts that raged. Visitors were also able to carry mail out of an area in conflict because letters sent through municipal and state mail could be intercepted and result in harassment and possible arrest. When Pope John XXIII requested that North American religious communities send missionaries to work in Latin America, many American sisters and priests volunteered to serve. Maryknoll with its home base in Ossining, NY helped prepare sisters, priests, and laity for missionary work throughout the world. My congregation, the Dominican Sisters of Sparkill, had already responded to a request for missionaries for Pakistan in the mid-1950s. Pakistan was a very different situation: Christians were a tiny minority in a Muslim majority country. Christians were poor and lacked the means to educate their children. Our Sisters studied Urdu, the language of the people. They gradually started schools to educate students of all faiths. Other Sisters studied nursing so they could provide health care. The needs of the poor cry out to heaven across the globe.

In terms of missionary work in Latin America my congregation sponsored one sister each year to go on a Parable Tour to Central America. The Parable Conference for Dominican Life and Mission (1976-2008) was a national collaborative organization sponsored by Dominican priests, friars, sisters, and laity. The conference offered trips that allowed participants to learn how Dominicans had interacted and impacted the lives of indigenous people. My congregation advertised the Parable Tour and the sisters interested in going submitted their names. Mine was chosen at a drawing so I went on the Parable Tour of Guatemala and El Salvador in August 1991. I wanted to learn firsthand what was happening in these countries and also to be able to communicate directly in Spanish. The interviews were mostly in Spanish so I had a head start in taking notes; when translated into English I could add whatever I missed the first time around. Could it be as bad as the news that we received about civil wars and massacres? I hoped that direct contact would reveal that things on the ground were improving. One thing for sure: this was no holiday excursion. Prior to leaving I had to apply for a US passport, be fingerprinted at One Police Plaza by the NYPD so I could get a Good Conduct Certificate, secure a letter from the Cardinal Archbishop of New York attesting to my good character, and get a number of immunizations (polio, tetanus diphtheria, typhoid, and gamma globulin). We also needed to bring anti-malarial medication to take once a week. I realized how important that medication was when we visited a community in San Salvador. In the hazy sunlight of late afternoon mosquitoes were so visible that I could barely concentrate on what the community leader was telling us. All that I could think was, "Which of these mosquitoes is the culprit carrying malaria?" And even more important, "Will the anti-malarial medication work?" so convinced was I that I would be the next victim.

I readied my Nikon camera and lenses, bought color slide film, and a guidebook. Even though our trip had loftier goals I needed to do background reading. When discussions of real life issues weighed me down, I could at least read about the cities/regions that we visited. We were scheduled to visit a rain forest famous for the *quetzal*. Even though sightings were rare, I was convinced that I would see this bird with its brilliant red and green feathers native to the region. As our van approached the area, our leader announced, "We are running late so we will not stop at the rain forest." No one complained, but I was so disappointed. "*Señor quetzal*, I know that you are out there. I so wanted to see you and appreciate your fabled beauty. I am so sad not to be able to make your acquaintance." I would have to content myself with representations/pictures.

We had our itinerary, the list of twelve participants, and airplane tickets. Our group of ten sisters from different religious congregations and two lay persons met the tour leaders, a Dominican sister and a Dominican priest, at the Miami airport to embark on a two week pilgrimage of Central America. I brought raisins, salted nuts, and hard candy for sharing, and a jar of peanut butter, a personal mainstay when traveling abroad to provide protein because while my spirit is willing, my gastrointestinal tract is not

Each day's schedule included Mass and prayer to nourish us spiritually. By day we met with civil rights leaders in each locale and stayed overnight at convents or retreat houses. To my amazement, every meeting began with the indigenous leaders saying, "Thank you for coming to be with us. There have been numerous death threats against us." Shivers ran down my spine as I thought, "How could I be so crazy to come here? We have more than our share of violence in the Bronx." I wondered if I had known that earlier if I would have volunteered. At this point there was no turning back, so I took a deep breath and hoped we/they would be safe. The leaders spoke of the web of fear and threats of violence that they faced every day. It was not unusual for them to be followed and harassed even in the capital. Their towns/villages had witnessed untold atrocities. Local leaders were in great danger. Some went into hiding, but when/if they returned to see their wives and children they risked capture followed by torture and death. It was really important for us to be there to hear their stories so we would tell the world the truth. Sad to say, truth was hard to come by in countries in the midst of civil war.

Our first day trip was a four hour ride by van from Guatemala City to Santiago de Atitlán over a variety of roads. Surfaces were paved in the city yielding to packed dirt with a continuous series of ruts as we wended our way around the lake to the village. Someone had suggested bringing our bed pillows to help ease the slow, bouncing advance around and through humongous pot holes. The ruts were so frequent that those of us in the rear seat of the van came close to hitting our heads on the ceiling of the van. We tried to lift each other's spirits as the van slowly crawled to our destination. Santiago de Atitlán, located at the far end of a beautiful lake surrounded by trees, was a bucolic setting viewed from afar. We arrived on Friday, August 2, market day. There were many people gathered in the town square including teenagers intent on seeing and talking with each other, much as they would in any public place around the world. Scores of people milled around. In the background was a ferris wheel, part of the celebrations that had begun on July 25th for the feast of St. James the Apostle.

We visited the sixteenth century church dedicated to St. James (*Santiago*) on the town plaza. Inside to the right of the entrance there was an altar dedicated to the memory of Father Stanley Rother. This name was new to me. I learned that Rev. Stanley Rother had volunteered to go to Guatemala in 1968. He was a diocesan priest from Oklahoma City and his experience working a farm before he became a priest proved invaluable in his new mission. He learned Spanish and then Tzutuhil, the language of the indigenous Mayans, and assisted in translating the New Testament into Tzutuhil. By 1973 he offered Mass in Tzutuhil so the people could worship in their native language. No stranger to physical labor, Father Rother repaired the church and rectory, dug a well, built a parish hall, and worked to improve the output of the local farms (*fincas*) by introducing new crops. As he taught the people that they were made in the image and likeness of God and that God sent his only begotten Son, Jesus, to suffer and die for all people, his parishioners were energized. At the most solemn moment of the Mass when the priest elevates the host, Fr. Rother recognized that the ever increasing sound that enveloped the church was all the persons' vocalizing their individual prayers of intercession. He scheduled weddings and First Communions on St. James' feast day so all the community would be present. He would also take a picture of each couple so they would have it as a memento of their wedding day.

Violence spread throughout Guatemala in the 1970s and 1980s reaching even this remote area. Under the leadership of General Romero Lucas García, President of Guatemala (1978-1982) *la doctrina de la seguridad nacional* was promoted to resist the efforts of the Guerrilla Army of the Poor. In the name of fighting communism, the government was determined to rid all organizations of subversive elements. Massacres of entire communities, the result of labeling the people as water and the guerrillas as fish, were the government's method of doing whatever was necessary, even removing the water to get the fish. The military was complicit in all of these efforts.

Father Rother continued his pastoral work: he offered Mass, baptized, forgave sins, witnessed weddings, counseled couples, mediated disputes, offered solace and comfort to the sick and suffering, anointed the seriously ill, and buried the dead. When ten men from his area disappeared, Diego Quic, a leader and respected catechist who chose to remain in Santiago de Atitlán with his wife and two sons, sought sanctuary at the rectory. One Saturday evening as he approached the rectory four men wearing hoods seized him and threw him into a waiting car. As Diego was dragged away, he was screaming, "¡Ayúdeme! ¡Ayúdeme!" (Help me.) Those who heard his cries were frozen with fear. Despite efforts to report the kidnapping to the police in San Lucas and searches of nearby fields, Diego was never seen again. That made eleven members of their community who were kidnapped and presumed dead.

Father Rother became a wanted man, labeled by the military as a subversive. Stanley Rother was a mild man who chose to preach the Gospel and had no desire to be involved in politics. When he visited a parishioner who was in prison, the authorities questioned his act of mercy. The rectory had always been a haven for those in need. He opened the church as a sanctuary so workers could stay overnight and not risk capture while returning home. Wives and children were left destitute when their husbands/fathers were killed. Father Rother quietly raised money from abroad to help them in their time of need. These acts of charity were labeled as subversive by the military. In a December 1980 letter addressed to the people in Oklahoma City, Father Rother shared why he needed to be with the people of Guatemala despite threats against his life, "This is one of the reasons I have for staying in the face of physical harm. The shepherd cannot run at the first sign of danger." When he learned that his name was on a death list, he returned to Oklahoma for a while maintaining a low profile so his words would not lead to harsher treatment of his people. He felt compelled to return to Santiago de Atitlán and arrived in time for the Holy Week services, the remembrance of the passion, death, and resurrection of Jesus. Mindful of death threats every night he slept in a different room of the parish buildings hoping to evade death. Despite these precautions, on July 28, 1981three masked men dragged him from his room. Father Rother could have fled, but the young man who had knocked at his door would have been beaten and killed. He did resist, not wanting to be taken and tortured to extract information about his people. The fighting lasted a few minutes; finally shots rang out and Father Rother dropped to the floor with fatal wounds to his head. As the news spread, they brought Father Rother's body to the church. Two Masses were offered that day and a third on the following day so the area bishops, priests, and people could pray together. So great was the love of the people for their parish priest who willingly gave his life for his people that they requested that his heart and a vial of his blood stay with them. While his body was returned to Oklahoma for burial, his heart and blood were interred under the floor of the church sanctuary. [2]

Since his death in July 1981, many have worked to have Fr. Rother recognized as a saint by the universal Church. The official process for declaring Fr. Rother a saint began in 2007. On December 1, 2016 Pope Francis declared him a martyr, one who gave his life for the faith. On September 23, 2017 Fr. Stanley Francis Rother was pronounced "Blessed" in an apostolic letter from Pope Francis delivered by Cardinal Angelo Amato, prefect of the Congregation for the Causes of Saints at the beatification Mass attended by thousands. Rother is "the first

---

[2] http://fatherstanleyrotherguild.org/index.php/biography Accessed 11/17/2015. Brett, Donna Whitson and Edward T. Brett. *Murdered in Central America: the Stories of Eleven US Missionaries*. (Maryknoll, NY: Orbis Books, 1988).

recognized martyr in the United States, and the first US-born priest to be beatified."[3]

After visiting the church, we met Renata Eustis and Kathy Ogle, Witness for Peace long term volunteers, who were the first permanent presence of this organization in the Guatemala countryside. I was familiar with the organization, Witness for Peace, founded in 1983 and their work— being with and for the people, communicating with the outside world, and advocating for the needs of the people. Their task was to monitor human rights noting all that the indigenous people did to maintain peace and work for justice, and to report the actions of the military and/or government that denied the people their rights. They told us that in 1980 the Guatemalan army had confiscated land to establish a military base in Santiago de Atitlán supposedly to stop subversives, but sadly the military presence brought violence. Just eight months before our trip, on December 2, 1990 soldiers who had been drinking shot a young man. Someone ran to the Catholic Church and rang the church bells. Thousands of people, men, women, and children, gathered in the town plaza; waving white handkerchiefs they walked to the army post. The mayor was prepared to speak with the commander, but the soldiers opened fire shooting directly into the crowd. The people scattered, but it was too late for the thirteen who were killed and the twenty-two who were wounded. Because of the soldiers' brutal actions widows and parents lost children and other children were left orphans. We walked the route that the people had taken; to the left of the dirt road were thirteen simple wooden crosses each bearing the name of the person who was killed. It was a stark reminder that human life can be snuffed out at a moment's notice. As Renata and Kathy told us, within a few days a petition was circulated insisting that the government investigate the massacre and punish those who were responsible. The petition bore 15,000 signatures or thumb prints of all who demanded that the army post be closed. The world learned about this massacre and reaction was swift: the United States and Germany cut military aid to Guatemala. Finally the Guatemalan president recalled the army. The people formed a Committee for Security and Development that organized neighborhood

---

[3] https://www.ncronline.org/print/news/people/fr-stanley-rother-beatified-oklahoma-city Accessed 11/25/2017.

watches (*rondas*) to patrol overnight between 8:00 pm and 5:00 am. Over time the Committee focused less on security and more on water systems, garbage collection, and celebrations (*fiestas*).The Ombudsman for Human Rights assisted the people with the original petition and later on May 23, 1991 when the army tried to return. What was evident was the people's willingness to take non-violent action and stand together against the army.

At day's end we traveled by boat to the opposite side of the lake. Returning on that boat were Father Stanley Rother's father and his sister, Sr. Marita (Elizabeth Mary) who had come for the commemoration of the tenth anniversary of Father Stanley's death on July 28, 1981. Their son/brother was buried in Oklahoma, but his heart remained among the people he had so lovingly served. I relaxed with our group enjoying the boat ride knowing that we would not be revisiting all those ruts. Once back in the van, we stopped at a scenic view to take a few pictures. I was bending down doing my, "This picture will be the best of the day" routine, when I felt something biting. By the time I got back into the van, I realized I had red ants all over my sneakers and biting their way up my leg. It was awful trying to get rid of them. They were a greedy bunch! It's a good thing I didn't become an entomologist.

The beauty of the sunset and the quiet of this country setting remain with me to this day. I will always remember my visit to Santiago de Atitlán. What we saw and heard gave me a better understanding of the high price that missionaries and ordinary people pay to claim their basic, God-given human rights. I vowed that I would learn more about Guatemala and those who endured martyrdom as they brought the good news of the Gospel to humble people in city and country. My activities were insignificant by comparison with the sacrifices of the missionaries and the Guatemalan people. I spoke to groups in New York City and Long Island, showing slides and sharing stories that helped to capture the beauty and strength of God's people in Guatemala. At school I also displayed table runners and wall hangings that used the colorful hand-woven textiles made from brightly colored thread. These are woven by the women, each of whom learns the distinctive designs passed down in each family from mother to daughter. Vibrant colors capture one's imagination: so much beauty created anew each generation. I gave many of these weavings to my friends who admired their intricate designs. Santiago de Atitlán now has a cooperative where these hand-woven treasures are sold directly to customers and shipped for sale to other cities and countries. I have continued to make donations to Witness for Peace and the Guatemala Human Rights Commission so I can learn what is happening and support the efforts for social justice. Endemic evil is not overcome quickly. It will take time and sacrifice, but I believe that love will ultimately overcome hatred and that social justice will become a reality.

We happened to be in Guatemala for the celebration of the feast of our founder, St. Dominic. Each village church brought their statue of St. Dominic to the church in Cobán so there were many representations of St. Dominic. Each statue was clothed in fabric as we do for the Infant of Prague statue. No doubt the garment is changed so that allows more persons to show their devotion by sewing and dressing the statue. People placed lighted candles and fresh flowers in front of each statue. They were blessed during Mass and the people from that village would carry their statue back to their village church. I had never seen anything like this. It was like having a convention of St. Dominic's all in the same place.

At one point I was looking for a lavatory. Someone directed me to a public building across the street. As I climbed the stairs to the second floor, I came face to face with an elderly indigenous woman, shorter than I with graying hair pulled back tightly into a bun. Before I could say anything, she embraced me. I had been thinking that she had every right to dislike a light skinned, blue eyed American because we had invaded Guatemala in 1954 and our government often supported military leaders that had little or no regard for the indigenous people. But, no, this woman smiled and hugged me. I was surprised to be welcomed so warmly. If only I/we could welcome the stranger as she had, how many barriers would be overcome! Truly this world would be a better place.

At week's end we flew to San Salvador, the capital of El Salvador, a country drenched in the blood of martyrs. I had been following the events in El Salvador and had taught students about those who gave their lives in love for the poor especially Archbishop Oscar Romero of San Salvador who was shot and killed on March 24, 1980 while offering

Mass at a hospital chapel. It was from this airport in San Salvador on December 2, 1980 that four American women were driving home when forced off the road, taken to a deserted country road, raped, killed, and buried in shallow graves. A Jesuit residence for the University of San Salvador that could be seen and observed from a nearby military command post was the scene of the massacre of six Jesuit priests, their housekeeper and her daughter on November 16, 1989. Over 40,000 Salvadorans were killed during the Civil War; they were teachers, labor leaders, human rights activists, catechists— lay people who taught catechism, led Scripture classes, identified with and helped the people who were poor and oppressed by a government all too willing to condemn anyone who encouraged others to stand up for their God-given rights. In the eyes of the military those who affirm their human dignity as sons and daughters created in the image of God, were their enemy. Their deeds cried to heaven.

Because of all I knew, going through Customs in El Salvador was scary. I had asked my medical doctor in New York for samples of medications to bring to El Salvador. Before I left I had typed a summary of the names and quantities of the medications on St. Helena Commercial High School stationery; Sr. Jean Thomas, the principal, signed it and imprinted the official school seal to give it credibility. I presented the list as I went through Customs; they had no idea what to do. Three different officials each viewed the letter and finally they waved me through. I was shaking as I joined our group outside for the van ride to the retreat house where we would be staying. My light blue denim skirt got caught and ripped as I climbed into the van, a permanent reminder of that day at the airport.

Teenage boys in military uniforms, carrying high powered weapons stood watch outside the residence. They were there to monitor activities at the retreat house, not to protect us. We had to walk past them every time we entered or exited. I composed a short song to give me courage as we moved past them. Overhead the whirring sound of helicopters reminded us that the military was very active and probably observing our every move. We were not alone. As highly educated American religious Sisters with passports from the USA, we were high profile visitors. What of those born in El Salvador who lived and worked among the poor? It reminded me of the Nature series on PBS where predators stalk and divide prey from the herd until the kill is made. I experienced palpable fear in El Salvador. We saw that the military were heavily armed and I knew that they acted with impunity. No one was safe from the dragnet that they cast when seeking so-called trouble makers. After years of civil war during which they slashed and burned villages, destroyed crops, killed cattle, and drove peasants from their homes, the military and their conservative politician friends enjoyed absolute power. Who could withstand such force? And yet ordinary people did stand up to them and when denied their simple livelihood, fled to neighboring countries.

We visited Archbishop Romero's residence adjacent to the chapel where he was shot while offering Mass for the Sisters at the cancer hospital. There was a simple bedroom and another space with a hammock. I imagined his taking a siesta when time permitted. On the wall behind the hammock was the white alb he wore that day, drenched with his blood that had turned brown. I was touched by the simplicity of that scene. Had he composed the Sunday sermons there that were broadcast by radio so all could hear his words of encouragement? His was the only voice that recounted the violence visited upon the people. Like a Litany of Saints he named the peasants who died at the hands of the military. Shortly before his death Monsignor Oscar Romero had pleaded with the soldiers not to obey orders to kill their fellow men/women. In his words,

> *I would like to make a special appeal to the men of the army, and specifically to the ranks of the National Guard, the police and the military. Brothers, you come from our own people. You are killing your own brother peasants when any human order to kill must be subordinate to the law of God which says, "Thou shalt not kill." No soldier is obliged to obey an order contrary to the law of God. No one has to obey an immoral law...In the name of God, in the name of this suffering people whose cries rise to heaven more loudly each day, I implore you, I beg you, I order you in the name of God: stop the repression.*

The church preaches your liberation just as we have studied it in the holy Bible today. It is a liberation that has, above all else, respect for the dignity of the person, hope for humanity's common good, and the transcendence that looks before all to God and only from God derives its hope and its strength.

From *The Church and Human Liberation*, March 14, 1980.

That afternoon we visited the cathedral where Archbishop Romero is buried. The cathedral was being renovated and everything was covered with dust. The tomb was covered by *votos*, scraps of paper with petitions for healing and thanksgiving for prayers answered. With the sound of workmen at the far end of the cathedral and sunlight streaming through open windows, we stood together at his tomb and prayed. It was a solemn, special moment. I tried to concentrate for this was "holy ground" as the hymn we sang reminded us, but the heat and humidity were unbearable. As perspiration trickled from my head, down my back, all the way to my feet, all I could think of was getting a cold drink. Given all that the Salvadoran people have suffered, how could I be so distracted by my personal discomfort? "The spirit is willing but the flesh is weak" (Mt 26:41).

The following day we were in our van going for an overnight visit to a newly developing town for refugees returning from exile. At a certain point in our trip the paved blacktop roads changed to bumpy, dirt roads, another sign that the US government cooperated in sustaining the Salvadoran government. Military guards denied us permission to go to our original destination. I remember thinking that I would gladly have returned to the capital, but finally we were allowed to proceed to different places, *Nueva Esperanza* and *Ciudad de Romero*. At *Nueva Esperanza* we slept in two houses. Five of us each had a bed in the room that served as the nurse's office; the others were in the infirmary. I remember putting all my things high off the floor in case insects or snakes found their way in. I had never camped out and I wasn't taking any chances. Latrines were a short distance away, but one hoped not to have to use them in the dark of night.

That evening there was a fiesta during which families were reunited, couples danced, and all shared a meal. A generator lit the common area where the townspeople gathered. We got word that a lieutenant of the resistance wanted to speak to us. We gathered outside the designated cabin. Guided by the flickering light of one large candle set on the ground we sat on crude benches that formed a large rectangle. It reminded me of story time at a children's summer camp. We waited quietly to hear an officer of the Sandinistas speak. No doubt he was a husband and father, but that night he spoke of fighting for his people. I was eager to hear directly from a leader who could tell us what the so-called rebels were doing. We understood that the rebels had strong roots in the community; no doubt some of their loved ones were in this very settlement. Who among us would have homes, livestock, and crops destroyed and not fight against those who were responsible for such horror? The government claimed that violence against civilians was punishment for attacking the government forces. Such actions brought undue hardship for civilians, especially women and children. Violence against non-combatants literally creates the next generation of fighters.

The Salvadoran government and for that fact many in our own country said that the FMLN (Farabundo Martí National Liberation Front) was evil, but here was a tall, thirty-ish young man in uniform speaking to us about their ongoing campaign to save their country. It was a brief talk. He wanted us to know how very important it was that we contact our elected officials by letter or visits so they would know that the FMLN was defending their country from the violence visited upon his people. There was something magical about this setting. Shadows danced gracefully as the lamp's light flickered. Suddenly out of nowhere came a lanky young man to speak to us. I would be hard pressed to identify him, a fact that was in his favor lest someone want to do him harm. Afterwards I went up to him and said in Spanish, "I have written letters to our president asking him not to send money and weapons to El Salvador. Sad to say, our president and Congress continue to send military aid. I do not agree with their policy and think that it is wrong to support the Salvadoran government and military. I will continue to resist actions that cause war and increase suffering." The FMLN had been labeled as socialists, communists, and anti-democratic, hell bent on destroying the country. That night we met a man willing to risk his life for his loved ones who, if/when peace accords were agreed upon would probably move into politics as a leader of his people. For us he disappeared as he had come: another shadow fading into the darkness of night.

The next day we had a tour of the newly formed village and heard about its genesis. April 2, 1991 they had begun the move to this location after nine years in Nicaragua. Their history was complicated: these people came from different Salvadoran communities that had been attacked in 1980 by the government forces. Repression was followed by assassinations. Whole families were killed in front of their children. An archbishop helped them to leave; Catholic churches were open to refugees 1980-1981. A woman told us about her family that had stayed in the basement of a church in San Salvador near the place we were staying. She recounted how very difficult it was to be crowded together, sleeping on the floor in the poorly ventilated basement. They had long waits to use the one and only washroom. Food was scarce. People got sick. In February 1982 they moved on to a refugee camp in Nicaragua. They formed a cooperative with Nicaraguans, were able to plant basic grains, but had no way to earn money. The USA blockade of goods to Nicaragua resulted in a scarcity of goods not only for the Nicaraguans but also the Salvadorans in the refugee camp. They formed Christian base communities (CEBEDS). At weekly meetings they prayerfully reflected on readings from the Bible. Their reflections bolstered their profound desire to return. When the Sandinistas lost the election in February 1990, a campaign was waged against the Guatemalan refugees. Propaganda spread untruths such as accusing the Guatemalans of being FMLN. In July 1990 a study determined that 303 persons wanted to return. The first assembly of the heads of families in August 1990 created a *Comité de Retorno* that sent a letter to the government and the UN expressing their desire to return to El Salvador. They continued to meet weekends in Managua to organize. They encountered many obstacles; even the UN was not receptive. Demonstrations culminated in a twelve day vigil in front of the embassy; that resulted in other embassies (e.g., Argentina) putting pressure on the government to help the displaced Guatemalans. March 1991 they were allowed to go to *Casas Viejas,* but the land was dry and uneven with many rocks. They sought an alternative location where they could be together as one community. April 2nd six families began the move. They were detained by the army for four days because they needed *un salvo de conducto*, similar to the way our group had been detained. After four days they decided to walk only to encounter barricades that soldiers had erected to block the road. People removed the rocks and used a bullhorn to speak to the people of San Miguel. Gloria drove the first truck, but the soldiers shot at the second truck blowing out the tires. This area had many trees that they needed to build homes and little by little common buildings. They needed potable water; they were able to dig two wells that gave them *agua dulce* (literally, sweet water). It took a month for the other families to get to the new community, named appropriately, *Nueva Esperanza* (New Hope).

The afternoon of August 11th we visited another new settlement, *Ciudad de Romero*. They had endured the horrors of the "scorched earth policy"—from March-May the army burned their houses and killed their animals. They fled to the mountains and to Honduras. The six months that they lived in Honduras they were caught between the Honduran and Salvadoran armies. Food was scarce; there were times when they only had mangoes to eat. Young and old suffered from malnutrition and required medical attention. The UN Commission on Refugees arranged for them to go to Panama. They settled in northern Panama where they had larger tracts of land; they built a house for each family and a school for the community. The disadvantages were that it rained for 11 months straight and they were far from the city of Colón. The roads were so terrible that it was easier to travel twelve hours by canoe on the Atlantic Ocean. Despite the disadvantages they remained in Panama for eleven years. In March 1990 they heard about the success of *Segundo Montes* and decided they wanted to return. In June 1990 they requested permission from the government of El Salvador and the UN to repatriate. The government was intransigent. Their leaders had to walk four days through the forest to get to the embassy to secure permission. It took nine months of negotiating and demonstrating in front of the embassy and through the capital, San Salvador. They demonstrated in the streets and sixteen members staged a hunger strike in front of the embassy. Finally they were given permission to leave January 24-26. When they crossed into El Salvador the military had a big banner: The Army Welcomes You and Will Take Care of You. They knew from past experience that was too good to be true. Sure enough five army tanks blocked the road when they were going to a Mass. There was not enough land for them to survive so they negotiated with the government to move to the location that we were visiting. Finally on March 24, 1991 they celebrated their arrival at *Ciudad de Romero*. They constructed houses and planted crops. At first they had to walk quite a distance to get water, but now they have wells. Their dream is to be self-sufficient raising their crops and in the future when war ceases, to return to fishing. On May 8, 1981 six hundred soldiers came carrying flashlights; some dressed as clowns pretending that they were friends and trying to make them forget the horrors. But the people knew that the soldiers' hearts were the same and they did not want them near their settlement.

Late afternoon on August 11th we visited the site where the four North American women had been killed. On this quiet country road the Salvadoran military brutally murdered these women for the crime of working with the poor. Dorothy Kazel, Maura Clarke, Ita Ford, and Jean Donovan were on their way home from the airport on December 2, 1980 when they were intercepted and taken to this dark country road. We saw the place where they were buried in shallow graves after they were assaulted and killed. In our time of prayer there was only one man leading a cow that passed by. It was dark when they were attacked, but in daylight I turned to see mountains in the distance—such a peaceful, beautiful place, but also a place of violence visited upon women who had dedicated their lives to accompanying the poor women and children of El Salvador. When we visited, their bodies had long been recovered and buried elsewhere, but here was the site of their martyrdom. They had chosen to share their lives with the poor who had endured so much violence. They felt the limitations of our humanity: hearts of flesh that ached for those suffering as did Jesus and these, God's people. They were steadfast and continued serving those who suffered, believing that God was with them even unto death. Their martyrdom was a scandal to those who thought they should have remained in the USA living a middle class life and not be bothered by those who were caught between the guerrillas and government soldiers. Their willingness to give their lives caused me to reflect. I am a Sister for many years, striving to love the poor but afraid, so afraid of being touched by violence. I could not see myself going to jail the way Dorothy Day did so many times in the USA when she demonstrated for peace and justice. I certainly could not picture myself rejoicing while suffering persecution. "Dear God, I have far to travel. Please enlighten me and strengthen me to do all that you want of me in life. May the Beatitudes (Mt. 5:1-12) become a reality for all who seek justice and charity in our time."

Of all the Salvadorans who spoke to us, I was most impressed by Rubén Zamora who at that time was the Vice President of the Assembly. He spoke calmly and intelligently. He did not rant or criticize. He proposed that the history of El Salvador could be seen as cycles of crisis. Each crisis had three common elements: 1) an increase in the level of popular mobilization during which they were able to overcome internal, ideological differences to work together; 2) a change in US policy toward El Salvador (except in 1971-1972) that produced destabilization of the military; and 3) a coup d'état when society relies on a sector of the military to counter the force of the military, a process of ridding the bad only to install new horrors. He told us that his country had entered a new period for popular organizations like the trade unions that formed coalitions to work for change. Zamora thought that the USA finally realized that reliance on the military alone did not work as evidenced by the death of the Jesuits. President George H. W. Bush's administration (1989-1993) was more pragmatic and not obsessed with Latin America. The US was also supporting negotiations that proposed reliance on political means. Negotiations were essential to counter the force of the military so democratization could be effected. The UN negotiator, Alvaro de Soto, was a professional who had the confidence of the General Secretary with whom he conferred on a regular basis. As Mr. Zamora spoke, I wondered if he were Jesuit educated and thought what a superb academic he would be. His was not an easy life in El Salvador, but despite threats against his life and the bombing of his home, he persisted in working for a political solution to the concerns of warring factions. It gave me hope that such an intelligent, balanced man was working to bring about peace. I could not foresee the future, but he would indeed be a professor and more interestingly, Rubén Zamora would be El Salvador's Ambassador to the USA, a post he assumed in April 2013 when he presented his credentials to President Barack Obama. The qualities I noted in him on our visit have proved invaluable in terms of current issues like the massive increase of children migrating to the USA from Central American countries plagued by gang violence, poverty, and corruption.

Our week in El Salvador included a visit to the University of Central America. We celebrated Mass in the chapel where the Jesuits and their housekeeper and her daughter are memorialized. I dreaded going there for I knew that they were murdered by the military whose post overlooked the priests' residence. We entered the priests' residence, a simple house with quarters for the cook and rooms for the resident priests. The backyard where they were executed with a shot to their heads now has pink rose bushes that the housekeeper's husband planted in honor of his wife and daughter who were also killed. I was deeply touched by this man's creating a place of beauty on the very spot where violence and hatred robbed him of his family. The work of educating Salvadorans has continued. Violence disrupts but does not derail the journey toward peace. As one presenter told us, "The history of Salvador is written in the blood of women, children, priests…" Those words were powerfully borne out by the witness of those who have been killed: Archbishop Oscar Romero, the four North American women, scores of priests, catechists and thousands of men and women seeking a better life.

On one of the last days of our week in El Salvador we had an appointment at the US Embassy. We walked into a building that was well fortified with heavy concrete barriers at the entrance. It reminded me of Spanish fortresses that the Moors had built in southern Spain to intimidate and discourage anyone from attacking. Once inside we were directed to the basement. "Who meets people of importance in the basement?" I thought. The young woman who met with us was an aide, someone far removed from the US ambassador. We were so eager to speak for the Salvadoran people: our minds and hearts were filled with stories of those who had given their lives. The aide listened as we spoke. We stressed the need for negotiations to work for peace so the years of conflict could come to an end. She gave us no hint that peace negotiations were indeed being pursued. I felt that our brief meeting was discouraging at best and probably pointless. Our representatives in El Salvador were more interested in security than the safety and well being of the Salvadoran people. There was no hint, not the least indication that the peace process was a priority. I felt that we had wasted our time going to the embassy and I realized that my own government was on the wrong side aligned with the rich and powerful against ordinary people. How did we/they get it so wrong?

I was depressed as we left the embassy. I had thought that our visit would be taken seriously, that the embassy would certainly respond to the information that we shared. They may have lived in a fortress but surely they would welcome information about the common people. I sincerely felt that our voices would be heard as they are in a democracy, but El Salvador was a militarized country receiving foreign aid from the USA. Our embassy was not interested in hearing about the suffering and injustices visited on missionaries, catechists, women, and children. They wanted to maintain order and allow businesses to flourish. Order is good when it allows people to live and work, and children and young adults to study and grow. I don't want to live where violence affects every aspect of life: where and how I live and everything I can do. That embassy visit showed me the huge divide between ordinary people and the leaders who represent us in foreign lands. I am proud to be an American citizen, but that day I was saddened to learn how our representatives in foreign countries are only interested in promoting "American" interests. That day was a real eye opener. I realize now that I had an idealized view of my own government thinking that they represented me and my views. The USA is a wonderfully diverse country but there is no guarantee that government officials represent my views. Governments have agendas and who is to say who determines their priorities? It helped me realize how really important it is to learn about issues and how important it is to advocate for people and their wellbeing. Nothing can be presumed, not here in the USA and definitely not in other countries. The more that communications, travel, and media connect peoples across the world, the greater the need to know what people need, for what they yearn, and how these dreams can be fostered by education, health initiatives, and freedom of expression. I took too much for granted. After my Central American trip I returned to the USA a wiser woman even though that included a definite cynicism about our leaders.

Chapter 7

SISTERLY LOVE

A recovering addict was telling her story to the group at Covenant House's Catskill facility. As the evening progressed the stories were so sad—young people caught in a web of addiction fueled by feelings of isolation, anger, and abuse. Our faculty group from St. Helena's was there overnight as part of our training to help teenagers who were experimenting with drugs. We were split up into pairs to be in different groups. I was trying my best to listen and to empathize with each person as he/she spoke. These young people like the teenagers I taught were sharing their life stories. I was thinking, "Is this what our students are doing?" What could I possibly say to show that I accepted each of them and could empathize with them? When I finally got the courage, I spoke of my sister, Joan and how she died so young. I had looked up to her all my life; we even entered the same religious congregation. That night I spoke about losing Joan and how sad and devastated I had been. Shortly after, a man who had also been silent for the greater part of the night began to speak. He said that he could identify with much of what I said. That of course is the aim of any group: to provide a safe place for each person to share his/her story and to feel accepted and supported by the other members. I was astonished because I had felt so apart from all the people whose stories I had heard; I was even thinking that my going there was a mistake. I felt that I had so little in common with the other people in the group that I could not wait to get out of that room. But my struggle to live after losing Joan was similar to those who had broken up with friends and lovers, who felt isolated and who turned to drink and drugs as a way to comfort themselves and to fit in with others. Who was Joan and how did we relate?

When I was born in Union Hospital in the Bronx, the third daughter of George A. and Margaret J. Willemse, my older sister, Joan was out buying a baby blanket. She was not allowed to visit because hospital rules did not welcome young girls, even ten year olds like her. It was many years later that I heard this story. I was really touched to know that my older sister was thinking of me even before she saw me.

Ten years older than I, Joan was and always would be my older sister, not just because she was older but also because she was wiser and more capable than I. That was easy to accept when I was growing up. Almost everyone I knew in the family was older than I so she was up there with aunts and uncles, though not quite a grandmother or great aunt. Joan was the eldest so she had to explore territory and claim possession long before I ever would: navigating boyfriends, high school, curfews, and gaining independence from our mother. She was a bright, serious, intense young woman. When our father died two and a half months after my birth, she was ten and felt his loss deeply. Joan was the oldest child and closest to him in temperament and talents. Like him she was serious and intense.

Joan enjoyed being with our father and followed in his footsteps when she too became a skilled shuffleboard player. Another familiar story was that our father could mentally tally the sum of the groceries he was buying and tell the clerk if he were a few cents off. Joan was born during the Great Depression that had cast a shadow over our parents in terms of limiting their education and their job opportunities. While our parents were lucky to finish high school, Joan would be the first of our family to attend college— Fordham University on a full scholarship for Chemistry. No doubt about it, Joan Marie Willemse had a great future ahead of her.

There were glimmers of greatness that I witnessed like the fountain pen in the top drawer of my mother's bureau. It was engraved with Joan's name and was a special award. Somehow the cap got separated from the pen so it could never be used. There was an Inquisition to discover the culprit who rendered the pen useless. When questioned, I denied playing with it, but it was obvious that I was guilty. That day I determined never to tell another lie, a promise that I have tried to keep these many years. It was not worth the trouble trying to remember what I said; far easier to tell the truth from the beginning. Honestly, it is really hard to tell the truth all the time. I would be afraid of the consequences/punishment if I had done something wrong. Some people are so slick that they make whatever they say the truth; it's as if they create a truth that lives up to their expectations. There are also those who tell you what you want to hear. That has struck me as weird: how does anyone know what I want to hear when I am uncertain about or may not even have thought seriously about something? Such people would have to be great guessers if such a word exists. Moral of the story: truth is hard to find and really hard to discern.

Joan could be a hard task master. We had returned home from the library one summer afternoon. I was excited to be with Joan and to have many new books to read. By the time we climbed up to our fifth floor apartment, we were both ravenously hungry, or so I thought. Before Joan would let me eat, she decided to teach me the proper way to arrange cutlery when setting a table. Her timing could not have been worse. I was so hungry that I wanted to stab her. Sure it was good to teach me this nicety, but couldn't she wait until we ate something? I wasn't going anywhere. It was a teachable moment of sorts, but I think it would have been better to have a captive audience with food in her stomach than to have a kid sister with a growling stomach, dying of hunger.

On another occasion Joan decided to give me piano lessons. I was so proud that she was giving me all this attention. She stressed the importance of learning the notes and what they signified: FACE and Every Good Boy Does Fine. As she talked, I noticed that the notes had numbers: one to five. Why learn the hard way when the numbers matched my five fingers? All was going well until the day she turned the page and there were only notes and no numbers. Joan could not understand why I could not play that piece. When I told her what I had done, she got angry, "You mean you don't know the names of the notes?" "No, I used the numbers," I replied. She gave me time to relearn all the pieces and she blacked out all the numbers. My next lesson I went from child prodigy to bumbling idiot when there were no numbers. Joan got so angry that she tore the Thompson Beginner's Piano Book from top to bottom—end of piano lessons. She scared me so that even though I tried on two other occasions once when I was a freshman in high school and another when I was an adult to learn piano, I never succeeded. Was Joan's reaction the reason I could not master the piano? The image of her ripping the book is with me still. I came to terms with my inability by concentrating, really concentrating so I could be the best listener ever especially of classical music that features piano concertos. My mother and Joan were the pianists in the family. I would follow another route.

Joan looked out for me when I was young. She brought me to my first dentist appointment. She wanted me to have my teeth checked because that had not been part of survival mode in the Bronx. In fact that would be something that would only be scheduled by my mother after she remarried and we lived upstate. That dentist's eyes appeared to look in two distinctly different directions. How could he drill and fill teeth when he had multi-visioning eyes? I never asked him directly but it bothered me every time I had an appointment.

Aquinas High School had an operetta every spring and as I got older, Joan and Geri brought me to see them. The singing was good and everyone loved the costumes and all that transpired on stage. When Geri graduated in June 1952 Joan and I waited outside the gate on a long line with all the graduates' relatives. Each graduate had two tickets so our going meant that my mother did not attend her daughter's graduation. Geri told me recently that our mother chose not to go to Geri's graduation when Joe Brady encouraged her not to go. In his mind, she had attended one graduation (Joan's) and there was no reason to go to another. That was a devastating blow to Geri. At not quite ten years old, I only knew that I was so lucky to go to the graduation with Joan. I was proud of Geri and also proud to be with Joan. When we finally got into the auditorium, I remember how everyone was tall. I was so short compared with the adults. When would I ever be tall enough to see over other people's heads?

September 7, 1952 Joan entered the convent, a sure fire way to achieve a new, exalted status. Nuns were special: they wore habits that set them apart. They vowed to live poorly sharing their life and possessions with their community; to obey God, the Rule of St. Augustine and the Constitutions of the Dominican Sisters of Our Lady of the Rosary;

and to live chastely foregoing marriage and children. It seemed like a perfect match when she was given her religious name, Sr. Joan Dolores. Her feast day, September 15 Our Lady of Sorrows would be celebrated in place of her birthday. At the time it was just Joan's new name and a pretty one at that.

I tried over the years to give Joan gifts that she needed and would like. On one of our first visits when she was in the novitiate in Sparkill, I brought a glass jar inside which I had placed a caterpillar on a bed of grass. The lid was perforated so the caterpillar could breathe. I knew that she liked science so she would warm to a caterpillar whose best days were ahead of him. That first Christmas I went to Woolworth's, the famous five and ten cents store. I chose plain white stationery with envelopes. Even as I searched for the perfect gift, I had an ulterior motive: I wanted Joan to write to me.

Learning to bake was my ticket to stardom. I baked batches of cookies (chocolate chip, snickerdoodles, and peanut butter) and several tomato soup cakes, a family favorite for its delicious flavor thanks to a combination of ground cloves, cinnamon, allspice and raisins. Joan shared these with the other sisters in the novitiate and later when they were away studying during the summer at Villanova and Catholic University. I had finally succeeded. These bake-offs occurred in the summer when it was hot and humid. No matter, if I could make Joan happy, it was worth the effort. One time we were going to visit Joan at Saugerties, the vacation place for the Sisters just north of Kingston, NY on the west side of the Hudson River. The day before our visit, Joan called to say that her plans had changed and she would not be going to Saugerties on Saturday. I was crestfallen. At first I thought that all my efforts had been for naught and that all that baking was in vain, but then I bounced back. If we could not go to her, then I would find a way to get the baked goods to her. I wrapped cookies in waxed paper in groups of two or four, then packed them with the wrapped cakes and shipped them using the USPS. I have no idea how they arrived: intact or smushed together into piles of cookie crumbs. Those were delicious cookies and cakes so I figure that Joan and company must have enjoyed them no matter what state they were in. After all it would only be a physical change not a chemical change. Whether eaten by hand or with a spoon, those baked goods were delicious.

Our band remained in Sparkill after profession for a Formation Program. It consisted of taking college classes along with doing charges and having evening classes with Sr. Evangelist Marie, the Formation Director. We moved over to the 4th floor in the Motherhouse. There were so many of us that rooms were at a premium even for the college professors many years our senior. Suddenly I was told that I would be sharing a room with my sister on the third floor. That sounded great. Unknown to me Joan had been assigned to share a room with another sister; Joan went and asked the Prioress if she could have her own room. Her reaction harkened back to all the years when we lived on East Gun Hill Road and she and Geri slept on narrow beds in the living room. They had no privacy and with only one bathroom they had to stagger showers and bathroom time among four women and one child. Closet space was almost nonexistent, but then they had few clothes. Joan knew only too well how lack of privacy affected her psyche. I remember how she strongly identified with our younger cousin, Peggy Ann when she was a teenager, the oldest of six siblings, living in a railroad flat. She said, "Peggy needs privacy." Joan knew this from experience.

Meanwhile I was thinking that sharing a room would be a great opportunity to get to know my big sister. The room was narrow, with a curtain that divided it in two. Each of us had a twin bed, bureau, desk and straight back chair. When we awoke in the morning it was Profound Silence so we got washed and dressed, went to the chapel, and after breakfast stopped briefly to pick up books and mantle. I taught fourth grade at St. Agnes School so I was on the run. Joan was a science professor at St. Thomas Aquinas College so she was even busier than I. We seldom saw each other. She rarely got back to our room before 9:30 pm when Profound Silence began. I was thinking that now that I was an adult Joan and I could get to know each other. We grew up in the same family, but ten years difference in age was a huge divide. I scarcely knew her. I had all those developmental tasks that an infant, toddler, child had to surmount while she was racing through childhood and heading into adolescence and young adulthood. On rare occasions someone came to visit. I remember Joan speaking with Sr. Dolorita who had come up to Sparkill for a wake. They spoke in low tones and I was not invited to join the conversation despite my being only feet away. All those conversations that I imagined between Joan and me did not take place that year.

One advantage of our room was that it faced the lake and there was a door through which we could climb out onto the top of the porch—no furniture or railing so only a quick peek around. One evening Joan was back in our room before Profound Silence. Conversation turned to star gazing. I told Joan, "I have no idea where any stars are." "You mean to tell me that you don't know the North Star and …?" she responded. Next thing I know we are both on the porch looking up at the stars. It was a moonless night so the stars were glowing brightly. After a few minutes, I said, "Joan, I cannot tell which star is which. I cannot see the patterns and to tell you the truth, I have no desire to know." Joan reacted as if I had just spouted heresy. She could not believe that her sister knew nothing about the constellations especially when she was teaching the Sisters in my band Astronomy. It would have been more diplomatic to feign interest, but I could not tell which star or constellation was which. Rather than appear inept, I said that I had no desire to learn. With all there is to learn in our world, why waste my energy on something for which I had no aptitude? Joan definitely did not appreciate my honesty that night.

Not long after on a cool, crisp September morning we were at morning prayer in Sacred Heart Chapel when the fire alarm sounded. (On August 28, 1899 fire destroyed ten of eleven buildings and left our Sisters and the 350 boys and girls of St. Agnes Home without a place to live. That part of our history made a lasting impression on us.) Sisters who were group mothers left the chapel to help evacuate the boys from the dormitories. The fire started on the third floor of St. Agnes in the room next to ours. That sister scared me and I dreaded meeting her in the common bathroom and here she was responsible for the fire. Besides being spooky we learned that day that she hoarded all kinds of things. It was an accident waiting to happen.

Once the fire was under control I ran upstairs to try to retrieve Joan's Master's thesis on the desk against the shared wall to the other sister's room. After a long wait I was relieved to find that the fire had not touched our room, but then I got involved in throwing down to a truck below soggy, burnt items from the room where the fire started. There were puddles on the roof, remnants of all the water the volunteer firefighters had aimed at the room, and I slipped and fell. By the time I went over to St. Agnes School, I was a mess with black smudges on my habit, and I was late. Given all that we knew about that fire long ago, we got off easy that day. God's angels were at our side.

To say that I understood why Joan would not speak to me when we shared a room would be a falsehood. Here I was physically closer to her than when we lived in the fifth floor apartment in the Bronx, but it felt as if she were far, far away. She may have timed her arrival home to forestall the need to speak. Profound silence began at 9:30 pm and lasted until after morning prayer and breakfast. During that time we had to refrain from speaking except in an emergency. Joan would not violate that rule with a younger sister lest she scandalize me. She may also have been so busy at the college that she could not have arrived sooner. Joan taught many science courses, some of which were new to her. She was often a few chapters ahead of her students. She worked in the science laboratory and spent hours in the library seated at a carrel surrounded by books. After evening prayer and recreation I would go upstairs, change into nightgown/pajamas, review my class work for the next day's teaching, take a shower, and go to bed. That year was a supreme disappointment. It was a classic case of "so near and yet so far." That summer Joan returned to Villanova to complete work on her master's degree. By the following August I was missioned to Our Lady of Grace Convent in the Bronx so our days of being roommates came to an end.

Throughout the novitiate and a year of Formation I tried to keep open the avenues of communication between our parents and Joan. She probably saw more of my mother and stepfather in those three years than at any other time in the convent. Joan's schedule was unpredictable. Compared with many of the other sisters, Joan was a youngster so she was often called upon to drive another sister to the city and she would be a no-show for my parents' visit. As young as I was in religion (most of the Sisters had entered many years before me), my life was more predictable so my parents would get to visit with me and not necessarily with Joan.

Joan's birthday was March 18. When I was a novice I wanted to let Joan know I was thinking of her even though we could not speak or be with each other on her birthday. I did have access to the refectory so I placed a small black and white snap-shot of Joan under her plate; she was dressed in full habit, seated in front of a cake with lit candles grinning from ear to ear. It must have been a celebration after she got her B.S. at Fordham University for it was taken outdoors at the summer home of Aunt Dorothy and Uncle Bill in Wallkill, NJ. As the Sisters turned over their plates, Joan would see herself. I wasn't in the pantry to watch her reaction, but those who did said that she blushed. Oh, yes, I had printed at the top of the picture, "Happy Birthday!"

As postulants and novices we had choir practice on Sunday afternoons to prepare for major feast days (Christmas, Easter, Pentecost) and the afternoon before a funeral. Our band loved to sing. Sometimes we practiced and sang from the choir loft located at the back of the church accessed by climbing up steep steps. In summer and early fall the choir loft was an oven—no fans and only one window. One afternoon we were up in the choir loft practicing. I did what any sensible person would do: opened the white plastic collar to get air. Joan was at the organ and noticed right away. Instead of smiling she made a face that signaled I was doing something wrong. It took the pleasure out of the afternoon.

Choir practice became a favorite activity when Joan was the accompanist for the choir director, Sr. Ann Catherine. The liturgy was still in Latin as were most of the hymns. We really liked singing in two parts (soprano and alto) and even liked singing the Requiem Mass. The summer of 1962 after our reception of the habit, four of the senior sisters died. We were singing the Latin Requiem every week or two. I am sure that Sr. Ann Catherine and Joan had a different take on all the practices, but for us novices it was serious entertainment. The opening lines speak of rest and light, two qualities we hope those who die will experience. The Sequence, *Dies Irae*, has powerful images of the Last Judgment pictured as a "day of wrath, day of anger." It was long and emphasized the anguish sinners need to feel. Throughout the Requiem there is a sense of awe before personal judgment, but even more at the final judgment at the end of the world. There are references to Jesus' forgiving sin and welcoming those who repent. The final segment, *In*

Paradisum, brings tears to my eyes when I think of loved ones being welcomed like Lazarus into paradise. These are some of my favorite excerpts:

Requiem: Introit

Requiem aeternam dona eis, Domine, et lux perpetua luceat eis.

Grant them eternal rest, Lord, and let perpetual light shine on them.

Sequence: Dies Irae

Dies irae, dies illa
Solvet saeclum in favilla,
teste David cum Sibylla.

Day of wrath, day of anger
will dissolve the world in ashes,
as foretold by David and the Sibyl.

Quantus tremor est futurus,
quando judex est venturus,
cuncta stricte discussurus!

Great trembling there will be
when the Judge descends from heaven
to examine all things closely.

Lacrimosa dies illa,
qua resurget ex favilla
judicandus homo reus.
Huic ergo parce, Deus,
pie Jesu Domine,
dona eis requiem. Amen.

That day of tears and mourning,
when from the ashes shall arise,
all humanity to be judged.
Spare us by your mercy, Lord,
gentle Lord Jesus,
grant them eternal rest. Amen.

Communion: Lux aeterna

Lux aeterna luceat eis, Domine,
cum sanctis tuis in aeternum,
quia pius es.
Requiem aeternum dona eis,
Domine, et Lux perpetua luceat eis,
cum Sanctus tuis in aeternum,
quia pius es.

Let eternal light shine on them, Lord, as with Your saints in eternity, because You are merciful.
Grant them eternal rest, Lord, and let perpetual light shine on them, as with Your saints in eternity, because You are merciful.

In Paradisum

In paradisum deducant angeli; in tuo adventu suscipiant te martyres et perducant te in civitatem sanctam Jerusalem.	May the angels lead you into paradise, may the martyrs receive you at your coming, and may they guide you into the holy city, Jerusalem.
Chorus angelorum te suscipiat et cum Lazaro, quondam paupere, aeternam habeas requiem.	May the chorus of angels receive you and with Lazarus once poor may you have eternal rest.

The Latin Requiem uses an economy of powerful words. As serious as the words are, we really liked singing it. We were young and not concerned about our own mortality. The Mass for Sr. Maria Ignatia, a former Prioress of St. Agnes and beloved by all, was one funeral we would not forget. I wrote to my parents, "Sr. Maria Ignatia's funeral last Monday was quite impressive. Wearing our black choir mantles, we were part of the *Libera* procession before Mass. There was something so inspiring about her funeral... All I could think was that Sister had come home and we, her earthly family, gave her the warmest, most sincere farewell possible on her return to her heavenly home and her heavenly family."

We felt the mournful quality of these words when Sr. Rose De Lima, the aunt of Sr. Frederick Marie, a fellow novice died. Singing her requiem was personal. While we did not know her aunt, we felt truly sorry for the loss that our novice suffered. I don't remember if she was able to spend time with her family. Even if she did, it had to be a really difficult time. I am sure that she had looked forward to seeing and talking with her aunt especially after profession of vows which was nine months away. For reasons unknown to us her aunt was taken a matter of months after her niece received the habit and long before profession of vows. Sr. Rose De Lima had cancer and had suffered severe pain for over two years; no doubt she was ready to meet God. I wrote to my parents on July 29. 1962, "A nun's funeral is different—there's sorrow in losing one of our own, but the fear of death is swallowed up in the joy of what's ahead for the one we've lost. A nun's funeral is beautiful and even more impressive than her Profession." These lofty words sounded good, but I doubt that our novice viewed her aunt's death this way. In fact it would not be long before I would learn that our thoughts are not the thoughts or plans that God has. Will we ever know why? Sometimes I would not even ask the question. Rather than risk an explanation I could not handle, it was easier and less threatening not to ask.

My sister, Joan, age 32, was experiencing strange symptoms. Visually her world was on a slant. This presented major difficulties when walking. Her doctor had her admitted to New York University Hospital. I knew she was undergoing tests but she told me not to reveal this fact to our mother. It put me in an untenable position. My loyalty was to my mother and to Joan, but Joan could not bear having our mother visit her in the hospital. When I heard that Aunt Dorothy and Uncle Bill had visited Joan, I was really annoyed. Granted Dorothy was Joan's godmother and they were very close; I could not understand why Joan would not even tell our mother about her hospitalization. I did see my parents around that time, but kept Joan's secret. It was not uncommon for Joan to be so busy that she barely got to see them on the days they visited me so they accepted my explanation without asking questions that I would not have been able to answer. When Joan was released from the hospital she returned to the Motherhouse. Shortly after on April 28, 1964 I wrote to my parents and explained that Joan had been in New York University Hospital for tests April 8-21. While tests ruled out a tumor, the doctors were not certain why she saw the world on a slant. Because fatigue aggravates neurological conditions, they ordered her to rest every day and to limit her activity. That meant a break from teaching at the college and no work on her thesis. Shortly after I wrote again to my parents that Joan gradually resumed teaching.

Another opportunity to play diplomat arose when Joan could not accompany me on my visit home which meant a different, unknown Sister would be my companion. My parents were more concerned about Joan than about my explanation so I succeeded in smoothing troubled waters.

While Joan spent the summer of 1964 at Villanova University, I was able to help her complete her thesis. Between working at the switchboard in the morning and minding the boys in Angel Guardian Group I devoted free time in the afternoon to working on the forty-two graphs for Joan's thesis. Before computers this meant hand-printing each graph times three, a total of one hundred twenty-six pages, in India ink. Sr. Rose Edwin, my able assistant, helped enormously as we labeled and inserted the graphs into the main thesis, numbering pages and such. Joan was very grateful that we could help her. We managed to get the copies to Joan in time for her to defend her thesis in the morning and take the Comprehensive examination in Chemistry the afternoon of July 30th. She was a success in both of these so finally she could relegate research dedicated to the formation of tin crystals to the far reaches of her brain and concentrate on her new love, Astronomy. No doubt Joan felt that her name was written in the stars. Well, I thought that. Joan was just happy to have completed these requirements for a MS so she could return to Sparkill and go to Saugerties for two weeks before returning to the college to teach for the fall semester.

One day in early September Joan was at St. Helena's for a meeting. As we washed our hands in the communal bathroom, I looked at her in the mirror. "I am so glad that I knew you when you were nobody before you became such an important somebody," I said. Joan smiled. Without a doubt Joan had emerged as one of the leaders of the Chapter of Affairs, someone who had read, thought deeply, and was able to communicate clearly how and why change could occur. During the Chapter when feelings had run high as they discussed making the habit optional, I heard that Joan had said, "Sisters, can we agree that every sister needs to be clothed?" Laughter rolled through those assembled. Once the tension broke they were able to proceed. More importantly, Joan and the Government Commission members were able to explain the principles of subsidiarity and collegiality upon which the changes in governance were based and to suggest new practices. It was an extraordinary opportunity for the delegates and our elected leaders to work and pray together for five days a week over four weeks. The delegates were living there so they also had time to socialize and time to reflect. I was sorry not to have seen Joan in action. It had to be such a wonderful experience for her. She was known as an intelligent, capable woman, but the Chapter showed her wisdom and ability to lead. Joan could not have been more appreciated.

When I went home to visit my parents in Staten Island, my stepfather was tethered to an oxygen tank. Since he retired in April 1969, Joe Brady's health had steadily deteriorated. On a previous hospitalization in May when he was struggling to breathe, I saw how strong the will to live can be. When he was hospitalized in mid-September, I was visiting a different man. He was depressed and seemed to have lost the will to live. He had had major health problems exacerbated by years of smoking two packs of cigarettes a day since he was a teenager. In 1957 he was diagnosed with cancer of the mouth. He stopped smoking cold turkey. Surgery saved his life, but the after effects were life-changing. From that day forward he had great difficulty eating for his tongue had lost mobility. It affected his speech, his appearance, and his ability to eat. When he returned home, he remained in their bedroom and fed himself standing at his bureau on which was a framed picture of his deceased mother. I worried that he would never be able to join us for dinner, but Joe Brady was a fighter. He returned to work and with my mother's help— she faithfully ground up meat with gravy or sauce and cooked vegetables until they were soft so he could ingest his meals. Gradually we could understand him when he spoke and accepted how he looked. I admired my step father's fighting spirit, but that Sunday in September Joe Brady was a man who had lost the will to live.

On Monday, September 22 my mother received a call from Staten Island Hospital notifying her that Joe Brady had died shortly after 9:30 am. She in turn called his children and my convent. So began our family's mourning the loss of Joseph P. Brady, husband of Margaret, father of three children, and retired civil engineer for the NYC Board of Water Supply. Joe's children, Tom, Jiggs (Joseph), and Clare joined my mother and me for the wake. A group of Sisters from my convent drove from the Bronx to pay their respects. My sister, Joan joined us for the Mass of Resurrection after which she returned to Sparkill.

I had hoped that Joan would be of some help, but I realized at the funeral that Joan was so involved as Dean of STAC that she had even less time than when she taught full time at the college. The responsibility of caring for my mother would fall on me. After the funeral I wrote to

Mother Evangelist Marie for permission to drop the graduate Spanish course for which I had enrolled at Hunter College. This was the best decision I made because within three weeks all hell broke loose.

Life at school was its normal busy self. Our seniors had their informal Yearbook pictures taken outdoors on the St. Helena High School campus. On other days Sr. Eileen and I supervised class pictures taken on the steps of the school's main entrance and in other nooks and crannies. With over 300 students in each year, taking group and individual pictures was a major project. It was a great relief to have that over.

Wednesday, October 15, the feast of St. Teresa of Avila, one of my favorite saints whose life I had read in Spanish and English. Who knew this date would touch me more personally? I got a call that Joan was in Good Samaritan Hospital in Suffern, NY. She had had emergency abdominal surgery. I knew better than drive myself to see Joan. Sr. Eileen Gannon drove me to the hospital. When I could see Joan, she had a tube draining brown fluid from her abdomen up and out through her nose. In that setting, dressed in a hospital gown Joan looked much thinner than when dressed in the habit. While my experience of hospitals was limited, I knew that the drainage tube was painful. It appeared that whatever she needed was often uncomfortable for the patient. I experienced mixed emotions. Joan had always been strong willed and capable of handling any situation. Now she was a patient and I needed to be there for her. How could I help her? Would she even accept help from me? When she was 25 she had had an appendectomy and recovered splendidly. At age 37 she was young but this surgery was more complicated and she had a harder time. I had not known how she had suffered from colitis over many months. Her favorite food was bananas for they supplied magnesium and were a source of nourishment. In the days following the surgery she told me that she had not slept well and had had disturbing dreams. I could not help but think that our father, George had been hospitalized and died when he was 37. I did not mention this to Joan, but I am sure it was on her mind.

I visited Joan at Good Samaritan Hospital but this time healing was agonizingly slow. I resolved to be positive. She would not find negativity in me. I wanted to convey that she would get better, that the hospitalization was a setback but not a life-changer. I had a lot to learn. I was shaken by Joan's surgery and her hospitalization. My friend, Eileen Gannon would be my helper as I faced the prospect of Joan's time in the hospital. Joan would never talk to me about health issues. I think she did that with her dear friends, Sr. Catherine Maher and Sr. Ann Magdalene. When I met the two surgeons, Dr. Wagner and Dr. Rast, I was a bit intimidated by the older, taller doctor and more comfortable with the younger, shorter doctor. This was no surprise because as a child I was afraid of the husband of one of my mother's friends but comfortable with his son who was as tall as the husband. Dr. Rast also explained things very calmly and scientifically and reminded me of Joan and her love of science.

Everyone at Sparkill was praying daily for Joan's recovery. Despite a capable surgical team and prayers rising to heaven, Joan was slow to heal. Even when the tube was removed, she was not able to eat. In fact she had many problems that no one anticipated. I arrived one afternoon to find Joan stretched out *sans* hospital gown on a bed of ice in an attempt to bring down a high fever. It was shocking to me and had to be humiliating for Joan who was such a private person. Every ten days to two weeks there was a major setback. Over the next eight weeks I spent hours waiting to get into the ICU to visit her. Around us life went on. I marked papers, entered student grades on computer cards, laughed at the way my name appeared on each card, Sr. Judith Bra. How did that escape attention? One afternoon one of our older Sisters was in a room down the hall. The nurse told us that she was talking out loud so we asked what she was saying. In her mind Sister was lining up the children as she had done so often for First Communion showing them how to fold their hands. Eileen and I looked at each other. What will we be saying when we are old and sick? Somehow we thought it would not be such holy words.

Thanksgiving eve, Eileen and I went to Staten Island to bring my mother to her brother's house in the Bronx so she could spend the holiday with Aunt Margie and Uncle Henry and their children. I discovered that the day before Thanksgiving is one of the worst traveling days because no matter where you go, there is unrelenting traffic. Eileen and I stopped at the convent to eat and then headed up to the hospital. We arrived to find Joan awaiting another surgery. This had to be an emergency for no one operates on a patient the night before a national holiday. I went in to see Joan. I was barely in the room when she told me to get out. I could not believe my ears. We had just traveled all over New York to be with Joan and she did not want me in her room? I was upset. Other sisters were there, Sr. Marie Jean and Sr. Adele from the college. They went in for a brief visit. What could anyone say to help Joan? She had to be at her wit's end. Over a month in the hospital and now another surgery; this was not good. Add to that the fact that she remembered only too well how our father, George, had died. I have no doubt that she was thinking of him and how it could also happen to her. That had preyed on her mind for quite some time. Joan went up to surgery late Wednesday night. She survived the surgery but was back again in ICU. The ICU at that time was such tight quarters; you could barely fit two persons in to see the patient for short visits. Joan at least had a window so she could see the sky and distinguish between day and night.

A few days after that surgery Mother Evangelist Marie and the Secretary General, Sr. Regina Rosaire came to visit. I stepped out for a moment. When I returned Mother was sitting on the edge of Joan's bed. Between gritted teeth, Joan spoke. Mother leaned over thinking perhaps that she had words of wisdom. Instead Joan repeated, "Please get off the bed." Mother stood up and soon said her farewells. Sr. Regina Rosaire had spoken with Eileen in the hall. "Doesn't she realize that her sister is dying?" Apparently I appeared more optimistic than the situation warranted. When Eileen told me what she said, I replied, "If there is even the slightest chance that Joan will make it, I am going to act as if she will recover. After all, she's bounced back from other emergencies. Who's to say she won't make it?" As Joan overcame so many crises and beat the odds, I had this strange feeling that she was invincible like a gambler believing that the next roll of the dice will bring the big win.

We had driven up to the hospital almost every day for two months. When there were emergencies, we would stay overnight at our convent in Suffern. Joan was in the ICU more often than she was in a room and time to visit was restricted to a few minutes each hour. We were in the waiting area so much that someone approached me and spoke to me thinking I was a nurse. It scared me a bit until I realized that I was wearing a nurse's uniform with the black veil. I knew little or nothing about nursing so I referred her to a real nurse. We got friendly with one nurse in ICU. She asked, "When is your mother coming to visit Joan?" After some days, I brought my sister, Geri who had flown in from Boise, ID with her two youngest children to help my mother in the weeks after Joe Brady's death. Geri emerged from the hospital and said, "This is the last time that I will see Joan." "Geri, don't say that. We don't know. Joan could pull through." I replied with a feeling of panic. No matter what I said, Geri was convinced that Joan would die. I on the other hand, chose to be optimistic. One of us would be right, the other wrong. I preferred to err on the side of recovery and life. If Geri were right then I would deal with that when the time came.

I only brought my mother to the hospital one time. Joan had made it clear that she did not want my mother to come. I was willing to comply for her sake and I also did not want to upset my mother any more than she was already. I believed that God could save Joan and that she would recover. Why expose my mother to so much anguish? All things considered it was better for my mother not to visit. As it turned out, it was also better for Joan not to be agitated.

The Sisters were storming heaven with prayers for Joan's recovery. Many believed like me that God would save her for her sake and for the sake of the congregation. Joan had been such an enlightened leader at the Chapter. She received the highest number of votes to serve on an interim Community Council. We needed Joan at this important juncture when we were moving from a hierarchical structure of authority with appointed superiors/principals to a new method of communal governance with the Sisters' voting for the President and on the local level, choosing coordinators, formerly superiors, to serve and relate to the Sisters more compassionately.

There were many persons who helped Joan and me in those long weeks of her hospitalization. Fr. Walter Murphy drove up from Richmond Hill, Queens to take Eileen and me out to a late supper one evening at 10:00 pm. His buoyant spirit did for us what I had been trying to do for Joan, lifted our spirits. Daria Holcomb, a nurse in the ICU, was a competent nurse providing medical care for my sister and emotional support for me. Daria had a warmth and sense of humor that raised our spirits when real life conditions had me feeling low. My cousin, Betty-Ann Campos had married only days before Joan's first operation. Betty-Ann and Amador Campos visited Joan when she, a registered nurse, and her surgeon-husband returned from their honeymoon. Their visit offered support and sound advice. Just seeing them was a comfort.

On December 8th they did a tracheotomy. Joan was no longer able to speak. She was growing less responsive. She did not have the strength to overcome all the assaults on her body. I would stand quietly by her bedside praying that God would care for Joan more than even the medical staff or we. Joan seemed far away. Those days relieved me of the burden of believing that Joan would surmount all the physical assaults on her body and spirit that I had tried to believe all those many weeks. I could finally admit that Joan was near death. I loved my sister and wanted her to be safe where suffering and pain could no longer ravage her body, and that her spirit would live on. She was too young, too intelligent, too loved to leave us, but we could not realize our hopes nor could we bargain with God to bring her back to good health. As awful as her passing would be for me, her friends, our relatives, and our Sisters, we were powerless to counter all that she had suffered. The best we could do was to pray that she would pass on to a better place where pain and disease could no longer ravage her and that she would enjoy God's presence, face to face. If resurrection is real as our faith states, then Joan was the fortunate one. How could God not love this young woman who had spent her life in loving God and loving acts toward others, who worked tirelessly so others would learn, who poured herself out in service to others? Joan was my sister with all the complex relations that loving one's sibling entails. I had determined early on that there was no competing with Joan's intelligence; she was smarter than I. I also chose a different major so we could not be compared. The fact that my mother and Joan were unable to maintain a loving relationship was awful to admit. I resolved even as a child to love my mother so strongly that she would never feel that hurt again. Joan had been a loving Sister who served God all her life and emptied herself so that others might live, learn, and love.

Sunday, December 14th was a cold, hazy, sunny day with snow flurries. I attended Mass at the hospital chapel. The Epistle that day began with the words, "Rejoice in the Lord always! I say it again. Rejoice!" (Phil 4:4) Tears streamed down my cheeks as the words flowed on.

> The Lord is near. Dismiss all anxiety from your minds. Present your needs to God in every form of prayer and in petitions full of gratitude. Then God's own peace which is beyond all understanding will stand guard over your hearts and minds, in Christ Jesus. (Phil 2:6-7)

It was the Third Sunday of Advent, Gaudete Sunday, when this theme of rejoicing in the nearness of God's presence was proclaimed by those who believed. The priest wore pink vestments to show that our period of waiting for Emmanuel/God with us was nearly over.

After Mass we returned to Joan's bed in the ICU. Outside that unit the hospital was decorated for Christmas with colorful decorations and red poinsettias. Dr. Wagner came to Joan's bed side. I had never been with someone when they died. I did not know what to do. He said quietly, "Hold your sister's hand." I held Joan's hand and prayed. The tracheotomy tube was removed shortly after noon. There were a few more minutes of slowed breathing and then silence, the empty silence of death. I had been at Joan's bedside almost every day, but this was different. Standing there I knew that Joan was no longer with us. Death is not reversible. Joan's life ended that day. As we moved ahead and the world celebrated Christmas and then New Year's, Joan could not be part of that future. Her life was circumscribed by her birth in 1932 and by her death in 1969. If I screamed or cried, I could not change that fact. In the future I might think that despite our sorrow and loss, Joan would have wanted to tell us, "I am no longer here. God has called me and I go to be with the God who loves me since eternity." After eight weeks of suffering, of watching Joan's struggle to recover, we surrendered Joan into the hands of God. God was blessed that day when the Father/Son/Holy Spirit welcomed Joan Marie Willemse/Sister Joan Dolores home.

Toward the end Dr. Rast had asked if they could do an autopsy. I answered, yes. The fact that Joan was a scientist was a strong factor in my agreeing. Joan had not been able to heal and an autopsy could provide helpful information for other patients. Sr. Ann Magdalen, Joan's friend and a registered nurse, objected. She said that the Mother General needed to give permission. I reacted like a mother tiger. I was Joan's sister, her next of kin. This was my domain, not that of a religious superior. Joan's autopsy might supply answers to the nagging question, "Why could Joan not heal?" It would be a way to answer our questions, advance science, and help other patients.

I had said to Eileen that I could not imagine how I could survive Joan's death. It was barely three months since my step-father had died. I also feared not knowing what to do nor how to conduct myself at the wake and funeral. I feared death for those I loved. It was so final, so silent, and so life-changing. Joan's death made me feel especially alone and vulnerable. I think this revealed how much I had come to depend on Joan, not in the sense of doing things for me. No, it was the opposite; she was someone for whom I did whatever and however much I could. Granted, Joan was at Sparkill and I in the Bronx, but every time I went to the Motherhouse I would see Joan. When I was on retreat and living in the north wing, I would go through the basement to visit her in S109. That was no small feat for it was dark with few lights and the way was circuitous. Suddenly the person that I most loved and hoped to see even briefly was no longer there. This became very evident when I went into her room and helped go through her things. Someone else must have done most of that task. I only wanted two tiny deer, part of a Christmas gift I had given her and the Hummel Christ Child. They are with me and appear every Christmas to remind me of Jesus' birth and of my sister, Joan.

After Joan's death Eileen drove me back to the Bronx. She helped me to notify family members, a task that I found totally draining. It was one thing to call and say there was hope which I had done over eight weeks. It was quite another to say that Joan had died. The congregation arranged the details of the wake and funeral. That first night when we returned to St. Helena's some of the Sisters were there to welcome us home and to say how sorry they were. I was afraid that I would not be able to sleep so Sr. Bridget O'Sullivan (Ann Eileen) volunteered to sit on a chair in my tiny room until sleep came. There was that moment just after awakening when my mind still thought that Joan was alive, but then my heart had to admit that no, Joan was gone. It was the first of many days when I awoke with joy only to realize that I had suffered an irreparable loss.

Eileen drove me to Staten Island to get my mother. At the Motherhouse our sisters were especially kind—embracing her and saying how sorry they were. My mother welcomed them as if they were her daughters. In the course of the wake many spoke of Joan's accomplishments. I would have foregone all that if only, if only Joan were alive. In deepest sorrow worldly honors cannot fill the gap that death creates; our loved one is not here. How can praising a sister's kindness, intelligence, wisdom ever compensate for her real life presence? It was a flimsy way of saying, "I'm sorry for your loss." I thought that would be a comfort, but speaking of Joan's accolades only reinforced the reality that she would no longer be able to achieve nor to assist our community's transition and growth into the future. Prayers helped as did the Mass offered by Rev. Walter Murphy on Tuesday evening. I valued his homily and was able to reread it in the days and months ahead when life returned to normal and Joan receded into memory. The Mass of the Resurrection was offered by Msgr. John J. Considine who was Joan's confessor and also the priest who witnessed the marriage of my mother and step-father in 1952. We had selected the Scripture readings and the hymns and my cousin, Sr. Barbara helped organize those who read and carried gifts at the Offertory. My family was well represented: our cousin, Captain Cornelius Willemse, Jr. was there in full dress uniform. My aunts and uncles came to support my mother and me. Geri had been with us in October when Joan was in the hospital, but could not come again. I learned how comforting is the presence of our Sisters who came to the wake and the Masses.

A wake for our Sisters is an occasion for Sisters to gather to console the family and friends of the deceased and to meet each other. It is both somber and social. The Sisters' joy is witness to our belief that God has called our Sister; now she is with the Spouse to whom she professed her vows and in whose hands all our lives rest. Joan was waked wearing her Dominican habit with the signed original copy of her vows in her hands in a simple, unadorned casket. Joan looked so small in the casket. To either side of the coffin were white lilies. Standing in front and to the side of the coffin was an honor guard, two student leaders in academic cap and gown from St. Thomas Aquinas College where Joan had taught and was Academic Dean at the time of her death. Just before we left the wake all the Sisters and then friends and family pass before the coffin to bid Sister a final farewell. There were so many Sisters. I could not help but notice older Sisters who were ready to die. Why had Joan been taken at such a young age, in the prime of her life? Later at the graveside in our cemetery up the hill behind the Motherhouse, I looked at the newly dug grave. I could not help but wish, "Take me. Joan is too young. She is needed. No one would miss me as they will miss her." Those thoughts were just that: thoughts that burst through as I tried to maintain a calm composure on one of the saddest days of my life. I was left to ponder what Father Murphy told me, "When one door closes, another opens."

Joan's untimely death left me depleted. At St. Helena's classes were in session, but when the Christmas break arrived, Sr. Lillian McNamara (Brendan Mary) invited me to spend Christmas with her and her mother in Florida. That was a God-send: it got me away from winter and my normal routine. After a short plane ride I found myself in warm Florida where poinsettias grew outdoors. The warmth, the complete change of scenery, and the kindness of the McNamaras saved me. During that week I went by bus up to Tampa to visit my Uncle Neal Willemse and Aunt Helen. This was a first for me; my older sisters had visited them many times, but they had moved to Tampa when I was a baby and were not nearby as I was growing up. Their son, Neal, Jr. took me out for the day on a commercial fishing boat. The Gulf of Mexico looked like the ocean to my inexperienced eyes. It was cold on the boat and waves were tossing us about. To add to my discomfort, I was near the bait, the smell of which triggered my getting wretchedly sick to my stomach. Trying to regain my composure I began repeating Latin declensions in an effort to distract myself and get back to normal. We were out on the high seas for what felt like an eternity. I could not wait to return to port so I could stand on terra firma. This was intended to be a special treat, but imagining the huge waves even now makes me queasy. I did not have the right clothing: just a light sundress, a nylon jacket, and sandals. I did not own jeans for we had only recently gotten permission to wear regular clothes as required. My guardian angel must have shuddered when he/

she saw me going on that boat. I knew that I could not swim, but that day I realized that deep sea fishing had never been nor ever would be part of my DNA. I will always cherish being on land rather than at sea.

The charter flight on which I returned to New York was filled with vacationers. They were all talking, comparing notes about the places where they had stayed and places they had checked out to rent or purchase. There was such a commotion in the aisles that the stewardesses had to announce, "Please clear the aisles so we can begin to serve refreshments." I had never seen such a rowdy bunch on a plane. It was a circus with the adults ignoring directives, talking loudly as if they were the only persons in the world, and their children doing whatever they pleased. For me it was a distraction for soon we would be back in New York City. The next day I would be teaching and life would return to normal. Father Murphy's statement, "When one door closes, another opens," was still on my mind. His words still remained a riddle. I needed time and experience to understand how sisterly love was wider and broader than my love for Joan. I witnessed firsthand how our Sisters had prayed and visited; they were there for me and my family. Sr. Eileen had proved how powerful the bond of friendship is by her tireless efforts to help me while Joan was hospitalized and especially afterwards. Without the Sisters I could not have survived. The next chapter in Sisterly Love was not yet written, but it would be lived by me and the Sisters in the years ahead.

Chapter 8

MOTHER DEAR

Christmas week— family visits, exchanging gifts, renewing friendships. As a teacher and administrator I was so grateful to finally have time to rest, recoup, and recharge. December 1984 was all these things and more. It had been a super hectic school year. I felt culturally deprived and resolved to see all the movies I could. I had it down to a system: follow the reviews, make note of the most appealing films, many of which were foreign films that would not be shown in the Bronx. That day I had gone downtown and saw two movies in different theaters, a bit of a stretch synchronizing times and locations. By the time I got home, I was starving. Why waste money on popcorn or lunch when I would be home in an hour? By the time I did eat I felt that I was filling an enormous sink hole.

On one such day Carmel Richmond Nursing Home called to tell me that my mother, Margaret Brady was seriously ill. How could that be? I had just seen my mother at Christmas and she had seemed fine. This news changed everything. My mother had been a resident in Carmel Richmond for six years. Of course she complained at first as she had after each hip surgery when she needed rehab, but Carmel Richmond run by the Carmelite Sisters was one of the best nursing homes in New York City. Somehow I had persuaded her to apply and she was placed on a waiting list. In 1978 my mother was cascading from one medical emergency to another so I reactivated her application, but it took more than nine months before there was a room. After the deaths of her husband, Joe Brady, and her oldest daughter, Joan, my mother was on a dizzying road to self-destruction. She seldom ate and was drinking, a combination guaranteed to bring her down. She had never been able to hold her liquor; it would make her sleepy and she would dose off. Now that she was living alone there was no one for whom she had to cook or to say, "Peggy, you've had enough." I had found her one day on the living room floor with a bottle of Seagram's Seven. That scared me. "Mommy, you can't go on like this; you will end up killing yourself." In desperation I took the bottle and said, "All right …you can have me or the bottle." Without a moment's hesitation she reached out and took the bottle. I wanted to grab the bottle and empty it into the sink. Angry and disappointed, I felt like hitting my own mother.

"Wait a minute," I thought. There must be someone that could reach my mother. She would not listen to me. Who could help? I am a relatively calm person, but I felt panic stricken. I wanted to get help for my mother, but I also did not want to give those who thought ill of her any ammunition. Then I thought of her cousin, Frances Scoppa, ten years older than my mother. Frances and her husband, Mario were family in the best sense of the word: relatives who cared about my family. They would understand. Frances and Mario Scoppa lived in Scarsdale; they had even visited my parents when we lived upstate. They were not just family but friends. I think that Frances' mother, Bella, had had a drinking problem so she would know what I was up against and perhaps, how to stop my mother's self-destructive behavior. I planned to call her when I got back to the Bronx. Before I could make the call, Mario Scoppa called to tell me that his wife of more than fifty years had died in her sleep. The shock of such a sudden death stopped me dead in my tracks and I selfishly thought, "There goes the one person who could have reached my mother."

I had arranged for a homemaker to spend a few hours four days a week with my mother. They got along well and she helped prepare food for my mother. My mother responded well to having company, but there were still the long evenings. She had too much time on her hands. This was tempting fate to have my mother under her own supervision.

My mother had cared for Joe Brady for the seventeen years of their marriage. Five years after they were married, he learned that he had a cancerous growth in his mouth. After surgery to remove the tumor, his face and appearance were drastically changed and it was hard to understand him when he spoke. Worst of all his tongue lost mobility so eating was a challenge. When he first returned from the hospital he stayed in their bedroom and ate standing at his bureau. To ensure that he got enough nourishment my mother would grind up roasted meat, mix it with gravy and cook vegetables until they were soft and serve them with a cream sauce. She prepared meals that he could eat like chicken croquettes and corned beef hash. Gradually my step father returned to eat with us at the table. We adapted to his changed appearance and were able to understand his speech. Joe Brady was a fighter; he gave up cigarettes cold turkey when he got the cancer diagnosis. My mother bore the brunt of his physical changes: her handsome husband was disfigured, it was difficult to understand his speech, and preparing food that he could eat was a challenge. My step father lived twelve years after that surgery so he was a survivor. Smoking two packs a day for over forty years caused emphysema and that severely restricted his breathing. He was hospitalized in May 1969 shortly after he retired. It was so difficult for him to breathe there in the hospital that I thought for sure he was dying. Watching and listening to him struggling to breathe was agonizing. To my great surprise and relief he did return home but tethered to an oxygen tank. His will to live helped him defy the odds. He taught me that life however fragile is stronger than death. When the chips are down, one needs to fight and not surrender. His time at home with my mother was short; by September he was back in the hospital. This time when I visited I found a different man. Joe Brady was depressed, wilted like a flower bereft of sun and water. He told me that he felt like a mere shell of a man. I tried to cheer him up, but he knew better than I. The next morning I drove back to St. Helena's to teach. At 11:00 am a Sister brought me a message to call my mother who told me that my step father had died that morning in Staten Island Hospital. As I drove out to Staten Island I experienced a whirlwind of emotions. He did not want to live like a cripple confined to home, dependent on oxygen. Joe Brady's death not only ended his earthly life; it put my mother at risk. As difficult as it must have been caring for a sick husband, Joe was always there. When the love of her life departed, she found it immensely difficult to be alone.

I had no sooner arrived at my parents' apartment than I heard my step brother, Tom speaking with my mother in the living room. I felt a sense of relief. As Joe's eldest, Tom was a steady, dependable person. He would know what to do. But then I listened to their conversation. He asked to see his father's will. What was this all about? They had not even made the funeral arrangements. Surely this could wait until later. But no, he was there to protect his sister, Clare Anne's interests. When Thelma, the mother of Tom, Jiggs, and Clare Anne had died in 1950, Joe Brady had designated his young daughter to be the beneficiary of his pension. Joe Brady must have told Tom so he was acting on his sister's behalf. After all his years as a civil engineer for the Board of Water Supply of City of New York his father had chosen the option for his pension to be inherited by a designated beneficiary. For years I had heard my mother telling Nana how concerned she was. "If he should die without leaving me his pension, how will I support myself?" The jobs my mother worked offered no pension so she would only be entitled to Social Security and that would not be sufficient for her to live. Only after Clare Anne had graduated from high school and married outside the Church did Joe actually make Peggy the beneficiary. At the time mere hours after Joe Brady's death, I thought Tom's actions were heartless. Surely he could have waited.

The wake was relatively quiet. Tom, Jiggs (Joseph), Clare Anne, and I were not on our home turf and Staten Island was off the beaten track so we were more or less on our own. Sr. Veronica Marie drove the convent station wagon from the Bronx so Sisters from my convent got to the wake. My older sister, Sr. Joan Dolores only arrived the morning of the funeral. She and I would carry the gifts of bread and wine up to the priest at the Offertory. I was so glad that she was there. I felt so shaky that I gave her the cruets and I took the paten with the host. Later as we drove to Calvary Cemetery in Queens I felt so very sad. Strange, I had not counted on feeling so sad. Joe's children were quiet, lost in their own thoughts. At the cemetery I looked at my step brothers and sister; each was married with children. I had no offspring and I felt so alone. That day prefigured how I would be an orphan when my mother would die. I had chosen to live the life of a consecrated religious and would not marry or have children because I was a spouse of Christ. But at that burial as I gazed into the sky and watched traffic on the Brooklyn Queens Expressway in the distance, the enormity of my sacrifice came home to me. When I would be laid to rest in the distant future, there would be no children to mourn me. It felt like an infinite chasm between life and death. I would miss my step father, Joe Brady for I had loved him far more than I could have admitted. Despite his flaws he had been a good father to me and I will always remember him as a man of intelligence and great wit who valued family above all else. I could never have dreamed that his passing would affect my mother so deeply. She would be a boat set adrift, unmoored and unable to cope with the absence of her true love.

I thought that when Joe Brady died, my mother would enjoy her new-found freedom. All those years caring for a cancer survivor and the months when he became increasingly depressed had severely limited what she could do. Joe Brady retired in April and until September when he died was seriously ill with emphysema. Every day he listened to the news on CBS radio. Bad news once was difficult; all day, every day it filled the mind and flooded the heart with sadness. Joe Brady's death freed him from sickness even as it robbed my mother of her will to live. "Mommy, you have many years ahead. You can do whatever you want. A piano? Sure you can buy a piano." The next week I found she had bought a new Steinway piano that replaced Joe's chair in the living room. She could have volunteered, been active at Good Counsel Parish…anything where she would be with people. The highlight of her life was the day that she was mugged returning by bus from the bank in Stapleton. The mugger followed her and took her bag containing the money she had withdrawn from the bank as she was walking uphill, just before she arrived at the house. When her story appeared in *The Staten Island Advance* instead of being angry, she was thrilled to see her name in the paper. I realized how vulnerable my mother had become. One Sunday I drove home from Sunday Mass by way of Wagner College so we could see the changing colors of the trees hoping to distract her with the beauty of nature. My mother barely looked. She could not appreciate what she had not seen.

She even ignored Timmy, a kitten I brought home one Sunday thinking he would be the perfect companion. This was an answer to prayer, or so I thought. My mother loved cats; surely her heart would melt when she saw him. He would make the empty apartment a home. He would rouse her cat loving nature and be her buddy, jumping up on her lap and purring contentedly. And at night he would curl up beside her in bed. Yes, Timmy would be the perfect companion. Timmy would also allow my mother to resume her role as caretaker just as she had done all those years for Joe Brady. That was my plan, but it did not work out as I had imagined. In the months that followed I could not fathom the cat's strange behavior: taking food from his dish in the kitchen, running into my mother's bedroom and disappearing under the bed. When I visited on weekends, Timmy viewed me as an intruder. When my friend, Eileen came with me, she too was one more stranger. Timmy would hiss at us whenever we got near. There was one unfortunate incident when Eileen was closing the convertible bed so we could sit on the couch. Suddenly shrieks sounded: Timmy had jumped into the space behind the bed and he was nearly crushed. His hiding out nearly cost him one of his nine lives.

The odd thing about Timmy was how he related to other cats and people. When I drove my mother out to visit my step-brother, Tom and his wife, Ann and their eight kids, Timmy went along. When I returned after a few days I thought that they would tell me about the neurotic cat, but no, the scaredy cat became someone else. Instead of hiding, hissing, and attacking, Timmy let the children pet him and play all sorts of games. He loved being with the children. He was in his element in a strange house surrounded by enough kids to scare the best of cats. He was so happy that I was tempted to leave him there. On another occasion when my mother was hospitalized, the owner of the house, Betty offered to care for him. She brought Timmy downstairs. When I stopped in after visiting my mother in the hospital I anticipated horror stories, but Timmy had adjusted to being with Betty and Don and their cats. He was a family man and needed other cats and people around him.

As New Year 1985 approached my mother at age 77 had a score of ailments, none of which seemed life-threatening. Arthritis was her main complaint and over the years she was confined to a wheelchair. She had settled in over the six years she was at Carmel Richmond Nursing Home. She received such good care, had made friends, and had a lovely room. I knew that she needed more care than a homemaker on weekdays and my visit on the weekends could provide. I was kept busy buying new clothes after she gained weight and picking up incidentals like Mink Hair Spray. "Mink?" I asked my mother over the phone. "Who ever heard of that brand?" I really thought she was joking, but no. "An aide told me about it. She said it is really good." I had my hands full shopping and lugging everything I bought that would make my mother happy. As I showed her the purchases, she waited until she could pounce. "Did you get the hairspray?" she asked. "Well, no. I couldn't find it but I brought you the brand that I use." That was not good enough. Who would think that I would be on the losing end of a competition for approval with an aide?

Peggy really wanted a recliner chair so one Saturday Eileen and I drove my mother to the Staten Island mall. We wheeled her into Macy's and took the elevator to the furniture department. There were recliners of all sizes and colors. As it turned out, my mother chose a chair with wooden arm rests so she could get out of the chair by herself. I was glad she was with us for I might have chosen one of those overstuffed recliners made for Paul Bunyan types. I had not adjusted to the fact that my mother needed a chair that fit her small frame and her limited ability to move. After that purchase my mother had one more wish: a certain perfume whose name was new to me, but which my mother admired on another aide. "What is its name?" I asked. She did not remember so we proceeded to roll through the aisles sniffing all the fragrances. It would have been funny except that I was so exasperated. Finally we landed at the right counter. Clinique Elixir— a lovely scent. I learned something new that day and my mother was as pleased as punch with her outing.

For six years my mother lived at Carmel Richmond Nursing Home and I thought that she would spend many more years cared for by well trained nurses and aides. She made friends whom I met when I visited on the weekend. She even had a best friend: a lovely woman, kind and compassionate, with whom she spent many hours each day talking and laughing. They had a lot in common. One time she wanted me to meet someone special, a man. The nursing home residents were mostly women so attracting a man was quite a feat. We went to the shop for coffee and cake. He was nice looking, older than my mother, but he could barely hear. So there I was with my mother and her boyfriend screaming so he might hear me all the time wondering what the other residents and their visitors were thinking. Would I be thrown out for disturbing the peace? And why am I wasting my time visiting a complete stranger when I had come to be with my mother? I don't remember why but he faded from view rather quickly. But that day my mother was so happy that she had a male friend. Like her mother before her, there was still life in the old girl…. Just when I thought all was well, I got that phone call from the staff, "Your mother's not doing well."

January 1985 was a bitterly cold month in New York City. Winds howled, temperatures plummeted, and there were warnings to stay indoors. Even for those dressed warmly, especially the elderly and those with heart conditions, outdoors was a dangerous place. I remember the piercing cold as I drove from the Bronx to Staten Island almost every day that month. A few times I stayed overnight with one of our Sisters who was training to be a pastoral minister and who lived near Carmel Richmond. Who could forget arriving at Sr. Eileen Donovan's residence with my overnight bag? "Do you need anything?" asked Eileen. "No, I think I have everything," I replied. That was until I discovered that anything liquid (deodorant, toothpaste, shampoo) was frozen solid. They had been safe and sound in the car. "Eileen," I asked, "could you give me some …?" Of course she graciously gave me room temperature versions of what was a block of ice in my overnight bag.

One Sunday afternoon I headed out over the Whitestone Bridge. The windshield was streaked so I tried the windshield wipers but there was no fluid. No problem; I pulled over when traffic permitted to get Windex from the trunk. It too was frozen solid. Alternate plan: I used some snow from the side of the road, but that was a temporary fix. I had to drive another forty minutes straining to see through a streaked, dirty windshield. It really added to the tension of the day.

My mother was bedridden as the days went on. I found myself thinking back, remembering all I could of her past. My mother was widowed at a young age when my father, George Willemse, had died November 13, 1942 shortly after I was born. At age 35 my mother was a widow with three daughters, Joan age 10, Margaret Germaine (Geri) age 8, and Judy, 2 ½ months. The family had already dealt with our paternal grandfather's death in mid-July, but who would have expected his 37 year old son to follow him so soon?

Who was my mother? She was the oldest child of Agnes McDowell Langknecht; her mother, Agnes would marry and outlive four husbands, but her father died at age 25 after scaling and falling from a rotted telephone pole. Margaret and Dorothy, fourteen months younger, were both Langknechts; their sister, Frances Scanlon was five years younger than my mother. My uncles, Howard, Alfred, and Thomas (Henry) Esch were quite a few years younger so my mother was their big sister. Life was hectic; money was scarce because my grandmother was searching for another husband on a fairly regular basis.

I only remember her last husband, Louis Wienecke. They lived on Middletown Road in the Bronx in a one story house divided into two apartments: one for his grown children that faced the street and the other for Agnes and Louis toward the back. Louis was a tall, portly man whose main pleasure was listening to the radio. He looked at the radio so intently that it prompted my grandmother to urge him to buy a television. I was scared of Mr. Wienecke because he was a big man who seldom spoke. Their living room had two rocking chairs: one large and one small. I loved to sit in the smaller and rock the larger chair. That was fun until my grandmother stopped me. Apparently there was a superstition that rocking an empty chair brought bad luck like the admonition not to open an umbrella in the house. My grandmother was the chief cook and bottle washer as well as the guardian of the coal-fed furnace in the basement. Agnes was vivacious, funny, personable, and very interested in men. It was second nature for her to notice men for she had been on the lookout for husbands all her life. Sometimes I went down to the basement with her when she shoveled coal into the furnace. The red-hot flames danced this way and that. It was hell barely contained in a furnace. I was scared the flames would leap our way and she would get burned. She seemed fearless though I heard later that one of her sisters, Bella, had been so badly burned by a coal-fed furnace that she was in constant pain for the rest of her life. Agnes had a joie de vive that rivaled none.

My mother told me that they had very little when they were growing up. One Christmas her mother asked the children, "Which would you like: a nice dinner or a gift for Christmas?" They answered that they wanted a gift thinking that they would probably get both. After all it was Christmas and they had always had delicious dinners, but that year, true to her word, Agnes cooked and served canned beans and frankfurters. They lived in the South Bronx along with many families of Irish and German descent. It was common practice to leave their apartment doors unlocked during the day as the children ran upstairs and down or across to a neighbor. Many families would pack up and move from one apartment to another apartment house at the end of the month to get cheaper rent. They were always one step ahead of the bill collector.

As the oldest my mother must have shouldered responsibilities for the younger children. Agnes' older sister, Nellie took a shine to my mother. A maiden aunt, Nellie worked downtown and on her free time would help out with her younger sister's children. She even paid for my mother to take piano lessons. That seemed like a great thing, but my mother told me many times that she had to play the piano at her own graduation from elementary school. What could have been a source of pride caused her to resent that she couldn't even enjoy her own graduation. She felt used. Too bad someone did not make her feel special and appreciated for her musical ability.

As a young girl my mother admired the Dominican Sisters who were her teachers at St. Luke's Elementary School in the Bronx. She told me about one of the nuns who had "snappy, brown eyes." The tone of her voice and the rapt expression on her face said it all: she wanted to be just like that nun who was beautiful, engaging, and a model of the best a nun could be. She applied to the Dominican Sisters of Blauvelt and was accepted as a postulant. The day after her seventeenth birthday, Margaret left home in the Bronx to become a Dominican Sister of Blauvelt, a town in Rockland County and the site of the Motherhouse where the Sisters did their spiritual basic training. I never knew this when I was growing up. One day I found a black and white photo in the top drawer of my mother's bureau of a young woman dressed in the white habit of the Dominicans with a crown of thorns on top of her veiled head. That was fascinating and creepy. There was no name, no date on the photo. I never asked who this Sister was. It would have let them know that I was looking around in my mother's bureau, a place that was off limits. For all

I knew the Sister in the picture could have been a friend of my mother's. It never occurred to me that it was my mother. As a child I knew that Sisters did not marry or have children. The young woman in the picture could not be my mother, or so I thought. A few years later after my mother remarried I heard my step-father cast it up to her when they were in the kitchen one night relaxing over drinks, smoking, and talking. He made it sound like a sordid affair, that my mother was attracted to a good looking Monsignor and left the convent shortly after. That sounded unreal. Was he kidding? No, he was trying to goad my mother. She did not respond. I thought that he had his facts wrong, but if it were true, he was downright cruel to say that to the woman who had waited ten years before remarrying, and when she married him, moved upstate far from family and friends, and cared for him and his youngest child, Clare Anne. In Catholic families it was an honor for a daughter to become a nun or a son, a priest or brother. As wonderful as it was for young adults to give their life to God if/when that Sister were dispensed from her vows and returned home, it was a great disappointment. Personally I loved my mother too much to accept the scenario my step father suggested so I blocked out his comments and hated him for making up this wild story about my mother.

The strange thing is that my mother never spoke of her years as a Dominican postulant, novice, and professed sister. That part of her life ceased to exist as if it were swallowed up and no longer existed. My aunts, uncles, and grandmother knew about this, but no one ever mentioned the convent and my mother in the same sentence. Many years would pass before sisters that left the convent could look back on their experiences as something positive. For whatever reasons the person left, the fact remained that she had dedicated herself, body and soul to God, lived in community with few pleasures, and worked everyday serving God's people. That was heroic and deserved to be remembered and celebrated. As Americans we remember veterans who protected our freedoms. Why should we do less for those who taught our children in Catholic schools and colleges, worked in hospitals nursing the sick, and demonstrated love of God and neighbor in so many ways with orphans, the elderly—in short, men, women, and children in need— all this while they prayed and meditated every day of their lives?

Very little evidence remains of my mother's time in the convent. My curiosity led me to speak with the archivist of the Dominican Sisters in Blauvelt. All she found in a folder with my mother's name were three papers: one a summary of the years my mother spent in Blauvelt and the Bronx (May 24, 1924—Feb. 14, 1929), and two separate handwritten pages: one, a request to become a novice and receive the habit of St. Dominic along with her religious name, Sr. Mary Charatina of St. Thomas Aquinas; the second, to be approved for profession of vows a year and a day after the reception of the habit. Three pages, so few, so little evidence of a young woman willing to give her life to God, brave enough to leave family and home behind, and cast her lot with a group of religious women. It is difficult to know how my mother felt, what she did, and even what prompted her to ask to be released from her vows.

I learned that as a young professed sister, my mother needed extensive dental work and had some medical issues. In June 1928 there was a swelling in her neck and the doctor recommended that she get X-rays before he could remove the goiter. The Sister in charge at Blauvelt sent her to Our Savior's, one of their convents in the Bronx. The superior at that convent accompanied her to the doctor appointments. By the end of January 1929 Sr. Charatina requested a dispensation from her vows. February 14, 1929 she signed the official forms, removed the habit, and left the convent wearing lay clothes. When I asked what my mother did, Sister said that she probably helped with the children when she was at the Motherhouse for the Blauvelt Dominicans like us in Sparkill had a home for children (girls). The archivist added that my mother took classes because she needed to complete her high school education. I've pondered these few facts. When my mother was at the convent in the Bronx, her mother would have been able to visit Sr. Charatina. I heard that an Aunt Margaret had died and left my mother some money. If that were true, my grandmother may well have pressured my mother to leave the convent. It was the only way that my mother could give her the money. My grandmother was always in need and she was a clever woman.

I never spoke with my mother about her being a nun, not even when I was considering entering the convent myself. Perhaps I thought that asking someone who left the convent would have jinxed me. If she thought being a nun was so great, why did she leave? Honestly I do not know. I sensed that speaking with a former nun was not the best way to proceed. Besides I wanted to give God a chance to woo me and did not want to be unduly influenced by someone who had lived as a Dominican Sister for almost five years and then chose to leave the convent. Because I was a huge help to my mother I could not imagine her being an objective advisor. She stood to lose a great deal if/when I entered the convent or for that fact when I graduated from college and began to teach. It was inevitable that I would leave to teach, marry, or set up home in another place. White Sulphur Springs was not a destination of choice for someone looking for work. Cows, horses, and chickens thrived there, but any college grad would have had to leave the area to find a job. As the saying goes, the grass was definitely greener…

Two months shy of her 22nd birthday, my mother was back living with her mother and five siblings. The convent was no piece of cake, but returning home must have been a major let-down. As her daughters reached their teens and went out to work, Agnes expected them to hand over their earnings each payday. It was a tiring, boring life. The only way out was to marry.

Only fourteen months between them, Margaret and Dorothy were sisters and over time, close friends. In the few photographs that I saw, my mother was a dark-haired, attractive young woman. Dorothy was the real beauty who knew how to use her charms. She married an older man, Harry Johnson and they enjoyed life. Dorothy and Harry Johnson were godparents for my older sister, Joan. At some point Dorothy was hospitalized after a miscarriage; after that she never had a child. When that marriage ended by death or divorce, I know not which, Dorothy worked in a bank where she met William Sorger. Dorothy told me how she had noticed this handsome young man who worked in the same bank. When they finally met they went to a local diner. She had no memory of what they ate that night, only that they talked for hours. They had much in common: both of them were single after having been married. Bill had married a teenage girl and soon realized that they had nothing in common; their marriage ended in divorce. Conversation flowed so naturally that they knew right away that they were meant to be with each other. Before they knew it, the sun rose and it was time to return to work. When Bill was drafted into the US Army and doing basic training, Dot rode the bus to his base in the south, stopping in the restroom at the last stop to change into a fresh dress, fix her hair, and reapply lipstick and perfume so she looked her very best. Dot and Bill married in 1943 just before he shipped out to fight in Europe. He fought first in northern Africa and then his unit advanced to Italy. It was tough fighting; the Nazis made the Allied advance supremely difficult. Bill's division had fought so bravely that they were up front and center when they celebrated the liberation of Rome by the Allied Forces. Shortly after, Bill suffered a head injury that removed him from active duty. The details of his wounds remain a mystery. Like many other soldiers he did not speak about the war and certainly not about his injury.

Bill was tall and blonde, handsome, athletic (he loved and played baseball well into his forty's), and totally in love with Dorothy. My mother was jealous of Dorothy's good fortune. As a child I noticed that Bill was different from all the men in our family. He helped out at home, waited on his wife, and catered to her every need. Aunt Dorothy would ask demurely, "Bill, Honey, would you get me another glass of wine?" Bill ever the loyal husband would gladly get her anything she wanted. Needless to say, my mother wished she had a man like Bill.

First things first, Margaret Langkneckt had to meet a man. How she met my father, George I do not know, but she did say that on their first date they went to the New York Botanical Garden. She had a bad cold and could barely speak, but as they walked inside the conservatory magically, amazingly she could speak again. She may well have looked upon this cure as a sign from heaven. This must be the man she was meant to marry. A short courtship ensued. In later years the date of their wedding was not celebrated, but their first child, my older sister was born on March 18, 1932. Aunt Dorothy and Harry Johnson were Joan's godparents; Dorothy was very close to Joan as she grew even after she entered the convent twenty years later.

My mother remembered that the first dinner she prepared as a newlywed was pot roast but there was so much gravy that it looked like stew. In fact her husband, George was a better cook for he was born into a family that had a restaurant in Manhattan. Both he and his older brother, Neal helped out at the family business and no doubt learned a thing or two about cooking.

Once Joan was born, Margaret (Peggy) was busy caring for a newborn. The convent certainly did not prepare her for having a baby and a husband so I doubt that she relished all that goes into being a mother. My mother spoke about the time she was on a bus with her infant girl. A woman, a complete stranger, observed Joan and noting how serious she was, predicted that she was destined for great things. That must have made my mother and father glad. Even as a baby, Joan had a stubborn streak. One morning my mother was feeding her oatmeal. Joan closed her lips, shook her head from side to side, and refused to take another spoonful. No matter what my mother did, Joan would not eat. When lunch time rolled around, Mother reheated the oatmeal. Joan could not be fooled; she continued to refuse to eat the cereal. Joan was her own person at a very young age. On May 2, 1934 a second daughter was born. Officially she was named Margaret Germaine, but everyone called her Geri. Germaine was a strange name, but I think it was the name of the nun my mother admired. Geri had one defining characteristic: she was a screamer at home and wherever she went. Once, in total desperation, our father, George lifted his howling daughter and carried her to the bathroom. Without losing a beat, he turned on the shower and held her under the running water. Finally the water splashing over her head and shoulders shocked her into silence. I imagine that Geri slowly grew out of this deafening response to life, but my older cousin, Barbara told me that she loved going shopping for shoes with Joan and Geri. If/When the salesman touched her feet, Geri screamed at the top of her lungs. Barbara was secretly thrilled because no one else did that in public. Perhaps all that screaming paid off: by the time she was a teenager, Geri had a wonderful singing voice. It was great fun when my mother or Joan played the upright piano and Geri would sing. Who knew all that went into developing her beautiful voice and powerful lungs? My mother would also play, "Glow Little Glow Worm" slowly, then faster and faster. I got so excited: I would laugh and clap in time. As a child that was my favorite song.

We had sheet music for many popular songs. I especially liked Bing Crosby. I loved his singing and often heard him on the radio. When we got a television and I actually saw Bing Crosby in real time, I was so disappointed. He was not the youthful crooner pictured on the scores we had. No, he was an older man with a receding hair line. He sounded swell, but he had aged overnight before my eyes. How could that happen? It took me a long time to reconcile my idealized picture with the middle-aged man he had become. That was one time radio served me better than television.

Smokey Stover was my mother's greatest fan. He was a charcoal gray cat that lived with us on East Gun Hill Road. His primary task was catching and discouraging mice from taking up residence in our apartment. I considered him my playmate so I tried to get him to do gymnastics going in and out the spokes of my child-sized wicker chair. Once he realized what I had in mind, he made himself scarce. He was somewhat less resistant to my dressing him with my doll's clothes, though that was no real fun when his front paws slipped out. Soon he shed the dress and went his merry way. What an exhibitionist! While I was concocting schemes, he would manage to slip away, but every night he would wait in the foyer for my mother. When she turned the key of the apartment door, Smokey was there to greet her. That had to be a great way for my mother to make her entrance. Of course I was also there along with my sisters and Aunt Nellie. Working at the bank and traveling to and from home, walking to the station and taking the subway meant that my mother was exhausted. If we were distracted in any way, she could always count on our resident cat. One evening Smokey was on duty as official greeter but my mother never came. In fact that whole week he was disappointed every night. What had happened? Where was his favorite person? My mother had thyroid surgery and she was gone for a week. There was no way to explain that to Smokey; even if we tried, I doubt he would have believed us. He knew in the very marrow of his bones that his favorite human would walk through that door; nothing we could say would dislodge that firmly fixed notion. Of course, there did come a day when my mother returned safe and sound. Had Smokey been able to speak, he would have said, "See I told you she'd come. She's never failed me; that's why I love her best of all." He was ecstatic as he greeted her. He followed her from room to room not letting her out of sight. He never wanted to endure another week of separation.

When my mother married Joe Brady they had all sorts of decisions to make. I overheard them as they spoke in the kitchen of his large, rambling, country house. By the time they opened the door and shared their good news, I replied, "Certainly." It was obvious that they were both happy so I guessed I would be too. I felt secure because I would still have my mother and my god father would become my stepfather. It seemed perfectly natural. I did not think of all the consequences that night, but they certainly had to plan. The area where he had lived would soon be flooded to create the Neversink Dam, the last dam constructed in the Catskill Mountains to supply fresh water to NYC. They found a small house west of Liberty, NY where we would live. He measured the rooms and the furniture in his house and our apartment and determined which items would fit into their future home. That was relatively easy. The real change was who would join Peggy and Joe upstate. Most of the adults would move: Aunt Nellie to her furnished room on East 204th Street and my sister, Geri to a different furnished room in the same house as Aunt Nellie. It was probably a relief for Aunt Nellie who had devoted ten years to my upbringing and who looked forward to having time for herself. For my sister Geri who had just graduated from Aquinas High School it meant an abrupt change. She lost her mother, her family, and her home. She had business skills so she could work downtown in Manhattan, but emotionally she was cut loose. It became obvious when she visited us upstate with her sailor boyfriend. Geri would marry early and be stuck with a sailor husband who had bragged about marrying this beautiful girl though he had no real sense of loving and sharing a life with her. That premature marriage would end in divorce and left Geri even more alone in the world.

There was also our fur person, Smokey Stover. Surely he would come with us upstate. He had been with us almost ten years. He was an indoor cat and he would have to adapt, but his favorite human would be there. That's what I thought, but one day I heard my mother discussing with her sister, Dorothy that Joe Brady did not want us to take Smokey. Dot and Bill were not cat lovers, but Dorothy had an idea. They ate at Louis' Restaurant on White Plains Road and East Gun Hill Road every night after work and there were cats out back that were fed leftovers. Suddenly Smoky went from valued working indoor cat to outdoors in a strange place. It had to be awful for him leaving the relative warmth and safety of our apartment to being outdoors and having to contend with feral cats for food and shelter. The worst: he lost us and especially my mother. All I can say is that my mother loved Joe Brady more than anyone else: she gave up her piano with little fuss because it would not fit, but to put Smokey Stover outdoors with no one who knew him…I doubt that Smokey lasted long—friendless in a foreign place. Why did they not bring him to a shelter? Maybe someone would have adopted him for he had a beautiful dark gray coat. Even euthanasia would have been more merciful.

I always wanted to think of my mother as pretty. I was her third child born when my mother was thirty-five. My mother had dark, wavy hair increasingly sprinkled with gray described as "salt and pepper." She had a broad forehead, gray eyes and a lovely smile. Her beautiful legs and shapely, slim ankles were in full view at a time when women always wore dresses. I thought that she had perfect proportions like beauty contestants with well formed breasts, a slim waist and wide hips.

I also wanted to think of my mother as young. I wanted her age to be frozen so I could always have a youthful image of her. My maternal grandmother stopped counting her age at 39 like the comedian, Jack Benny. She lived long enough to have her children and grandchildren celebrate birthdays well beyond that magic number. What difference did it make? Why was youth such an asset? Was I identifying with society's glorification of youth? I wanted even more to think that my mother was pretty. This was important for I looked very much like my mother: I was short, my face resembles my mother's except for eye and hair color—my blue eyes and dirty blond hair more closely resembled my Dutch ancestry on the Willemse side of the family. I came face to face with this when I met my paternal uncle, Neal who visited me at Our Lady of Grace Convent in 1964. Uncle Neal's blue eyes were a mirror image of mine. To return to my objection to my mother's frequent comments that she was not pretty: if that were true, then I who most closely resembled my mother was also not pretty. I roundly rejected and resented when my mother made these comments. Couldn't she pretend for my sake?

Christmas 1952 my step-father commissioned me to buy his gift for my mother. He probably thought it was not manly for him to go into the women's store on Main Street in Liberty. He gave me money, dropped me off and waited outside while I went in all alone. I had never shopped by myself and certainly not in a specialty shop. In the Bronx I had gone with my sisters to Alexander's on Fordham Road to buy jeans and a spring coat each year. That store was a God-send for it had good quality merchandise at reasonable prices. You could rummage around, choose your merchandise, and even try it on. But here I was a neophyte who had to speak with a saleslady. I asked to see a nightgown, a gift for my mother. "What size and color?" she asked. Since she was newly married I said, "white," my idea of what a bride would wear. My mother had worn a tailored blue-gray suit for her second marriage ceremony, but in my mind brides wore white. The gown sets she showed me had lovely details at the neck and on the sleeves. There was a matching robe so it seemed perfect. When we opened gifts on Christmas Eve, each of us took turns so we could admire each one's gift. I was holding my breath, hoping that my mother would like the nightgown set. She exclaimed how pretty it was and I breathed a sigh of relief. The following week we returned to the same shop, this time together so she could exchange it for a color she liked (pink) and in a size that would fit. I don't remember being Joe Brady's personal shopper again, but it was a sweet idea on my step-father's part. I guess he thought that I would know what my mother liked. At that age I barely knew what I liked let alone what my mother would like. It would be many years before I grew into a capable shopper at ease with store clerks.

Liberty was far from the shopping capital of the world. If we wanted to shop for something special we would go to Middletown. We went there to buy a winter coat for me. With my mother firmly in command I tried on many coats. Finally a wine-colored wool coat was the winner. It reminded me of the coats worn by cadets at West Point with its added cape. My mother was so proud that I had a really stylish warm coat. I was too but I looked a bit lost in it. I guess the idea was that I would grow into it. It took a few years for me to grow and fill it out. It did serve me well for many years through the bitter cold winters in the mountains so it was a good investment and was the best coat I ever owned.

They say, "Beauty is in the eye of the beholder." If so, then anyone can consider someone else beautiful if she measures up to that person's idea of beauty. An example was my great Aunt Nellie. Compared to other women her age she would not have won any beauty contest. She was a buxom woman, had her grey/white hair swept up and away from her face in a bun, always wore dresses and sensible shoes like her contemporaries of the 1940's. What Aunt Nellie lacked in classical beauty, she made up for in personality and character. She liked to sing, talk about politics, and most important of all, she loved me. She and my mother shared many responsibilities after she came to live with us: preparing hot cereal in the morning before we went to school and cooking dinner at night and on the weekends. They would alternate: when one of them got distracted, the cereal was lumpy and did not taste so good. I suspected that my mother was the culprit for she was also trying to get dressed and put on make-up before she left for work.

More importantly, Aunt Nellie was interested in politics and was an avid supporter of the principles and policies of the Democratic Party. This was evident in her praise of Franklin Delano Roosevelt during the Great Depression. When my mother and Aunt Nellie had a glass of wine on a Friday evening, I could hear them as they discussed the merits of FDR's policies. My mother was critical of FDR but Aunt Nellie praised all that he had done to bring the country out of the Great Depression. I found myself agreeing with Aunt Nellie for her comments made more sense. My mother's comments were aimed more at making the discussion livelier. My mother complained about a time when her family was on public assistance. She remembered inspectors coming into their apartment and actually opening the refrigerator to see if there were beer; apparently government relief could not be spent on frivolous pleasures. My mother hated those anti-social workers. I suspect that creature comforts were few and far between so those men were not only snoopers, but also party poopers. The other comment she made was even more personal. The government would pay a dentist to remove teeth and then you had to get false teeth. They would not pay for more costly procedures to conserve teeth. She had an upper plate so I figured her criticisms were valid on that point. It also accounts for my mother's wanting to see where the dentist had worked when I returned home after a dentist appointment. I did not want to open my mouth like a horse being inspected. But now as I think of it, she was happy that I could go to a dentist. In the Bronx I only remember going once to a dentist and that was when my sister Joan brought me. What saved me was Aunt Nellie's insistence that I brush my teeth. As we know now, having good teeth is not a luxury; it is necessary for good nutrition and communicating. A smile is valued for sharing good times with friends and lovers. It is even more vital when one is in the business world. A toothless hag might get laughs on Halloween, but never when one works with people.

Joe Brady loved to watch the news. Every evening we would watch the news on CBS even during dinner. We could speak during commercials but not during the actual newscast. There was a weather forecaster, Carol Reed, whose good looks and cheery delivery made all forecasts even for bad weather palatable. Besides she always ended with, "Have a happy." She was an attractive brunette with a good figure. My stepfather started kidding my mother by saying how pretty Carol Reed was. Then he'd turn to my mother and say, "Why, Peggy, you're jealous." My mother got flustered and denied it. It became a standing joke in our family. To this day I remember Carol Reed better than any of the newscasters at that time. It helps to be pretty and to have a sense of humor.

January 1985 was a cold, windy month. It was my first year as Assistant Principal at St. Helena Commercial High School and I was also teaching two classes so life was busy. After school I would drive out to Staten Island from the Northeast Bronx alternating driving through Queens and Brooklyn on the Brooklyn-Queens Expressway and over the Verrazano Bridge or driving through the Bronx and Manhattan and taking the Staten Island ferry. Both routes were through heavily trafficked areas, but the ferry route had the advantage of being able to see the Statue of Liberty. It was always a thrill to see this lovely lady; imagine how our ancestors must have felt as they arrived in New York/New Jersey. Some days I was so tired, I would just close my eyes and rest. Before long the ride was over and we could disembark. A short ride to Carmel Richmond Nursing Home and I was there. I lived at a high level of dread all that month. How would my mother be? Would she even know that I was there? I hoped that I would be with my mother in her final moments, but knew that might not happen. As the days and then weeks crawled by, I found myself grasping for straws imploring the saint of the day to come to my mother's aid. Jan. 21, feast of St. Agnes, my grandmother's first name. Just a year ago Jan. 21, 1984 Sr. Gerry McGinn died. Gerry was a few years older than I, a lively, dedicated woman, greatly loved in our congregation, who died as a result of a flash flood in Colombia where she was doing missionary work. I wasn't so sure about St. Agnes, but I knew that Gerry McGinn would come to my mother's aid.

I alternated standing and sitting near my mother, watching the rhythm of her breathing. I told her that I was there and how much I loved her. One evening I was standing at the foot of her bed. There was a commotion—nothing visible to the eye but definitely something, someone(s) were thrashing about in the space behind my mother's bed, to the right near the wall. I sensed that it was a fight/tussle regarding my mother. Were they little demons fighting among themselves, tripping over each other to trouble my mother? It would have been comical if the danger had not seemed imminent. Even though I saw no one, I knew it was real. I felt that my mother was about to be attacked and there I was frozen in place. Was this a struggle for my mother's soul involving some unresolved conflict? Feeling afraid and powerless, I prayed to God, "Jesus, Mary, please help my mother. Do not abandon her in her hour of need." The feuding continued; they were like bullies planning an attack. I continued to pray placing my mother in God's hands. If ever there was a need for the God of mercy, this was surely such a time. No matter what my mother had done or failed to do, she needed God's mercy and love. Suddenly I sensed a bright light in the same place where before there had been conflict. A palpable sense of peace flowed toward my mother. As quickly as the struggle began so it ended and I knew that my mother was safe. God was with her. I felt drained but immensely relieved. I have been with other persons as they neared death, but I have never experienced anything like this. My mother was barely responsive, just breathing fitfully. Life was ebbing, but I knew that my mother was in God's hands. My/Our prayers for a peaceful death were answered. From that day forward I believed that even as my mother's physical strength waned, she was protected by Jesus and his mother Mary. God's Spirit would sustain her and welcome her into eternal life.

Friday morning, Jan. 25 I had a dentist appointment to complete work on a crown. I had spoken with the nurse at Carmel Richmond who told me that my mother's blood pressure was very low. It was risky, but I decided to keep the appointment. I arrived at the nursing home shortly after mid-day. One of the Carmelite Sisters asked if I had eaten. "No," I said, "I haven't but I would rather stay with my mother." Soon after, she brought me a turkey sandwich with mustard and a diet soda. It was many hours since I had had breakfast. I was grateful to eat though I would never have put mustard on turkey and I hated the after-taste of diet soda. The doctor came, checked my mother, and told me that it would not be long. Eileen Gannon arrived c. 4:30 pm. I was so glad to see her, to have company. I am as afraid of death as the next person. I spoke softly to my mother, "Mommy, you are in good hands. God is calling you home. Feel free to go. Do not be afraid." As much as I would miss my mother, she had to know that I was not holding her back. Eileen and I kept vigil: praying, speaking softly, hoping… We were witnessing the slow, inexorable shifting of my mother's body as systems shut down. It seemed like an eternity watching one breath in, another out, but her breathing was slowing down, losing its natural rhythm. Suddenly there was silence, no labored breathing, just silence, the awful silence of death. My mother's body was there but the woman and mother I had known was gone. My mother who always had a ruddy complexion was changing before my very eyes. It came as a shock to see a colorless copy of my mother's face.

After so many weeks of waiting for the inevitable, my mother's passing was strangely anti-climactic. Above my mother's bed was a copy of an icon depicting Mary our Mother holding the Christ Child. I had bought it for my mother after she went to Carmel Richmond so she would have an image of the Blessed Mother. It was a burnished orange, bright but not gaudy, reassuring as Madonna and Child representations always are. It came to me in a flash: God is our Mother. I could never think of God as Father without knowing in the deepest fiber of my being that God is also Mother. I had lost my father before I knew how wonderful he was so the concept of God as Father was never an easy fit. Now God had to be Father/Mother or God would not/could not be God.

I noted the time of my mother's passing: shortly before 6:00 pm when WQXR radio broadcast part of the Sabbath service from Temple Emanu-El in New York City. At each service there was a prayer offered by the congregation for all those who were mourning the loss of a loved one. I had listened to it many times over the years. It was strangely comforting knowing that they were praying the Mourner's Kaddish as my mother left this world. I did not know the English words, only that the congregation supported the loved ones who survived by lifting their minds and hearts in prayer.

Over the years I got aggravated with my mother when she would say, "You will miss me when I'm gone," but truer words were never spoken. The silence of death led to the depths of grief. The chasm between life and death is enormous. My mother had been a huge responsibility. Yes, from age ten I felt that I was responsible to: make her life easier by helping at home; ease her discomfort when Joe Brady demeaned her in words; bridge the gap between painful words spoken and the disquieting silence of the following day(s). I had tried to be the perfect daughter because I knew from their discussions how both my mother and Joe Brady were disappointed by their children and I resolved to do all that I could so they would be proud of me. I was both a child and an adult, too young to interact as their equal, but eager nonetheless to bring happiness into their lives. I did not want to resent what I had to do so as a young girl I dreamed up a grand scheme: I would pretend that I was working in a hotel doing whatever chore was at hand. I had a vivid imagination; playing such a game would make dreary duties fun. I could not fathom why my parents were so disappointed by their children. From my vantage point, Tom, Jiggs, Joan, and Geri were doing well. I did not like hearing bad things about them. Is this how I would be when I reached middle age? Life was so brand new to my child's mind and sensibilities that I could not understand their cynicism. Why were they not proud of their children? Would this happen to me when I got older, married, and had children? I did not want to follow in their footsteps. I did not mind when they were critical of living upstate. Compared to life in the city, living upstate was no joy. They had some friends with whom they played cards, but they were so intent on winning that Joe Brady said it took all the fun out of the evening. Most of our family was in the Bronx and driving to NYC took four hours. Everything/one was just too far away. When we drove on a country road from our home to Livingston Manor, there would be an occasional lone house or trailer. I thought, "How could anyone live here? What happens when there are disagreements or fights?" With so much space one could scream at the top of one's lungs and never be heard. I could not picture relationships being strong enough to survive let alone thrive so far from civilization.

Here I was some thirty years later having lost my mother. There were things to do: phone calls to notify my relatives, the first to my sister, Geri in Boise, ID. I had really hoped that Geri would come and had offered to pay for the flight. Her children were no longer infants/toddlers like the time she came after Joe Brady's death with Michael age three and Noel only one to be with and help my mother with practical concerns. Geri's job was important, but most people are allowed time off to attend a parent's funeral. It reminded me of my mother's not attending Aunt Nellie's funeral. For God's sake this was her mother. Despite all their differences over the years why would she not come… if not for her mother then to be with me, to be my emotional support? It was not to be so I relied on the family who wanted to be there: my mother's sister, Aunt Dorothy and her husband, Bill who lived in Mount Vernon; Uncle Henry and Aunt Margie who had welcomed my mother and me into their home for holiday celebrations, the family with whom my mother could chat, relax, and be her joyful self; and my younger cousins. I counted on my cousin, Sr. Barbara and my best friend, Eileen Gannon. Without them I would have crumbled. Eileen volunteered to call the Sisters at our convent for they knew and loved my mother; they had been praying and needed to know first. They in turn would notify the Motherhouse so a phone relay would alert all our convents; many Sisters would come to the wake, some to the Mass, and all would pray for the repose of my mother's soul. In a very real sense my Sisters were my emotional support. They would not abandon me as I felt Geri had.

Practical concerns after death are so strange, like choosing the clothing that my mother would wear. The world felt upside down. This was a funeral not a festive occasion, but custom dictated that I choose an outfit for the viewing. Deciding which Scripture readings and music/hymns were best for the Mass of Resurrection was comforting. Dan Entrekan, a professional singer with whom I had sung in a church choir for many years referred to a funeral as "a sacred send-off." Well I had to make this a grand farewell. My mother would be waked at Park Abbey in the Bronx and the Mass would be at St. Helena's in Parkchester.

I dreaded making the funeral arrangements. I asked my dear friends, Eileen Gannon and Judy Donaldson to go with me. They were my staunch allies to prevent me from doing anything extravagant. The funeral director was Bonnie Smith, a short, shrewd woman who with her husband had built Park Abbey on Unionport Road across from St. Helena Church in the 1940s. As we sat in her office I heard dogs barking, a strange sound in a funeral home. She had dogs in the back room and somehow they had a connection with another business she owned, a horseback riding academy on Pelham Parkway. "At least she's an animal lover," I thought. I brought the deed to a plot in Woodlawn Cemetery where my father, George Willemse and grandfather, Cornelius Willemse were buried. That cemetery was a block away from where we had lived and we sometimes walked there in good weather. It spooked me out especially when I read the engravings on the tomb stones and learned that children and mothers were buried there. They followed me home and at night inhabited my dreams. Bonnie Smith had a list of amenities that folks consider. She was rushing through them as fast as she could speak. To my surprise Bonnie was eliminating many items. A typical comment was, "Obituary (Death notice) in the newspaper? You don't need that." I grasped that I had to be alert or she would not have included a casket and who knows what else. Entering the room where caskets were displayed was enough to take my breath away. I wondered if some patrons chose the casket closest to the door; it was stately and the most expensive. As I chose a simple casket the words of a co-worker who had to make arrangements after her husband's sudden death came to mind. "I told them this is a casket. I don't want the finest wood or finish; it is not going to be on display in our living room." When those tasks were complete, we stood to leave. "I like your coat." said Bonnie. "It looks like it would keep you warm." "Yes," I assured her, "it's a down coat." She wanted to know where I had bought it and I told her Alexander's. It seemed so strange to be speaking with the owner of a funeral home about the warmth of my coat, but her job as funeral director meant that she routinely went to cemeteries and stood outside in the bitter cold. It made sense to check out my coat. Her final words that day were, "That is just what I need." In an odd way Bonnie reminded me of my grandmother: a woman who worked hard, spoke her mind, and had some quirky ways. She was strangely reassuring.

 The second stop that day was the florist next door to Park Abbey. As I looked at the pictures of floral pieces with so many different flowers and colors, my legs weakened and I felt as if I was going to faint. Just then the phone rang: Father O'Shea from St. Helena's. He knew my family, was close to my cousin, Sr. Barbara; his family had a home at Lake Tamarack, New Jersey where Barbara's parents lived. He had also offered the Mass for our grandmother's funeral in July 1974 and had included Barbara and me in the liturgy, a great comfort to me who loved Nana dearly. He spoke with me briefly that day and in the weeks and months ahead. When the full impact of losing my mother hit me, he would call me at the convent and chat. He would leave funny messages when I was not home such as, "Tell Sister that Robert Redford called." I remember asking, "Who's that?" not recognizing the name of the handsome actor. My sense of humor took a hit in those months of grieving.

I soon realized that wakes are for the living. At the viewing my mother looked peaceful and beautiful, something for which I was grateful since I had the image of her face after death etched in my memory. Even though I had said many times, "Flowers are such a waste of money," I had to eat my own words. This was my mother's final show and I wanted her to be remembered with beauty and color and delicate flowers, the complete opposite of death's mask in the midst of "a bleak mid-winter." I had a hard time explaining why my sister, Geri was not at the wake. A silly expression came to mind, "Put your money on the horses that are running." So I looked at those who were there: my aunts, uncles, and cousins, and the Sisters, oh so many Sisters who came to pay their respects. I was surrounded by those who cared and the wake became "a circle of love." I was surprised how important some things were: that my mother looked good; that so many Sisters and friends came—their presence meant the world to me. I had feared this moment for so long, worried that I would not get through the wake and services without folding. This last was probably no surprise to my family, but I had this awful fear that I would break down and cry inconsolably. There were moments of humor such as Fr. Haggerty's homily during a short prayer service at the wake when Father spoke gallantly of my mother's being reunited with her husband ("Which one?" I thought. "What if George and Joe both show up?"). The Sisters from my convent were a great support for they knew how I had loved and cared for my mother over many years. They had welcomed my mother to the convent for Thanksgiving dinner and other occasions. My mother was among friends and if she could see, she would have been happy.

As we filed past the coffin in those final moments of viewing the body, Aunt Dorothy leaned over and said, "I will always be here for you." The mere suggestion that she could replace my mother—for that is how I understood her comment—made me incredibly angry. No one could ever do that. I had to compose myself as we went to the church for the Mass of Resurrection. At the entrance of the church the priest welcomed us as they placed the white pall over the coffin, a reminder of how Peggy was embraced by God at Baptism and wrapped in the fullness of grace. Life comes full circle when at death we return to God hoping that God embraces us fully as the child that received the new life of grace Ahead of me was that incredibly long walk behind my mother's casket down the center aisle of the church... There were priests from St. Helena Parish and from the high school. The music led by Marilyn Martin, a professional singer with whom I sang in the choir on Sundays, included music by Georg Friedrich Handel, "I Know That My Redeemer Liveth" and an *Ave Maria* by Jacques Arcadelt. Music that I loved beat down the door of composure, sneaking in and touching my heart. I wanted the best music and Marilyn was able to sing solos as well as lead us in hymns that the congregation would sing. After Mass we followed the hearse in our own cars to Woodlawn cemetery. By some wonderful coincidence we drove past the apartment house where we had lived, 282 East Gun Hill Road. It felt right to bring my mother through the streets that she had walked as we traveled to her final resting place. Margaret Josephine Brady was laid to rest that bitterly cold day with prayers entrusting her to God. As powerful winds surged and waned, we huddled close together.

> Saints of God, come to her aid!
> Hasten to meet her, angels of the Lord!
> Receive her soul and present her to God the Most High.
>
> Eternal rest grant unto her O Lord,
> And let perpetual light shine upon her.
> May she rest in peace. Amen

We did not linger at graveside but hurried back to our cars. Our destination was Castle Harbor Inn where we would eat a warm dinner. My aunts, uncles, cousins, and close friends shared stories of my mother from bygone days. We could visualize my mother when she was healthy and played the piano, sang somewhat poorly, laughed and enjoyed happier days. I would remember how my mother loved deeply and needed desperately to be loved in return. Conversations with relatives and those who knew her at Carmel Richmond would help me to understand that my mother really loved me even when she was critical and less than satisfied. Like her elegant cursive script my mother was graceful and beautiful, endowed with intelligence and wit. I would need time and prayer to let her best qualities rise to the top like cream in a bottle of milk. We the living needed to focus on the complete picture of her life: an amazing amalgam of moments of pure gold amidst ordinary, mundane activities. Peggy would live as long as we could gather and share stories. I welcomed that meal during which I felt intimately the loving presence of my relatives and friends. By day's end as I paid the bill and bid my relatives good-bye, I was exhausted and relieved. My mother had truly had a grand, sacred send-off.

My mother's life and passing remind me of a favorite hymn that we sang honoring Mary, the Mother of us all:

MOTHER DEAR, O PRAY FOR ME ♪

By Isaac B. Woodbury (1819-1858) in 1850

Mother dear, O pray for me!
While, far from heaven and thee,
I wander, in a fragile bark,
O'er life's tempestuous sea.
O Virgin Mother, from thy throne,
So bright in bliss above,
Protect thy child and cheer my path
With thy sweet smile of love.

Mother dear, remember me,
And never cease thy care,
'Till in heaven eternally
Thy love and bliss I share.

Chapter 9

THE JOYS OF CONVENT LIVING

The short black line moved gracefully from convent to church. They walked two by two into the church, genuflected and took their seats in the front pews. The whole church could have been empty, but there they were up front ready for Mass. At the end of Mass the same black line moved from the church and then disappeared behind the walls of the convent. Their connection to the world came after breakfast when they went to the parish grade school to teach their class. This triad: the church, the convent, the school was the world of Catholic Sisters, not just the geographical world but also the religious world of Catholic Sisters in the mid-twentieth century.

Convent life in 1961 was very structured. We thought that the rules and customs we learned would be the same, as they had been for many years. Catholicism was a religion whose regulations reflected a rich tradition. We willingly spent many hours and days learning the intricacies of customs and practices that for us represented a rich, religious life. In the name of love we chose the life of a Dominican Sister. In our youth we enthusiastically embraced religious life because we treasured its goal: becoming a bride of Christ.

That decade would bring huge social and political change. Who could have imagined all that would transpire: the election of the first Roman Catholic, John F. Kennedy, as president of the USA in 1960; the sexual revolution; civil rights marches and protests that led to laws that guaranteed people of color equal access to education, voting rights, and housing? Political unrest led to violence that claimed the lives of children, young men, and leaders caught in the crosshairs of uncompromising bigotry: President John F. Kennedy, Dr. Martin Luther King, Jr., Malcolm X; and Robert F. Kennedy as he was campaigning for the presidency in 1968. Violence ended many lives, and I prayed that they would rest in peace. I also thought about myself: if shot, I would rather be killed outright than suffer prolonged paralysis. A swift death was far superior to being maimed and forced to live in a wheel chair like George Wallace, the governor of Alabama, who so famously said, "In the name of the greatest people that have ever trod this earth, I draw the line in the dust and toss the gauntlet before the feet of tyranny, and I say segregation now, segregation tomorrow, segregation forever." Some things are worse than death.

Upheavals in society did not always directly affect Sisters/nuns, but they affected the children we taught and their parents and families. In Middletown, NY we Sisters attended a community meeting regarding birth control methods. Health education curriculum was slated to change and we needed to know how that would affect our students. We also had relatives, especially our sisters and nieces who were facing these problems. Even in the novitiate when we had withdrawn from the world, our Novice Mistress, Sr. Cecilia had spoken to us and asked us to pray when the Cuban Missile Crisis occurred. Living a cloistered life did not mean that we were disconnected from world events. In fact, we were in a unique position to implore God to save us from folly. Our involvement through prayer acknowledged the frailty of human nature and the power of an all loving God working through people of good will. Inspired leadership was especially important in crises.

Convent life was known for what could be seen: habits that originated centuries before when ordinary women wore layers of clothing, covered their heads, and hid their bodies from view. Prayer was not so easily seen, but if one were near a convent or church, prayer could be heard and observed. Meditation could be puzzling like the time I was in New York University Hospital under observation and a nurse came running in to see if I were having a seizure. "No," I said, "I am just reading and meditating on Scripture." What was obvious was that we were unavailable many hours of the day and that most of that time we were in chapel/church chanting the Little Office of the Blessed Mother, praying the Rosary, attending Mass, and as just mentioned, meditating. It was accepted that we spent time before the Blessed Sacrament praying before the God of life and love. Our families and friends learned quickly that our time was not our own: that we had to ask permission to go to a wake or funeral, to visit the sick in the hospital or nursing home, and to visit our parents and siblings on rare occasions. The vow of obedience seemed to bind us to the convent, not free us to do for those in the world. If the superior thought an action was good, then of course we were directed to act. Our comings and goings were easily observed by neighbors for Sisters traveled in pairs.

A Sister at my first mission asked me to accompany her to a wake. She was from Ireland and dutifully read the obituaries in *The Daily News* to learn if anyone from "home" had died. Off we went to a local funeral home to pay our respects. We were kneeling and praying for the deceased man when Sister said to me, "I do not know this man. I thought it was someone else." I was her companion and along for the ride so to speak. How would she get out of this? Would she tell the widow and sons what she had whispered to me? We ended our silent prayer, made the Sign of the Cross, stood and walked over to the family. Sister said, "We are so sorry for your loss. Your husband was a fine man." The wife proceeded to tell us how her husband had died and leaning toward her we were compassionate listeners. After promising them our prayers, we returned to the light and noise on White Plains Road. Even Sister, a professional mourner, was shaken by the fact that this was a complete stranger. I learned something new that day: those who are grieving may well not know all those who come to the viewing, but they do appreciate prayers and kind words.

Over the course of ten months three of my third grade students lost a parent. At the first wake I tried to comfort the daughter by saying, "Your mother is so beautiful… I am sure that she is in heaven." Her older sisters spoke with us explaining how their mother had suffered as she endured treatments for cancer. Then one of them said, "The wake is a circle of love." I had never thought of wakes like that, but I saved that for future use. All I could think of was how this woman's youngest daughter would no longer have her mother's presence and advice as she grew. At eight, almost nine years old, she would have limited memories of her mother… Shortly after New Year's when a winter storm made driving perilous, we got word that the mother of another girl in my class had died. She was in a terrible car accident caused by icy road conditions. This was particularly sad because I had often spoken with her mother after school standing on the corner as she waited for her younger daughter to be dismissed. I had to hide behind a large sign so the principal would not see me because speaking with externs was discouraged. Both girls were excellent students and were a credit to their parents.

When I went to the mother's wake there was a closed casket, an indication of the gravity of the accident. It was my first experience of a closed casket and added to my discomfort. As I looked up, I was startled by a man coming toward me who had the same blue eyes as his sister. How could God not have protected this woman, the loving mother of two beautiful girls? She was so young and so dedicated to her daughters. At a time like that, I had to act as if my faith were strong. My affection for mother and daughters was genuine and I prayed that God would comfort them. I would miss those casual meetings, but her husband and daughters would miss her daily love and devotion. That incident made me realize how fragile life is: we are here now but we know not when we will be called (Mt 25:13). Sudden death is wrenching. How I wished that I could have changed that Sunday when the mother's car skidded and she was mortally wounded. I hated to think that this mother could be taken from her family so tragically and so irrevocably. How I wished that Jesus could call her forth as he did with Lazarus whose sisters had mourned his passing (John 11: 41-44). But no, there I stood with the father and brother united in a grief too deep for shallow words.

Yet another of my students lost her father in the spring. I did not know the circumstances or what caused his death. This wake was my first time seeing a deceased black man. What would I say? Would this wake be like others I had experienced? By the time I found the funeral parlor and parked, the family had left for supper. The proprietors let me in so I had a private viewing. I saw a young man in his thirties, robust, looking as if he could get up and greet me. How very sad that his daughter would no longer experience his love and care. I prayed at the bier, signed my name in the Visitors' book, and departed for home. My concern for his daughter would carry over into the future in our classroom with her peers where she would learn and grow. We would be her circle of love by day until she returned home and could be with her mother and family.

I had never experienced so many deaths of parents in one year. I wanted to help and did with my limited expressions of sympathy. I knew that no one could ever replace the mother/father each had lost. I questioned why these girls had to experience the loss of a parent at such a young age. I had no power to reverse what had happened, but I did what little I could: surrounded them with good experiences with other students so they would have happy days at school where they had friends and a teacher who deeply cared about them. Yes, they would learn and they would enjoy many happy moments with their classmates. School would be a good experience in their young lives.

Vatican Council II (1962-65) brought about many changes for Catholics. What we noticed first was changes in the liturgy. One dramatic modification was offering Mass in the vernacular. For centuries Latin was the Roman Rite's official language for Mass and the administration of the sacraments. I loved Latin and had wanted to major in Latin, but it was becoming a dead language for almost no one studied or spoke it. When the vernacular was approved, it was thrilling to have the priest lead prayers and for the congregation to respond in English. At Our Lady of Grace School our students went to Mass on First Fridays. At that time there was only the lower church. It was not large enough to accommodate all the students so my third grade had to go to Mass early before the rest of the school. First Friday arrived and my class was seated up front for the 8:00 a.m. Mass. The bell sounded and the priest and server came out of the sacristy to stand before the altar. I could not wait; my students were all primed for the English responses. But no, we were fooled. Father was saying the prayers, but it was not English. He was praying in Italian. The grandmothers scattered throughout the church were all responding and looking so happy. I was upset because we could not respond. I was standing on the side aisle trying to look calm while whispering threats to unruly students all in an effort to maintain order. I had known the Latin prayers, but Italian was another language altogether. The Mass proceeded: Scripture readings in Italian; Offertory prayers in Italian; the Canon in Italian. Finally we went to Communion; at least the host was still the same and Jesus came to us in the form of unleavened bread. I could not believe that my class would not hear English at Mass that day. We would have to go to the Sunday Mass and be sure that it was not in Italian. From that day forward one had to check the church bulletin to learn which language would be used for while English was the language of the majority there were parishioners, some of whom spoke Italian and others Spanish.

    My cousin, Sr. Barbara was stationed at St. Edmund's in Brooklyn and invited me to visit her on a school holiday, the feast of the Ascension. It was a long trip by public transportation from the North Bronx to Brooklyn. I brought a small briefcase that contained copies of the 3rd grade final exam in math and my Office Book. A series of math figures (circle, square, triangle, rectangle, and parallelogram) had not copied well so I had to go through sixty copies and draw each by pen. Barbara wanted to go to the beach and walk on the boardwalk. So off we went. It was a bright, sunny day with a slight breeze—perfect weather for a walk. We were laughing and talking and then had our lunch seated on a bench overlooking the water. What a delightful day. Of course we had to retrace our steps and take buses and trains all the way back home, but that was a small price to pay for a day with my cousin out by the water. We checked in with the superior as was the custom and all was well until I realized that I did not have the black briefcase. Where had I left it? I called Barbara thinking that she might have it, but no. What would I do? I could borrow an Office Book, but how could I get copies of the math exam? I was praying for a miracle; perhaps my guardian angel could find all the things that were lost or taken who-knows-where. That evening at supper the superior commented on my color. "Oh, yes," I replied, "we were in the sun waiting for the bus and I looked up so I would get color." When I got changed that night, my face was bright red. I doubt that the superior was fooled, but she did not have proof of our excursion. As the days ticked by I was thinking that I would have to own up to what had happened. We had no access to a printer; we could not even get out and go some place where we could make copies. Finally Barbara called: she had the briefcase with the tests and Office Book. "How," I asked her, "did you get it?" A man found it on the bench where we had sat and looked inside for identification. He knew there was a convent near the beach so he brought it there. The Sisters were not our congregation but they could see that it was a Dominican Office Book. They contacted the nearest Dominican convent and Barbara got my things back. I was so happy. Now, of course, how could I get it? It was a convoluted process: from Barbara to a Sister going to Sparkill, and then to another Sister who brought it to the Bronx and to my convent. When it finally was in my hands, I was so relieved. Our training in those days involved so much ingenuity, intelligence, and imagination that we would have been natural candidates for the CIA. And my angel? Well my angel was back in favor, but now had to make sure I did not leave things behind. And just in case, I began to pray in earnest to St. Anthony, the patron saint of lost articles.

Sr. Oliver became Prioress at the Motherhouse shortly after our profession in 1963. We soon learned that she was a hands-on person. She was a tall, amply built woman whose glasses slipped to the edge of her nose much like Benjamin Franklin in spectacles. We soon realized that she was a down-to-earth, no-nonsense person who wanted to get things done. What a wonderful change from the wishy-washy superior who never could make a decision even when the professional dish-washer was spewing water in the basement. My first contact with Sr. Oliver was when she decided to remove a stain from the concrete step outside the main entrance of Sacred Heart Chapel. The other Sister and I had no idea how to remove a stain from concrete, but Sr. Oliver knew just what to do. She used Muriatic acid and like magic, it sizzled and the stain disappeared. I stored that name (Muriatic); it just might be the solution to future problems.

The following year I told some of my comrades about the cleaning properties of Muriatic acid. I had the upstairs shower room as my charge so I thought the corners where it was damp would benefit. Diluted, it still cleaned the gunk from the corners of the shower stalls. Another Sister was so impressed that she decided to use it on the staircase that led to our rooms upstairs and the laundry downstairs. She had not thought of doing a patch test to see how it would work on that surface. She diluted it and mopped the staircase from top to bottom. As the mixture dried whatever sheen the stairs had disappeared. In its place there were white swatches like huge cataracts on each of the stairs and landings. Sure enough the superior arrived home and wanted to know, "What did you do to ruin the terrazzo floor? You would have to go to Italy to replace it." Needless to say I immediately resigned as consultant on cleaning affairs.

August 1963 between the first and second retreats in Sparkill my cousin, Sr. Barbara gave me a package containing three cans of soda. That probably sounds odd in this day and age when people have all kinds of beverages in the pantry and refrigerator, but that was not the case at the Motherhouse. With no access to a refrigerator I resorted to boarding school tactics. The water in the lavatory opposite Mother Kevin's office was icy cold. The toilet tanks had equally cold spring-fed water. There were so many Sisters on the retreat that I put all three cans in the tank of the toilet farthest from the door; it would be easier to get into one stall than have to wait for all three. After I fed the boys, I was eating supper when someone whispered, "You have to see Sr. Oliver. The toilet isn't working and she's in there with a snake." Once they explained that a snake would remove anything blocking, I got a bit uneasy. Sure enough, Sr. Oliver was in the lavatory with her sleeves rolled up fixing the toilet that would not flush. When the snake did not solve the problem, she removed the cover on the tank. "Look at what we have here!" she said. She removed the ice cold cans of soda and someone said that she put them on the glass covered desk of the Mother General across the hall from the lavatory. On my way to Compline I heard all that Sr. Oliver had done and my blood froze. My plan had backfired. What would happen? Would they send me home? I prayed Compline like someone on death row awaiting execution. After evening prayer I joined the sisters on line outside Sr. Oliver's office to ask permissions or to get a penance. My mind was full of words I dreaded saying, but one thing I would never disclose: who gave me the soda. Barbara was my cousin and I would never think of getting her or anyone else in trouble. As the line inched forward, out of the corner of my eye I saw my sister, Joan still wearing her black mantle returning from driving someone to the city. "Sure," I thought, "Joan is doing everything right and here I am about to be sent home." More time waiting in the dark, airless hall. Finally I am in front of Sr. Oliver. "Sister," I began, "I put the cans of soda in the bathroom tank." "Oh," she replied and after a slight pause, "Why did you put all three cans in one tank?" I wasn't prepared for that question so I stumbled some reply. "Don't you have soda in the refectory?" "No,

Sister, we never have soda." Sr. Oliver made a sound as if she found that hard to believe. "Sister, may I have a penance?" Then I made the *venia* and left her office relieved that I was still a member of the Dominican Sisters of Sparkill. I was so glad I had kept Barbara's role a secret. We lost the soda, but Barbara's secret was safe with me. Unknown to me, Barbara had spoken with Sr. Oliver earlier that day and told her that she had some things to give her cousin, Sr. Judith Mary. So my secret was no secret. Even better, they started to serve soda at the Motherhouse. We couldn't believe our eyes when it was served really nice and cold—what a lovely surprise. Sr. Oliver was a gem!

Those of us with a driver's license would drive postulants and novices along with the Postulant Mistress or Novice Mistress to dentist appointments in Rockland County. Occasionally we drove into Manhattan. I had gotten my driver's license at age 17 and had experience driving in Liberty, NY and on curving country roads like the old Rte. 17. Once I drove Sr. Oliver downtown on the FDR Drive, a three lane parkway with lots of traffic. With practically no city driving I was concentrating on driving safely. Sr. Oliver said, "Don't let all those cars pass you. Go faster." I had to laugh; I'm trying not to have an accident and she is telling me to be more aggressive. I picked up the pace and we got where we were going. These many years later as I drive on that same road, I can still hear her words and feel her encouragement. Sr. Oliver was an amazing woman.

Over the years I have met many amazing women. While they were mostly my teachers or professors, some were in positions of authority. I admired their selfless concern for the community and their ability to make sane decisions. They modeled for me what I hoped for myself: to live my life motivated by love and dedicated to serving others. They were different ages but they shared a common trait: joyful charity. Yes, they clarified issues, but more importantly they had a vibrant spirituality rooted in love of God. They cared about me so consistently that when they shared advice I knew that it came from a place of deep wisdom. Knowing them made me a better woman and inspired me in the various roles to which obedience called me: teacher, administrator, campus minister, and professor.

While I met sisters at different stages of life, becoming friends with Sr. Thomas More came at a time when we were both in Siena Hall Infirmary (2010-2012). As I recovered from multiple surgeries and hoped to be in good health for my Golden Jubilee and return to active ministry, Thomas was in her golden years and facing the challenges of later life. She was intelligent, knowledgeable, well read, and wise especially about congregational life and leadership. Most wonderful of all, she had a lively sense of humor so we talked and laughed when the absurdities or silliness of life threatened to bring us up short. Our friendship came late in life and I would have given anything to have known her longer. She loved life and her friends but many of them she told me, "were on the hill." When I asked where that was, she smiled and said, "In our cemetery" located up the hill from the Motherhouse. I remember another sister had asked her if she were scared of dying. Thomas More replied, "I have loved God as long as I can remember. How can I be afraid of the God who has loved me all my life?" Sr. Thomas More, I love you and hope that we will be reunited.

The Chapter of 1976 began with each of the delegates making a directed retreat. Previously hundreds of Sisters made a week-long retreat at the Motherhouse. The retreat master gave three conferences a day and offered Mass, was available for confession, and was generally far removed from every retreatant. A directed retreat meant each Sister had a spiritual director: a priest or Sister trained in spirituality. Before the retreat opened, we joked among ourselves, "When I talk about God, it will be a really short conversation. Then what will we do?" We had no idea what would happen. In the normal course of events we relied on conferences, Scripture, and being with God in silence to open our minds and hearts to God. We instinctively knew that talking about God and one's relationship with God would lead us to realms unknown, well if not unknown then to realms hidden from normal discourse. My spiritual director for my first directed retreat was Sr. Carol Johannes, an Adrian Dominican. We had never met, but it would prove to be a pairing made in heaven. I remember how nervous I felt before the retreat. What could I say about God and me? This was not talking about God in a theological sense; this was talking about my relationship with God. It felt so deeply personal like talking about one's sex life. (Now that would be a short conversation!) Or perhaps like the vow of poverty: possession of money was really limited. The first time we met our spiritual director consisted of a brief introduction and lasted 15-20 minutes. It was a way to calm ourselves for we were genuinely afraid of this process. Logically why would this scare us? We were vowed religious women who had pledged our life to God, who claimed Jesus as our Spouse, and who lived a life dedicated to the vows of poverty, chastity, and obedience. We had a reasonable knowledge of saints who wrote about loving and relating to God; we attended daily Mass and prayed communally and privately. Despite all this, we were scared.

Over the next seven days we observed silence, prayed privately and communally especially at Mass each day, and individually met with our spiritual director. Sr. Carol Johannes was just what I needed. In the course of that week I finally uncovered a sore that had not seen the light of day: I spoke of my relationship with Joan, my sister and her untimely death at the age of 37. It wasn't that I had not spoken of this before: my friend, Eileen had listened and shared my sorrow and distress when Joan had been ill and then when she died in 1969. What made this different was allowing myself to get angry with God. Now you might say, "That is normal. Why had you not done this after Joan died?" For reasons I could not articulate, I had never gotten angry with God. Maybe I was afraid. God is all powerful so I could have figured: get angry with whoever you want, but do not under any circumstance get angry with God. You might just need God's help so you'd better play it safe. It sounds silly now, but for all those years, seven to be exact, I never felt safe enough to even think of getting angry with God.

Admitting that I was angry with God was monumental. Tears, torrents of tears were unleashed. Why had God not listened to my prayers? "God, how could you have allowed Joan to die? It was so unfair. I had answered your call, given my life to you, and was working heart and soul for the people of God. Was this the way you cared for me? God/Jesus, you are a monster." I went through tissues like crazy. In fact I felt as if I were becoming unhinged, that I was going crazy. To unleash such deep seated emotion against the all powerful God was scary beyond words. But somehow I was able to do that. Besides Carol Johannes' expert spiritual guidance I had my friend, Eileen who understood how deeply I loved Joan and how her sickness and death had affected me. Experiencing such pent-up emotion was like breaching the walls of a dam and unleashing a flood of epic proportions. It threatened to undo me.

By week's end I knew that I needed to work more under Carol's direction. She was a spiritual director at St. Stephen's Priory in Dover, MA. Eileen and I arranged to go to Dover for a thirty day retreat in July. Over that month I met with Carol. Like the week in Sparkill, she would assign Scripture readings each day and I would pray and meditate using each reading as a springboard. We met each day for 45 minutes and I would share with her my experience of prayer. My fear at confronting God/Jesus gradually dissipated. With her help I was able to relate to God in a more realistic/human way. I had idealized my sister, Joan to such a degree that our relationship was unreal. I probably did the same with God. It was my way of dealing with a God that I feared would do to me what he had done to Joan: abandon her to sickness and death. Slowly, ever so slowly I could relate with God honestly. I had had my doubts about God's existence, but I had gritted my teeth and hung on for dear life. Even if I could not feel the presence of God, I would go on hoping in some strange way that not discussing a problem would make it go away. I had seen examples of this in my family: ignoring situations and pretending all was well even when anger and resentments had built up to the force of a pressure cooker. Denial had its advantages: not to admit that something is happening is tantamount to saying that in fact it is not happening. Years later I would read that patients use denial when dealing with cancer; it is in fact a superb way to deal with aspects of cancer, but of course it cannot heal or stop advanced metastasis. Denial only helps up to a point and by 1976 I had reached that point spiritually.

The month at Dover was a life saver. Not only was I rewired spiritually, I also had time to talk with Eileen. We had no responsibilities; meals were served and we each had our own room. There was time to read, to think, and to pray. It was a respite from teaching and a break in visiting and caring for my mother. Being on retreat was one of the few excuses that my mother would accept for my absence. Somehow she survived and when I returned, I resumed caring for her on the weekends: visiting her in Staten Island, shopping for food, cleaning the apartment, and taking her to church. My mother would have many health crises in the next few years so it was a blessing that I had put my own house in order. I was better able to face those events with greater calm and equanimity.

Chapter 10

THE HUNDREDFOLD

*P*eter the Apostle was not shy. He would ask Jesus questions that no one else dared. It comes as no surprise that he would state the obvious, "We have put aside everything to follow you!"

Jesus answered, "I give you my word, there is no one who has given up home, brothers or sisters, mother or father, children or property, for me and for the gospel who will not receive in this present age a hundred times as many homes, brothers and sisters, mothers, children and property—and persecution besides —and in the age to come, everlasting life" (Mk 10:28-30).

This passage comes right after the story of the rich young man who sincerely wants to follow Jesus and asks what else he had to do. Jesus encourages the young man to, "Go and sell what you have and give to the poor; you will then have treasure in heaven. After that, come and follow me." The rich young man could/would not do that. "At these words the man's face fell. He went away sad for he had many possessions...Jesus looked at his disciples and said, "How hard it is for the rich to enter the kingdom of God!" He uses an image that must have seemed ludicrous. "It is easier for a camel to pass through a needle's eye than for a rich man to enter the kingdom of God" (Mk 10:17-25). The disciples had passed through that particular gate and the image of a camel trying to fit through probably made them laugh except that this was a serious discussion. When they quibble among themselves, Jesus responds, "For man it is impossible but not for God. With God all things are possible" (Mk 10:22).

When I heard this reading in the novitiate, I felt proud of myself. After all, had I not left my parents, brothers and sisters, and the possibility of marrying and having children? Did I give much thought to the hundredfold? I had left home and some possessions to cast my lot with the Dominican Sisters of Sparkill. I was happy to sacrifice comfort and live in community not knowing exactly what that meant. Isn't it true that each new endeavor: making a friend, attending college, starting a new job, living in a new place means letting go of the familiar to embrace a whole new set of circumstances? There is no real understanding of what is new and unknown, just the willingness of a generous heart to embrace what is new hoping that it will work and prove to be good. It is probably better that we do not know all the particulars because we might never embrace change or set off on a new endeavor. We may have an imagined sense of what is to be, but a real, honest to goodness sense of all that will be is just not possible until living at that time, in that place, under those circumstances, and with those people. It is possible that the new situation will exceed our expectations, but the opposite is equally true. This new situation may be a disaster. Only time will tell.

As I got older I hoped that we would be rewarded in this life. When we left the novitiate to go on our first teaching assignments, we believed that this was God's will. God went with us, and as Scripture says, "If God is for us, who can be against?" (Romans 8:31) That epistle goes on to say, "Who will separate us from the love of Christ?...For I am certain that neither death nor life, neither angels nor principalities, neither the present nor the future, nor powers, neither height nor depth nor any other creature, will be able to separate us from the love of God that comes to us in Christ Jesus, our Lord" (Romans 35, 38). Now that was good news!

After novitiate and formation when we were missioned, i.e., sent to a convent where there was a parish school, we went forth to share with others the "fruits of our contemplation." As new members of an established local community we had to get to know these Sisters and how to fit in. Having young Sisters join a local community was both good and bad. Young sisters infused new blood, new ideas into an existing convent and school. We could be a liability if we caused trouble in the house itself or as one superior feared, reported malfeasance to the authorities in Sparkill. My superior in Our Lady of Grace Convent in the Bronx was someone who loved being in charge. When all went her way she would provide good things for the Sisters. One evening they served Miller Lite at supper. I have peculiar tastes: I have never liked coffee or for that matter, beer. Every Sister had to partake so I thought long and hard how to get around this. That evening I passed my beer to the sister to my right and she nudged her empty bottle my way. But for the future there had to be a better way. Finally it came to me: Miller Lite came in a bottle. Perhaps I could substitute apple juice? Our cook could enjoy the beer in the kitchen and I would have the juice. When Miller Lite was next served, the superior could not understand why I drank the contents of the bottle with great pleasure. From where she sat at the top of the table my bottle looked like every other bottle on the table, but if she had been closer, she would have seen that when poured my beer had no head. It was such fun to deceive that woman. A few months later they served martinis in the community room before dinner on a major feast day. I was stumped. I could not replicate the density of the clear liquid so when I did not partake, I was clearly on her bad list.

More important to me was that we had no access to the printer in the principal's office. That meant manually printing the exercises from the Reading Manual on wide rolls of white shelving paper using flow pens whose fumes I quickly learned cause abdominal pain. Downtown on Barclay Street I found a gel tray that could be melted in a pot on the stove, then poured back into the tray. I also bought a book with reading exercises for mimeographing: first press the original on the warm gel and massage gently so the image would be imprinted; then place copy paper one page at a time; continue the process to get about 20 copies. It was slow and tedious, but it provided meaningful work for the students when I was teaching one of the three reading groups.

There was a pear tree in the convent yard. It had beautiful white blossoms in the spring and lovely pears in the summer. How many pears could our convent of twelve Sisters consume? I invited my younger cousins to come and share our good fortune. One day, the superior returned from her day out earlier than expected. My cousins had bags full of pears and we guided them out the kitchen door so they were moving along the outside of the convent toward the sidewalk as the superior came in the front door and walked toward the kitchen. A close call!

During Lent we could not make or receive phone calls. There was one phone in a closet-like space where we could receive phone calls between 7:00-8:30 pm. Ash Wednesday the phone rang; a Sister told me it was for me. Who could this be? I had alerted my family that phone calls were not allowed. "Who is this?" I asked. A strange voice said that she was a Jehovah Witness calling from Brooklyn. My step sister, Clare Anne had converted to the Jehovah Witnesses after she married and moved to Rhode Island. Apparently she gave them my name and phone number so they could proselytize. The caller would not accept what I said, "I am a Roman Catholic nun and have no interest in converting." Even worse was facing the superior who found my explanation outlandish and was convinced that I was trying to circumvent the rule.

For some strange reason, I rise to the occasion when someone tells me that I cannot do something. My mother often used this tactic with me. "Judy, I bet you can't …." It always made me so determined to prove her wrong that I would expend extraordinary energy and I would get it done. The same carried over to religious life. In Our Lady of Grace the superior became convinced that we, the youngest, were having more fun at the end of the table during evening recreation. She decided to rearrange the furniture. Instead of two long tables where she sat at the top and farthest from the television, she had the tables placed across the room. I landed across from her with my back to the television. That reminded me of my step father's arrangement to watch television. His favorite wing backed chair was right next to the television so each evening we positioned a 4' high mirror at the opposite end of the room so he could see. What did I have that could achieve that same effect? It finally came to me. The next night I sat with my back to the television with the round mirror on a stand aimed at the television. Most nights I was marking quizzes so I did not want to be turned around with nothing to lean on. The mirror was a Band-Aid, but it got enough attention that the superior soon had the tables rearranged into one long line. I was back with my friends and life was good.

At Christmas our students brought all kinds of little gifts for their teachers. I could not believe my eyes: scented powder, gloves, candy, and all sorts of lovely things. Most would be saved for the annual Bazaar in Sparkill when we raised money for the congregation, but we were allowed to keep a few most of which we promptly recycled as Christmas gifts for our immediate family. My second year each class chose a mother who was a liaison with the teacher. When mine asked if there were anything that I needed, I said, "Yes, I need a black suitcase to use when we go away to Saugerties or to Sparkill for retreat." That year my class gave me a sturdy, black suitcase. We had to ask permission to use any gift. When the superior saw the suitcase with my initials engraved, she told me to put it in her office. I complied, but I was angry. "What does she want with my suitcase? She has all the suitcases she needs and besides, my initials are engraved on it." Months later I was assigned to work at the summer camp in Commack, Long Island. I would be away for six weeks. The superior was upset when I left by way of the front door with my belongings in large shopping bags. What would the neighbors think? I had no suitcase except a small one for papers. When I returned in August, the slightly dusty, black suitcase was in my room—delayed delivery to be sure, but very appreciated.

McDonell Camp in Commack, Long Island was far from Sparkill, but that was exactly where a group of us professed Sisters was headed in June 1964. Each year the St. Vincent de Paul Society sponsored poor children from Brooklyn, NY so they could have a ten day experience at sleep away camp. Each cabin housed up to 60 campers. There were five large cabins for children, a cabin for the Sisters who would work with the children, and another that was a chapel so the Sisters could have daily Mass. On Sunday we had an outdoor Mass with the children. That June Sr. Marie Jean, an English professor at STAC, headed up a small group of young professed. Our task was to "open the camp." It involved removing newspapers from sixty-one mattresses in each cabin, sweeping the dirt, removing dust and cobwebs from corners, windows, wooden floors, and washing surfaces to remove dirt and grime. It was heavy work on bright sunny days, but we got to speak at length over supper. As the days passed we got to know each other and best of all we had Sr. Marie Jean's input. She was smart, knowledgeable, and very down to earth. By week's end we had removed enough newspapers to build a bonfire and had seen enough spiders and ants to thrill an entomologist. We were also well on our way to solving the problems of our Dominican congregation. Those days were so different from life at the Motherhouse that I dreaded returning to Sparkill.

Three times I have been seriously tempted to leave the convent. The first, September 8, 1961 was the day I entered and my first night sleeping in the novitiate. Once we bid farewell to friends and family and were in the novitiate with a group of strangers, I had the greatest temptation to call it quits. I could almost hear evil spirits whispering among themselves, trying to persuade me to leave. "This is silliness. You have good friends and a loving family. Why leave all that for the strange life at the convent?" I could not believe how tempted I was on that hot, humid night in the novitiate. I only weathered that storm when I agreed to check it out. If it continued to be weird, then I would leave and start my own congregation.

The second time I was tempted to leave the convent was at the end of the week after we had prepared Bishop McDonell Camp for its annual opening. We worked hard, but we were energetic and had great team spirit. At supper we would discuss issues that were swirling about. It was so good to be able to speak and be heard; we weren't just newly professed Sisters. Our views counted, something that Vatican Council II encouraged. The thought of returning to the rigors of Formation at Sparkill was daunting. All I had to do was leave and I would experience normal conversation among equals. It was supremely difficult to return to "the more austere but happier way of life" as is written in the Rule of St. Augustine.

The third time was shortly after my sister, Joan died. Exhausted both physically and emotionally by two months' driving to the hospital after teaching all day to visit my sister who slowly and painfully lost her fight to live, I was totally spent. When Joan died I would no longer get to see her at the Motherhouse, to visit when we went to Sparkill for a meeting or retreat. I felt as if I had lost my home and yes, I felt like leaving. It made no sense. I had made final vows and been a Sister for eight years. Eileen Gannon and many other Sisters had supported me emotionally. How could I turn my back on them? This temptation was all the more insidious for it came at a time when I was barely standing and wondering how I would get through the next day, let alone the next few months of school. That winter was particularly long and dreary. Whom was I kidding? Sparkill might be better off if I left. It would have been hellish to return home and live with my mother who was facing her own demons. It was one thing to help her on weekends, but living with her? No, I could not endure that. When reason prevailed, I knew that the convent provided a sane structure and my work, teaching teenagers, gave me a reason to live.

During the two years that I was at Our Lady of Grace, I sometimes went to the public library, a block away from the home of Uncle Henry and Aunt Margie so I dropped in from time to time. Their daughter, Eileen made her First Holy Communion at St. Mary's Church; Sister Barbara and I attended the Mass and went out with them afterwards. Uncle Henry said, "Eileen, this is your special day and you can order anything that you would like." My uncle proceeded to show her the menu that had all sorts of breakfast specials. Eileen knew exactly what she wanted even before her father finished speaking. She said, "A hamburger with mashed potatoes and corn." Even though it was a restaurant famous for breakfasts they served Eileen just what she wanted.

Despite a thirteen year difference in age between my mother and Henry, they were always very close. When we lived on Gun Hill Road, Henry often came over after the Monday night novena at St. Ann's Church. He would arrive speaking in a convincing German accent, and he and my mother would have a beer as they sat and kibitzed. One Christmas Eve Henry stopped by and told me that Santa was on the way; he also read "The Night before Christmas" to me. He was so convincing that I thought I heard the hooves of Santa's reindeer on the roof above us. It was a perfect landing place for the sled and reindeer so this was totally logical. Only one thing: we had no chimney unless brick tissue paper taped to the wall counted.

The hundredfold came to me over the years as I lived with our Dominican Sisters in different convents, doing a variety of tasks, and responding the best I could to all that God asked and the community required. Living in community was sometimes challenging, but overall it taught me how to relate to people from different backgrounds. I witnessed how our sisters were generous and self-sacrificing. They showed me how to love the youngster who could not read, the teenager struggling to find her identity, the young adults eager to learn but desiring above all, friendship and love, and the adults trying to earn a living, hold their family together, and seeking reassurance as parents of teenagers. I hope that I have touched their lives with tender love and shared knowledge in a common pursuit of truth. I have grown older and wiser thanks to all those with whom I have lived and worked. As a younger sister I thought that it was I, Judith Brady who accomplished this task or excelled in learning, but now I realize that I have partnered with a loving God, my spouse, Jesus. Thanks to God I have been able to be and do, and when I failed or my efforts fell short, Jesus supported me, understood my foolish thoughts and forgave sinful deeds. I am not alone; we are not alone. God is with me. God continues to call me and show me the way. "I have called you. You are mine" (Isaiah 43: 1). Thanks be to God!

Appendix

Letter written by Sr. Joan Dolores to Sr. Judith Mary on May, 6, 1962:

Dearest Judy,

Tomorrow the Church shall name you Sr. Judith Mary and shall clothe you in the habit of a Dominican novice. What can one say to one's baby sister on the eve of such a day?

You are beginning a new life that is more significant than the most obvious and joyous change of garments. These are the sign of the new life—the religious life you shall begin, and pray God, continue till He calls you home to Himself.

It will be a life of much joy and much sorrow, work and prayer, contemplation and solitude, consolation and sometimes loneliness and even desolation. But above all, it is primarily a religious life—a life "bound to God," lived by one belonging to God.

What can I say then? "Pious" words come easily, the truths of the real God are often unutterable. The spiritual authors are far more capable than I of attempting such a task.

But I say this: remember who you are, and you will be safe—a woman who belongs to God, not as do the works of creation, nor even as souls in grace, but as one specially chosen to love Him in a more perfect way, and to be free to receive His love—remember this, and make your decisions accordingly,

I love you, dear baby sister, and I am happy with you today because I have helped you to come to God, which is the greatest blessing you could receive.

All I can say now is God bless you—today and always—with His joy, His peace, but especially His love—with all it shall require of you.

Be a good novice, baby sister, and I shall be happy.

Love and prayers,

Sr. Joan Dolores

Printed in Great Britain
by Amazon